Confronting Technology

Princeton Theological Monograph Series

K. C. Hanson, Charles M. Collier, D. Christopher Spinks,
and Robin A. Parry, Series Editors

Recent volumes in the series:

Steven C. van den Heuvel
*Bonhoeffer's Christocentric Theology and Fundamental
Debates in Environmental Ethics*

Andrew R. Hay
God's Shining Forth: A Trinitarian Theology of Divine Light

Peter Schmiechen
*Gift and Promise:
An Evangelical Theology of the Lord's Supper*

Hank Voss
*The Priesthood of All Believers and the Missio Dei:
A Canonical, Catholic, and Contextual Perspective*

Alexandra S. Radcliff
*The Claim of Humanity in Christ: Salvation and
Sanctification in the Theology of T. F. and J. B. Torrance*

Yaroslav Viazovski
*Image and Hope:
John Calvin and Karl Barth on Body, Soul, and Life Everlasting*

Anna C. Miller
*Corinthian Democracy:
Democratic Discourse in 1 Corinthians*

Thomas Christian Currie
*The Only Sacrament Left to Us: The Threefold
Word of God in the Theology and Ecclesiology of Karl Barth*

Confronting Technology

The Theology of Jacques Ellul

MATTHEW T. PRIOR

PICKWICK *Publications* · Eugene, Oregon

CONFRONTING TECHNOLOGY
The Theology of Jacques Ellul

Princeton Theological Monograph Series 243

Pickwick Publications
An Imprint of Wipf and Stock Publishers
199 W. 8th Ave., Suite 3
Eugene, OR 97401

www.wipfandstock.com

PAPERBACK ISBN: 978-1-5326-7145-6
HARDCOVER ISBN: 978-1-5326-7146-3
EBOOK ISBN: 978-1-5326-7147-0

Cataloguing-in-Publication data:

Names: Prior, Matthew T., author.

Title: Confronting technology : the theology of Jacques Ellul / by Matthew T. Prior.

Description: Eugene, OR : Pickwick Publications, 2020 | Princeton Theological Monograph Series 243 | Includes bibliographical references.

Identifiers: ISBN 978-1-5326-7145-6 (paperback) | ISBN 978-1-5326-7146-3 (hardcover) | ISBN 978-1-5326-7147-0 (ebook)

Subjects: LCSH: Ellul Jacques—1912–1994. | Technology and civilization. | Technology—Social aspects.

Classification: BR115.T42 P75 2020 (print) | BR115.T42 P75 (ebook)

Manufactured in the U.S.A.   03/10/20

For my children, Micah and Sophia, that they may grow up as digital natives confident in God's goodness and grace.

La Parole de Dieu ne peut être transformée en objet. Elle n'est jamais à la disposition de l'homme. Ou Dieu est présent, alors c'est la Parole de Dieu, ou Dieu est absent, alors il n'y a rien.

—Jacques Ellul, *La parole humiliée*

Contents

Acknowledgments

I WOULD LIKE TO express my gratitude to my supervisor, Revd Dr Andrew Goddard for his guidance, support and forbearance during this long-running research project. I am also grateful to my former colleagues within the Diocese of Guildford, for giving me financial support to study part-time.

My heartfelt thanks also go to my parents Ian and Jane Prior for their support and love, as well as to close friends who travelled with me on the journey, especially Philip Plyming and Rob Handley who both read and commented on my developing work. St John's Church in Farnborough, UK, supported a very busy vicar's husband in various ways during the writing of this work, and I'd like to thank Peter Gamston and Roger Panter especially for their eagle eyes in proofreading. During a spell of chaplaincy at Archbishop Tenison's School in Kennington from 2013 to 2014, I was reminded once again of the hard realities of city childhoods, and it would be remiss not to acknowledge the effect of that experience on shaping chapter 2.

I am of course hugely grateful to Wipf and Stock Publishers for their care and excellence in bringing this book to publication. But finally and above all I would like to express my gratitude to my beloved wife Esther for her love, prayer and deep spiritual insight as I have worked out my discipleship and my fascination with technology in conversation with Jacques Ellul.

Abbreviations and Notes on Translation

ALL BIBLE REFERENCES ARE in the NRSV. The standard abbreviations of biblical books are employed, as well as OT for Old Testament and NT for New Testament.

References to commonly cited books by Ellul within the text and footnotes refer to the volumes by means of an italicized abbreviation. The abbreviations are listed below. Full titles and details of exact editions used can be found in the bibliography.

I have cited French texts in English translation in order to enable this book to be more widely read, but all references given are to the French originals. In some cases, I agree with an accepted translation offered in a published work and simply employ that. In other cases, I offer a slightly different interpretation of my own. In still other examples, I offer my own rendering of texts which were untranslated at the time of writing (*Si*; *Théologie et Technique*) or are still untranslated (*Conférence*; *Genèse*).

French Texts

A temps	*A temps et à contretemps*
Apocalypse	*L'Apocalypse: Architecture en mouvement*
Ce que je crois.	*Ce que je crois*
Changer	*Changer de révolution: L'inéluctable prolétariat*
Conférence	*Conférence sur l'Apocalypse de Jean*
Défi	*Le défi et le nouveau: œuvres théologiques 1948–1991*, Collected works including Présence au monde moderne *(Présence), Le livre de Jonas, L'homme et l'argent, Politique de Dieu, politiques de l'homme, Contre les violents, L'impossible prière, Un chrétien pour Israël* and *Si tu es le fils de Dieu (Si).*
Éthique	*Éthique de la liberté*

Fausse	*Fausse présence au monde moderne*
Histoire	*Histoire des institutions*
Genèse	*La Genèse aujourd'hui.*
Nouveaux possédés	*Les nouveaux possédés*
Sans feu	*Sans feu ni lieu: Signification de la Grande Ville*
Subversion	*La subversion du christianisme*
Technique	*La Technique ou l'enjeu du siècle*
Théologie et Technique	*Théologie et technique: Pour une éthique de la non-puissance*
Vouloir	*Le Vouloir et le faire: Une critique théologique de la morale*

English Translations

Betrayal	*The Betrayal of the West*
Bluff	*The Technological Bluff*
City	*The Meaning of the City*
Freedom	*The Ethics of Freedom*
Hope	*Hope in Time of Abandonment*
Humiliation	*The Humiliation of the Word*
Money	*Money and Power*
Presence	*Presence in the Modern World*
Revelation	*Apocalypse: The Book of Revelation*
Sources and Trajectories	*Sources and Trajectories: Eight Early Articles That Set the Stage*

Introduction

Therefore, since it is by God's mercy that we are engaged in this
ministry, we do not lose heart. We have renounced the shameful
things that one hides; we refuse to practice cunning or to falsify
God's word; but by the open statement of the truth we commend
ourselves to the conscience of everyone in the sight of God. And
even if our gospel is veiled, it is veiled to those who are perish-
ing. In their case the god of this world has blinded the minds of
the unbelievers, to keep them from seeing the light of the gospel
of the glory of Christ, who is the image of God. For we do not
proclaim ourselves; we proclaim Jesus Christ as LORD and ourselves as your slaves for Jesus' sake. For it is the God who said,
"Let light shine out of darkness," who has shined in our hearts
to give the light of the knowledge of the glory of God in the face
of Jesus Christ. (2 Cor 4:1–6)

Why Do We Need a Theology of Technology?

THIS PROJECT BEGAN AS an enquiry into the theological meaning of technology, motivated by the experience of mission and ministry within the
contemporary church in the United Kingdom. I started with a focus on
the missional challenge of communicating the gospel in a culture where
it often seemed to exhibit a strange lack of power, in comparison with
the vast array of visibly powerful systems and devices available within a
technological society.

And yet training from 2002 to 2005, I was struck by a basic lack of
theological reflection upon the nature of technological power on the reading lists of my Theological Education Institution. Faced with this cultural
context at local church level, I thus found it all too tempting to assume that
technological power was an essentially neutral ally for an assumed task
called "mission," whether in practice that meant upgrading our church
communications hardware or maintaining attention on Sundays through

1

the latest worship software, downplaying geographical locality in favor of virtual networks or drawing funding from government sources to enhance social capital by assisting the technically inept.[1]

In the sparse Christian literature I could find, I noted a marked tendency to reimagine the Christian life using technological metaphors: connecting with God, rewiring our inner circuits, mapping the DNA of the church, even redescribing seemingly simple human activities such as talking to one another as "technologies."[2] When this literature looked up from the particular concerns of church leadership, the default position in popular treatments of so-called marketplace theology, scientific theology or social theology seemed to be the basic neutrality of technology: it is all a question of discerning the right use.[3] All this seemed quite hard to resist, although I had a nagging concern it merited further attention. I pondered hard at this point upon the Apostle Paul's words in 2 Corinthians. Might this seemingly uncritical embrace of technology run the risk of silencing the Word of God?

Times have changed, and popular Christian literature upon technology has become far more ambivalent.[4] However, often the apparent pressures of our missional context ensure that the concerns we bring are still narrowly instrumental. By way of anecdotal evidence, on explaining with a little embarrassment that my research has been concerned with a theology of technology, many ministerial colleagues have assumed I would be investigating the missional possibilities of crowd-funding, the evangelistic use of Facebook, the power of new apps for improving church administration, the potential for digital discipleship materials or whether the Vicar should take to Twitter.

That navigating this new terrain is absolutely essential for the mission of the church is a banal observation. There is no point in denying the vast potential of using new digital technologies: new opportunities for democratized access to information and learning, widened avenues for social interaction and global communication, efficient and ecologically sound working practices and last but not least, the boon this could all represent for biblical literacy and learning. Yet, as far back as 1964, the media critic and famous

---

1. These four areas were a major focus of my work in my curacy parish in 2005–2008.

2. See, e.g., Dixon, *Cyber Church*; Kelly, *Get a Grip on the Future*; Sine, *Mustard Seed vs. McWorld*.

3. See, e.g., Hood, *God's Payroll*; Strobel, *Case for a Creator*. A marked exception to the general picture I have painted here is Pullinger, *Information Technology and Cyberspace*.

4. See, e.g., Chester, *Will You Be My Facebook Friend?*; Hart, *Digital Invasion*; Lewis, *Raising Children in a Digital Age*; Brooks, *Virtually Human*; Brandon, *Digitally Remastered*.

aphorist of message and medium Marshall McLuhan put his finger on the naivety with which we commonly approach new technologies: "Our conventional response to all media, namely that it is how they are used that counts, is the numb stance of the technological idiot."[5] Granted, to some degree, the idea that technologies can "use" and change us, as much as we can direct or modify them, has recently gained currency in popular Christian writing.[6] Yet in this thesis, I have set out to go deeper, to probe what we mean by technology and how we might think differently, more theologically, about it.

I have pursued my concern by turning to the works of the late French sociologist and Reformed theologian Jacques Ellul, whose writings on technology date back to the 1930s. And here I found something interesting: not only a vivid awareness of the non-neutrality of technologies but even a sense of their radical ambivalence and moreover, the power they can come to hold over and against us. This was interesting, if a little disturbing: a focus on communication, like McLuhan, but also a wide-angled take upon fundamental questions of theological anthropology. What do we mean when we group together a diverse set of activities under the rubric of "modern technology"? And what particular questions do such activities pose us about what it means to be human now? To live, to love, to speak, to listen, to work, and to worship?

In this introduction, I will begin by considering briefly how Ellul's work contrasts sharply with two popular contemporary theological approaches to technology. This opening discussion will anticipate my substantial engagement with Ellul's polemical approach towards common theological accounts of technology in the chapters to come. However, before proceeding to that engagement, I will conclude this introduction with a brief overview of Ellul's biography. Although my concern here is with Ellul's texts, rather than with his life, any engagement with him needs to foreground how his life and thought are interwoven.

In the following opening chapter, I will unfurl my methodology in two senses. Firstly, I will set out there my reading of Ellul in dialogue with other readers of Ellul, including Ellul himself, his first reader, so to speak. Secondly, in so doing, I will outline the presuppositions behind the progression of my argument in the chapters to come. That is to say, the purpose of my first chapter is not merely to outline Ellul's methodological statements or to engage with important secondary literature upon Ellul,

---

5. Nicolas Car begins his well-researched recent Pulitzer Prize finalist on the Internet and neuro-plasticity by citing McLuhan. See Carr, *Shallows*, 4.

6. Many are aware of this at the obvious level, e.g., that the use of a mobile smart phone imposes forms of communication and that social media impose certain models of self-disclosure, e.g., Reinke, *12 Ways Your Phone Is Changing You*.

but to discover in his life's work an "apocalyptic theology of revolution"[7] for Christians living in technological societies.

In four cumulative chapters, I will then sympathetically explore and probe this theology before concluding, in a more critical vein, by assessing what concrete ethical resources Ellul offers for Christian ethical discernment in a technological society. This is a necessarily brief outline, and it will, I hope, become clearer as we go how my argument progresses.

Let us now turn briefly to survey two common paradigms within theological literature on technology: on the one hand, the creational paradigm of the cultural mandate and on the other, the eschatological paradigm of progress.

Technology and the Cultural Mandate

At its simplest, technology, according to the theology of cultural mandate is, in Freeman Dyson's words, "the gift of God. After the gift of life itself, it is perhaps the greatest of God's gifts. It is the mother of civilizations, of arts and sciences."[8] It is no doubt incontrovertible that "a world with penicillin and light bulbs is better than a world without, all things considered."[9] And what are these innovations, if not expressions of divine gift?

Founded in a reading of the early chapters of Genesis, the language of the cultural mandate has its Protestant roots in the Reformation, although it receives paradigmatic treatment in the social theology of the Dutch Reformed theologian Abraham Kuyper.[10] Indeed, in a recent work of Kuyperian urban missiology, *Why Cities Matter*, Jason Buzzard and Stephen Um argue from creation that God's original design is for urban, technological development:

> Because the Bible's first reference to a city is a city built by
> Cain the fugitive (Gen 4:17), we tend to think that cities are an

7. The phrase belongs to Fasching, *Thought of Jacques Ellul*, 116. See chapter 1, "A Faithful Betrayal."

8. Dyson, *Infinite in All Directions*, 270.

9. Brian Brock begins his account of Christian theology's capitulation to the icon of modern technology with this important affirmation in Brock, *Christian Ethics in a Technological Age*, 2.

10. I am of course aware of the vast tracts of natural theology in the Roman Catholic tradition, rooted in Thomas Aquinas. I will at points engage with it, most obviously because Ellul's work dialogues with it endlessly. However, I have sought here to clarify the paradigms I am responding to in this research. For an interesting harmonization of Catholic and Protestant perspectives on the "cultural mandate," see CAFOD et al., *Wholly Living*.

unfortunate product of the fall. This assumption is the result of
a misreading of the Bible's story line. The Bible teaches that the
city is God's idea, invention, and intention. . . . In essence, God
called upon humanity to continue doing what God himself had
been doing—to create. God gave man and woman the Cultural
Mandate—a calling to be fruitful, to multiply, to fill the earth,
and to cultivate and develop the garden. This mandate was ultimately an urban mandate, a call to create settlements where
people could live and work together to be fruitful, to multiply,
to develop, to cultivate, and to flourish.[11]

For the biblical city, they argue, in a move Jacques Ellul would certainly agree with, read "technology." The Reformation's validation of the
"secular city" from the Bible quite simply made the modern Western
political, economic and technological order we take for granted. "The
reaffirmation of the priesthood of all believers, along with the validation
of secular vocation, created a new ethic for urban life—one that would
help pave the way for urban advancements in technology, production, and
social life for future centuries."[12]

Although the good faith of the authors is not to be doubted, it is not
difficult to understand why such a theology of cultural mandate holds evident promise for churches emerging in Silicon Valley and in the shadow of
the Massachusetts Institute of Technology. And they are quite candid in their
concern to offer a theology which resonates with the realities of an urbanizing
world. The point is this: Christians need to be city and technology-positive
if they are to have any global impact today.[13] "As engines, cities take the collective talents, skills, and creativity of their citizens and translate them into
world-driving technology, industry, and cultural development."[14]

On this reading, to question technology runs the risk of both dualism and escapism, refusing a gift in creation and refusing to step up to
the gospel challenge of our generation. This is not to say that a Reformed
theology of cultural mandate is light on sin. However, it is concerned to
safeguard the goodness of creation and culture by pointing up instead
our *sinful misuse* of God's gifts. Tim Keller, an effective exponent of this

11. Um and Buzzard, *Why Cities Matter*, 19.

12. Um and Buzzard, *Why Cities Matter*, 26.

13. "Cities no longer shape just their surrounding regions—they now shape the
whole world. This new world presents Christians and the church with an unprecedented
opportunity to bring the gospel of Jesus Christ into every dimension of human life. God
is doing something new and big in our cities, and he's calling some of us to participate
in it" (Um and Buzzard, *Why Cities Matter*, 18).

14. Um and Buzzard, *Why Cities Matter*, 45.

tradition and an influence on *Why Cities Matter*, cites Kuyperian theologian Al Wolters with approval:

> The great danger is to single out any one aspect . . . of God's good creation and identify it, rather than the alien intrusion of sin, as the great villain in the drama of human life. This "something" has been variously identified as the body and its passions . . . culture in distinction from nature . . . institutional authority, especially in the state and the family . . . technology and management techniques (Heidegger and Ellul).[15]

In identifying Ellul in this way, Keller and many readers of Ellul assume that he tilts towards an unhelpful technophobia.[16] Yet Ellul himself claims that to call him a "technophobe" is categorically false: "Whatever the impression given . . . I have never written anywhere that Technique and its products are bad and that we should go without them."[17] In this thesis I shall argue that Ellul rightly rejects this charge against him. For Ellul, technology simply *is*. It is neither good nor bad but nor is it neutral. Moreover, it is important to note that technology was not his only topic: politics, revolution, language, money, sex, violence, Islam, the state of Israel, modern art, to name a few subjects, all come in for Ellulian treatment. However, he himself concedes, with his customary irony, that he may appear to be a "monomaniac"[18] insofar as the centerpiece of his analysis—no matter what the topic—is almost invariably what he calls Technique.

Though off-putting to some, it is this constant attention to technology that drew me to Ellul, and hence what most concerns us here is Ellul's writing on Technique. And what one finds on even a cursory reading is Ellul's direct challenge to the idea that we approach technology first of all as a good gift of God in creation, to be freely used. This is not to say that he considers technology to be intrinsically bad, or beyond redemption, although we will

15. Keller, *Counterfeit Gods*, 100, citing Wolters. There are striking similarities and differences between Ellul and the work of Martin Heidegger, perhaps the best-known philosopher of technology of the twentieth century. Heidegger published *The Question Concerning Technology* in 1954, the same year as Ellul's *Technique ou l'enjeu du siècle*. For a brief account of the relationship between Ellul and Heidegger, see Porquet, *Jacques Ellul*, 257–60.

16. The American "futurist" Alvin Toffler accused Ellul of being one of the most extreme of "a generation of future haters and technophobes" (Toffler in Greenman et al., *Understanding Jacques Ellul*, 21).

17. *Ethique*, 219, citing Rom 4:14; 1 Tim 4:4–5; Titus 1:15. Note also the preface to *Bluff*: "The first false conclusion is that of opposition to Technique. That is just as absurd as opposition to an avalanche or to cancer. It is childish to say that someone is against Technique" (*Bluff*, viii).

18. *Parole*, 164.

address below why this charge has been laid against him.[19] However, in stark terms, Ellul's starting point for understanding technology is not creation but fall, not Genesis 1 and 2 but rather Genesis 3 and 4. As my argument develops, I hope it will become clear that this opens it up to the gospel far more can than an unnuanced theology of cultural mandate.

As Ellul argues throughout his work, and as we shall explore, the argument from creation is often blind to its own legitimation of power structures which appear God-given but are in fact the necessary expressions of fallen culture.[20] And the argument that sin is the basic foe can tend, if not carefully nuanced, to produce abstract, individualized accounts of sin. Ellul's concern is thus with the concrete expressions of sinfulness in human culture rather than sin as an essentially spiritual condition.[21] Such structures, though "necessary," are never neutral, and therefore technology, as one of such structures, is no value-free gift placed in our hands, but rather a power that all too easily lays its hands on us. And in our day perhaps more than ever, it comes to us offering vast and ready power, an illusion we fallen human beings are particularly prone to.[22]

We have begun to trespass here upon the topic of eschatology, so let us now turn briefly to a second approach to technology, viewing it not from the beginning but from the end, not in terms of creation, but in terms of the Spirit's work of redemption.

Technology and Eschatology

Much Anglican theological reflection in the aftermath of the millennium was taken up with the theme of the *Missio Dei*. This was a time when the church was enjoined to "catch up" or join in with what God's Spirit is already doing, whether in the church or in the world.[23] More theological than the mere

---

19. See chapter 5 on creation below.

20. See, as a typical example, the introduction to *Ethique*, where Ellul outlines this concept of necessity.

21. Goddard, *Living the Word*, 72–86. This is what I will begin to explore in more detail in chapter 2.

22. As Archbishop Justin Welby's recent book, *Dethroning Mammon*, demonstrates, Christian theology has always been willing to see money as radically ambivalent without claiming that it is thereby wholly evil and beyond redemption.

23. "The Church takes its missionary form through receiving the gifts of the past and the future. At a time of substantial change, the Church of England needs to learn to be more an anticipation of God's future than a society for the preservation of the past" (Church of England and House of Bishops, *Mission-Shaped Church*, 90).

pragmatism of "keeping the message but changing the medium"[24] but more radical than the cultural mandate, such accounts are rooted in a history of viewing technology through the lens of eschatology and pneumatology:

> The missionaries of the Holy Spirit include the probation officer and the literacy worker, the research chemist and the . . . teacher, the psychiatrist and the designer, the famine-relief worker and the computer operator, the pastor and the astronaut . . . this surging diversity of creative *and redemptive* activity.[25]

This association of technology with redemption is of course centuries-old,[26] although it has become particularly marked in more recent theological accounts of technology as progress. For reconstruing technology through the lens of redemption leaves open the possibility that we might discern in particular technologies an unfolding revelation.

We are far here from the naivety of assuming that technology is neutral; the note of discernment is key. On this account, as we see in the work of one early writer on emerging church, Gerard Kelly, technology is a multivalent site of meaning, perhaps the most significant site for the mission of the church faced with "post-Christian spirituality."[27] For the most part, Kelly treads a fine line between critique and appreciation. Citing David Lochhead, he argues that the task of mission is locating "Pentecost in the cacophony":

> In a world of multiple voices, the Christian response of witness is one of pointing to and naming the signs of the Spirit in the multitude of voices. It is a task of discerning the Spirit, of locating Pentecost in the cacophony.[28]

However, despite his call for discernment, he ends up with a scarcely nuanced instruction to "embrace technology," on the grounds that in a postmodern world, technology has lost the allure of progress: "it has no such power, and is associated, rather, with play." Drawing on Mike Riddell and making much of the themes of personalization and decentralization in postmodernity, he argues:

24. Davison unfairly argues that *Mission-Shaped Church* amounted to little more than this banality. See Davison and Milbank, *For the Parish*.

25. Taylor, *Go-between God*, 38 (my italics). Yet Taylor dwells upon the possible downsides of the technological society, calling for a process of testing the spirits (55).

26. Hedley Brooke's "Detracting from Divine Power?," in Deane-Drummond, *Re-ordering Nature*, 43–64, traces the justification of technology to the early modern period, resulting in part from a contemporary desire to collaborate with God "to work for the restoration of a blighted world."

27. Kelly, *Get a Grip on the Future*, chapter 12.

28. Kelly, *Get a Grip on the Future*, 125.

> Postmodernists are the children of technology. They embrace it
> for the enhancements it can bring to life . . . and especially for its
> ability to increase the scope of play. There is no longer any ex-
> pectation that technology is somehow going to solve existential
> angst, but it may well provide better ways of escaping from it.[29]

For Kelly, technology is both redeemed and redemptive when viewed as essentially social, an agent of life enhancement and play. In the most ide-alistic accounts of the possible impact of technologies on human flourish-ing, technological development might make possible the emergence of a new humanity, the melding of the human spirit with technology.[30] For more measured, pragmatic accounts, genetic technologies, rightly used, might open a new path to reordering a fallen nature.[31]

Technology, viewed through the lens of pneumatology, is no longer a great "world-driving" power, a "megamachine"[32] that must arouse suspicion but merely something ordinary with the potential to humanize all our lives. When viewed in this light, the word "technology" itself must be detached from an oppressive meta-narrative and redeployed to deconstruct and lib-erate us from modernity. Much space would be required to fully outline, let alone critique what one might call the postmodernist position, for what is at stake here is nothing less than the central claims of this thesis: that technology is still best understood in terms of power, and that Ellul's con-cept of Technique (of which more below) is an important contribution to a contemporary theological account of technology.

---

29. Kelly, *Get a Grip on the Future*, 152. Although these citations are drawn from a now dated text, the point is that Kelly was one of the first to blaze a trail that very many have followed. For a recent call to the church to "embrace technology," in the guise of hyperconnectivity and the melding of online and offline worlds, see the provocative paper by Windle, *Eight Innovations to Leading Millennials*.

30. Erik Davis, an early writer on the spirituality of technology, presents American "techno-eschatology" in terms of Joachim of Fiore's "Age of the Spirit." See Davis, *Tech-Gnosis*. For a similar account of American techno-utopia, see the BBC documentary series, *All Watched Over by Machines of Loving Grace*, written by Adam Curtis.

31. The editors of a recent book on *Re-ordering Nature* provide an example of such a move, arguing for an eschatological "Christianity of the evening," leading to an "un-settled, nomadic ethics": "We want to suggest that the rise of uncertainty points us towards a Christianity of the evening, one which can only point imperfectly to the eschatological daybreak. The time in which we live, suspended between the incarnation and the eschaton is one that can only press forward in anticipation rather than rest sab-batically in its own self-completion" (Deane-Drummond, *Re-ordering Nature*, 318). In this vein, they see the technological revolution, especially in the science of genetics, as "as a revelation" of a kind, revealing in new ways the Christian ethic of the "precedence of love over law."

32. See Mumford, *Myth of the Machine*.

In defending the prescience and present value of attending to Ellul, Greg Wagenfuhr has recently argued, drawing on Ellul, that the very idea of post-modernity is itself a "phenomenal mistake."[33] Arguing that the Christian celebration of postmodernity is little more than fancy but ultimately dishonest intellectual footwork, he contends that late modernity is not so much a disruption of modernity as its highest form, the apogee of technological power. And rather than dethroning naked technological progress, the language of the postmodern re-clothes it in "the garments of little narratives" such as sustainability, democratization, human rights, and freedoms of expression and identity. The much vaunted uncertainties, diversities and liberties of our globalizing world, whether by accident or design, conceal

> the growing global uniformity necessitated by the laws of technique. . . . National, religious, racial, and gender identities are becoming increasingly superficial insofar as a person of any background, creed, or gender can operate a computer with equivalent performance.[34]

As Wagenfhur and many other keen Ellulians have noticed, we find in Ellul an alternative phenomenology and meta-narrative about Technique. It goes something like this: whereas throughout human history one can observe "une opération technique" which has had its place within an array of factors affecting civilization, today, Ellul claims that we now live in a "milieu technicien" where technique has become an integrated, total, and potentially totalistic, system.[35] In a careful survey of Ellul's key phrase "no common measure" ("aucune commune mesure" or similar) to describe the relationship between past and present, Goddard argues that Ellul thereby contends that modern Technique does not merely repeat the past, but constitutes a new environment, the very condition of modern life. Ellul summarizes his case in a late testimonial book, *Ce que je crois*, which establishes a chronology of three milieux, "le milieu naturel," "le milieu social," and "le milieu technician."[36] For

33. Greg Wagenfuhr explores this concept in "Postmodernity, the Phenomenal Mistake: Sacred, Myth, Environment," in Jeronimo, *Jacques Ellul*, 229–42. He is of course playing on words, implying it is a colossal misdiagnosis of a societal phenomenon. Wagenfuhr interestingly also contends that in Western societies, religious commitment has been relegated to the status of play. On Ellul, revolution, and post-modernity, see chapter 2 in Tomlin, *Provocative Church*.

34. Wagenfuhr in Jeronimo, *Jacques Ellul*, 238.

35. Goddard, *Living the Word*, 136. Critics of Ellul's sociology often attack this notion of a novel "technical milieu," as it is axiomatic to Ellul's sociology.

36. See *Ce que je crois*, part 2. Ellul develops this historical metanarrative of three periods: the pre-historical (where human embedding in a natural milieu predominates), the historical (where human embedding in a social milieu predominates), and

Ellul, "The crisis of modernity is seen to be of much greater significance than that of any previous historical crisis. It is not a political or economic crisis but a crisis resulting from a change of milieu."[37]

For Ellul, we live in an unprecedented "technical civilization," incommensurate with the past, but technical progress is not in itself a sign of God's in-breaking rule in the age of the Spirit. As many readers have noted and as we shall explore, Ellul operates with an apocalyptic framework. "Ellul's eschatology is directed by an apocalyptic narrative where God's kingdom breaks into a world enslaved by its own technological creations."[38] That is to say, if we are to think of technology in terms of power, we must think of it in terms of principalities and powers, in terms of what I will call an apocalyptic exousiology.[39] And this is no mere intellectual exercise but a discernment of the spirits, vital to the mission of the church.[40]

Given the vast scope of this polemic, which it will take the whole course of this thesis to unpack, let us briefly turn now to introduce Jacques Ellul.

Who Was Jacques Ellul?

There is little space here to rehearse Ellul's biography, to see how in Goddard's words, "Ellul's life and his thought are intricately interwoven. He wrote out of what he lived and he lived out what he wrote."[41] Although it is extremely important that Ellul's life and work are closely intertwined, Goddard's excellent biographical study, building upon other accounts, has ably

the post-historical (where the human embedding in a technological milieu predominates). Techniques play a role in these first two periods: in the first, paradigmatically, in the making of tools; in the second, paradigmatically, in the building of towns. Indeed, elsewhere, Ellul describes the "technical operation" as a constant in human history, the mundane process by which we use methods to achieve ends, that is, the process by which we seek utility. However, the transition from the first to the second is marked by an increasing complexity in human artifice. And yet it is only in the third period that technique becomes the dominant factor, a period he describes as marked by the rise of the "technical phenomenon."

37. Goddard, *Living the Word*, 146.

38. Burdett, *Eschatology and the Technological Future*, 113. See his chapter 6 on Ellul.

39. I will briefly outline my understanding of the genre of "apocalyptic" below (66–69). Scott Prather defines the rarer term, exousiology, as a "shorthand for a Christian theology of the powers," noting that the phrase was apparently first coined by Yoder in relation to the Pauline theology of the *exousiai* in Ephesians 6 (Prather, *Christ, Power and Mammon*, 4n15).

40. 1 John 4. See chapter 6 below on this theme.

41. Goddard, *Living the Word*, 2.

demonstrated this already. However, some brief biographical background will set the scene for what follows.

Growing up in poverty and having to support his family for a number of years, Ellul was academically bright and sought a career in the history of law, obtaining his doctorate in Roman law in 1936 before taking up a teaching post at the University of Strasbourg. Ellul's early life experience had led him to interrogate the reasons for poverty and deprivation and it was by reading Karl Marx that he had come to understand the world. He would indeed for many years combine teaching Roman law with expounding Marx's thought.

Ellul's early interest was nourished within a movement known as French Personalism, which began in the years between the world wars, seeking to protect and restore the importance of personhood over and against the perceived threats posed to it by power structures, whether political, economic or cultural.[42] Through the influence of a fellow Bordeaux Personalist, Bernard Charbonneau, Ellul did not simply accept Marx's work wholesale but adapted it, with Technique crucially taking the place of Capital.[43] We will consider how this critique developed in the next chapter, but a brief summary will offer some helpful context here.

For Ellul, Marx had argued that the division of labor required by capitalism led to the alienation of workers from their labor, leading to a radical disempowerment. However, starting from this point, Ellul contended that in the late twentieth century, what now alienates is not solely exploitation of workers by the power of Capital, but the power of a technical system controlled by fewer and fewer expert hands. Moreover, Technique operates not only as a system but as an ideology which attempts to fascinate and console all the while it escalates the powerlessness of the mass of people: in Ellul's polemical phrase, it almost universalizes the experience of the Proletariat, while sweetening it with the opium of technology. "The proletarian of the technological society is a rootless person, dispossessed of himself, hypnotized by technique, and all in all satisfied with his lot."[44]

We will allow this brief and inadequate summary to stand for now, as we will explore the influence of Marx upon the method and content of Ellul's thought in the first chapter. What is important to note at this point is that while variously disagreeing with Marx, Ellul does not set out to refute

---

42. Goddard, *Living the Word*, 21–30. For more on the influence of personalism on Ellul's reading of the Bible, see chapter 2 below.

43. See also chapter 1 in Porquet, *Jacques Ellul*.

44. Ellul in Rognon, *Pensée*, 60.

his work but actually proclaims it as "prophetic" by drawing us to the biblical roots of Marx's call for freedom from slavery and alienation.[45]

The genesis of this *theological* engagement with Marx lies in Ellul's dramatic conversion to Christ in 1930, largely in isolation from the church.[46] Ellul's Christian thinking was shaped in his early years by encountering the Bible as the living word of God, under the influence of the theology of first John Calvin, then Søren Kierkegaard and finally, Karl Barth, to whom Ellul was introduced by another important early mentor, the French Reformed theologian Jean Bosc.[47] Dismissed from his teaching post by the Vichy regime on account of his political activities in 1940, Ellul spent four years farming a small holding in a rural area to the east of his native Bordeaux, during which time he was active in the French resistance. It was also during this time, as early as 1943, he suggests, that he conceived of an academic project to interrogate the impact of technology in the modern world from both a biblical and sociological perspective. Rather than offering a synthesis, Ellul resolved to hold them in tension by writing separate works of sociology and theology, in dialogue with one another.

For instance, on the inside cover of the French editions of Ellul's book, his works are listed in separate categories, sociological and theological, reflecting the almost holy demarcation between Ellul's work as a social historian in the Marxian tradition on the one hand, and his work as a Christian theologian influenced by Karl Barth on the other.[48] The term "dialectic" immediately points us in a philosophical direction. Indeed, Ellul had much to say about his dialectic of theology and sociology, and no treatment of Ellul can proceed without attending to it. Yet by way of approach, we must first attend to key questions of definition: what is Technique and what is technology in Ellul's writing?

Technique and Technology

The perceptive reader will have noticed already that I have slipped between these two words. Let me thus be clear. I work from the position, shared by many readers of Ellul, that although "technology" is one possible rendering of

45. See especially the opening chapter of *Ethique*. For a fuller summary of Ellul's reapplication of Marx, see Rognon, *Pensée*, 225.

46. Goddard, *Living the Word*, 9.

47. Ellul declares many times that his early enthusiasm for Calvin soon waned. Whilst he never lost respect for Calvin's achievements, Ellul marks his distance from Calvinism as a system (*A temps*, 72).

48. There is no categorical pairing of works, but perhaps the linkages suggested by Rognon (*Pensée*, 22–23) are most appropriate.

the French word "technique," Ellul increasingly comes to use "technique" in a reified sense as if it were a force, a power in history. Indeed, this reification suggests that Ellul imputes to Technique an autonomous agency, which justifies the capitalization of the term I shall follow henceforth. Let me explain.

In his seminal 1954 work, *La Technique ou l'enjeu du siècle*, Ellul offers a definition of Technique, or more exactly, what he calls a "characterology" of Technique. Firstly, Ellul argues that Technique is *artificial*, based upon the *rational* reordering and improvement of nature. Yet, Ellul wishes to push his analysis further than these two commonplaces. He proposes that modern Technique should first be understood as an *automatic* process, since efficiency imposes itself, meaning that Technique is now *self-augmenting*, following a technical rationality that is not consciously chosen.[49] It therefore becomes *monistic*, demanding and therefore creating the total integration of a range of technical processes, and finally, and inevitably *universalistic*, since Technique does not respect local boundaries but seeks to integrate everything within a universal system. Technique thus defined is *autonomous*, a law unto itself.

In the second of his so-called "technological trilogy," the fiendishly complex book *Le Système technicien* (1977), Ellul claims that these seven characteristics are the key features also of "informatique," or information technologies. At this stage, he claims, these new technologies have not fundamentally changed the game, for it is "an unwarranted assumption that everything would shrink because certain devices are now so tiny."[50] In the final "upgrade" *Le Bluff Technologique* (1988), at the end of a theological trajectory that takes in the earliest information technologies, Ellul finds his early analyses substantiated and even superseded by the degree to which the "technical system" has become unchallengeable by its increasing control of our language and our culture.

Indeed, for Ellul, a stickler for etymology, the growing tendency to speak of "technology" signifies the admixture of Technique and the word, and hence serves to justify the "technological system" as a new, and essentially mathematical, way of naming and therefore running the world.[51]

49. Ellul here anticipates "Moore's law," named after Intel co-founder Gordon Moore, who noticed that the number of transistors per square inch on integrated circuits had doubled every year since their invention.

50. *System*, 2.

51. The English translator of *Bluff* (interestingly the theological translator, Geoffrey Bromiley) notes that the nuance is easily lost in English. "Established usage in English makes it difficult to retain the distinction that Ellul himself always makes and emphasizes between la technique (technique) and la technologie, (technology). It should be remembered . . . that in the title Ellul has the stricter sense [of technologie] in view, that is, technology as discourse, study, or system" (*Bluff*, ix).

Technique has taken over our minds and our imaginations to the degree
that we all too easily accept Technique's unintended consequences while
overvaluing the goods produced. In their recent primer, *Introducing Jacques
Ellul*, which seeks to give renewed currency to Ellul's technology criticism,
Greenman, Schuchardt and Toly accurately summarize what is at stake in
Ellul's concept of technical autonomy:

> The erosion of reasoned human judgment and choice is central
> to Ellul's concern, and the result is a loss of a basic human free-
> dom by the imposition of a social convention. . . . Technique
> identifies and valorizes the single most efficient way to do
> anything.[52]

In the original French text of *Technique*, Ellul cites programmatically
the American mechanical engineer and technological apologist Frederick
Winslow Taylor, pioneer of the production-line method of "scientific management" (named Taylorism). "'The one best way,' that's exactly what our
technique today corresponds to. . . . There is strictly speaking no choice
when it comes to which is greater: three or four. Four is greater than three.
. . . The decision as to technique today is of the same order. There is no
choice between two technical methods: one is inevitable because the results
have been counted and measured, are visible and indisputable."[53]

By retaining in English the pithy descriptor "the one best way" and
elaborating on its meaning in the English edition,[54] Ellul meant also to al-
lude to the significance of America in driving Technique, an allusion which
in part accounts for Ellul's continuing popularity and relevance there today. Most of all, Ellul draws our attention less to artifacts and more to a
mathematical mindset which becomes almost unstoppable as it is applied
to every area of life.[55] In this way, to risk a technological metaphor, one

52. Greenman et al., *Understanding Jacques Ellul*, 25. In this generally excellent
book, there is an example of the confusion of reading Ellul only in English translation:
"The third chapter of *The Presence of the Kingdom*, 'The End and the Means,' expands
on [Ellul's] critique of modern civilization, especially what he calls 'technics'—which he
would later describe more elaborately as 'Technique' in a series of major books" (18). Of
course, Ellul uses the single French word "technique" in all his works, but what changes
(as the authors note) is Ellul's concern for technical autonomy.

53. *Technique*, 74.

54. In the foreword to the 1965 American edition of *Technique*, Ellul offers this
definition: "The term Technique, as I use it, does not mean machines . . . or this or that
procedure for attaining an end. In our technological society, technique is the totality of
methods rationally arrived at and having absolute efficiency (for a given stage of human
development) in every field of human activity" (*Technological Society*, xxv).

55. See Brock's treatment of Canadian philosopher (and Ellul enthusiast) George
Grant's concept of mathematecized reason, in *Technological Age*, 75.

might suggest that Technique is as much concerned with our own internal psychological "software" as with external "hardware" or tools.[56] As we have already noted, Ellul insists that modern Technique is incommensurate with past techniques, and therefore it is not simply a set of powerful tools that we decide to manipulate and use as we wish; it has become a power into which we plug ourselves, thereby enabling ourselves to be used.[57] The autonomy of Technique thus signifies its *reification* as an active power, and through that process we lose the freedom to control it. For Ellul, we become alienated, possessed by forces beyond us.[58]

Hearing the Word in an Age of Technique: Ellul's "Dialectic of Sociology and Theology"

At no point in Ellul's sociological writings do we get the impression that human reason can, alone and unaided, control Technique. We need to look to Ellul's theology if we want to see where that power might come from. There is an abundance of primary and secondary material concerning Ellul's "dialectic of theology and sociology," and this will be at issue in my first chapter.[59] Yet in a pregnant and programmatic comment which frames all that follows in this thesis, Ellul himself establishes a basic contrast between Technique and the divine Word:

> Technique seemed terribly dangerous to Charbonneau be-
> cause it called into question the natural world and humanity's

---

56. Erik Davis agrees with Ellul, though without passing judgment: "The popular New Age image of sacred technologies suggests that Ellul was right, and that the empirical and instrumentalist logic of technique has colonized the human spirit" (Davis, *TechGnosis*, 156).

57. Greenman et al. rightly draw attention to Ellul's summary concern in *Technique* (chapter 5) with what he calls "techniques de l'homme." Human techniques aim to accommodate humans to a technological society (*Understanding Jacques Ellul*, 22).

58. *Technique*, 95. In an interesting turn of phrase, the Jewish historian Yuval Harari suggests that in a digital age, "people just want to be part of the data flow, even if that means giving up their privacy, their autonomy and their individuality . . . when you are part of the data flow you are part of something much bigger than yourself" (Harari, *Homo Deus*, 449).

59. In my account of Ellul's dialectic, I focus on two key self-reflexive texts: *A temps et à contretemps*, a series of interviews with journalist Madeleine Garrigou-Lagrange, published in 1981 (in English translation as *In Season and Out of Season*), and Ellul's late testimonial book, *Ce que je crois* (1987, and subsequently published in an influential English translation, *What I Believe*, 1989).

relationship with nature. *It was for me insofar as it called into question our human ability to hear the word of God.*[60]

What is striking here, moreover, is how Ellul situates himself vis-à-vis his friend, the agnostic Personalist intellectual Bernard Charbonneau. A pioneer of ecological awareness in France, Charbonneau was primarily concerned with the changing relationship between humanity and nature.[61] Ellul agreed on the significance of Technique and while he shared Charbonneau's concern with ecological crisis, the primary mode of Ellul's concern was theological: with the relationship between speaking creatures and a speaking Creator. These two modes of concern are of course closely related. The philosophical theologian Peter Scott is one of the few British theologians in recent years to interrogate technology, primarily within the framework of ecological theology: "An example of the close relation between the separation of nature, humanity and God and the privatization of belief is technology. At first this seems unlikely: what has technology to do with God? Yet that is precisely part of the point: technology provides and supports a view of the world which makes God redundant."[62]

Scott clarifies rather starkly the broad question of the theological significance of technology that has engaged me in the works of Ellul. At root, from the beginning to the end, Ellul believed that Technique had overwhelmed our attention to God. The purported erosion of belief in the gospel facilitated by technology is also apprehended in the work of David Wells: "While [technology] has greatly enhanced many of our capabilities . . . it also brings with it an inevitable naturalism and an ethic that equates what is efficient with what is good. Technology per se does not assault the gospel but a technological society will find the gospel irrelevant."[63]

Starting from a similar apprehension, Ellul envisaged a principled separation of theology and sociology, precisely in order to enable their confrontation, to overcome their isolation one from another. The point was to make the gospel relevant to a technological society:

> There could not be two separate registers . . . a kind of relationship had to be possible. But what kind? I thought there might be a dialectical mode of relationship. Not that to a problem posed in sociological terms there is a Christian answer, but rather

60. *A temps,* 128 (my italics).

61. Charbonneau's contribution has been charted in detail in the work of Christian Roy and, most recently, Sebastien Morrillon. See Chastenet, *Comment Peut-on (encore) être,* 227–49, 286–306.

62. Scott, *Political Theology of Nature,* 14.

63. Wells in Dawn, *Reaching Out,* 10.

there is a dialectical counterpoint. . . . The study of Technique
was one of the main directions of my work, the other concerned
the insights the Bible offers and the way in which we can live
humanly in this context.[64]

These two areas of study were distinct, but this was a principled distinction for the purpose of dialectical confrontation. For this reason, simply
stated, I will be developing here a reading of Ellul which seeks to privilege
his theology in an attempt to interrogate technology today. In Ellul's mind,
and as we shall explore in chapter 1, his sociology could not stand alone
and it risked being dangerously misunderstood in isolation. Therefore, in
order to acknowledge Ellul's considerable contribution to thinking about
technology and the mission of the church, I argue in what follows that we
need not be too concerned with expounding and extrapolating from the
characterology outlined in *The Technological Society*, crisply summarized
above. Indeed it is all too easy for the contemporary reader to get bogged
down in the sheer density and ambitiousness of Ellul's analyses there.[65]
What is perhaps of most value for us today is what underlies these analyses,
the meticulous attention he gives to his social context.

In an era known in France as "the thirty glorious years" of sustained
economic growth following the end of the Second World War, Ellul paid
for his technology criticism with relative obscurity. It has only been in
the past few decades that many have recognized in Ellul a method for
understanding better the ambivalence of technologies and their role in
manufacturing contemporary problems: "Organized crime, social disloca-
tion, unemployment, globalization, international inequality and poverty,
divorce, abortion, the environment," as Goddard noted in 2002.[66] The fact
that this list seems so outdated is a reflection of the exponential technological growth of the past fifteen years, which has turned the attention of
Ellul scholarship towards the erosion of personal freedom in a culture of
digital surveillance,[67] the erection of global digital divides, the devoicing

64. *A temps*, 68.

65. Perhaps Ellul's clearest example is his argument that the medieval introduction
of the measurement of time by the clock submitted human life to abstraction and quan-
tification, an echo of Heidegger's concern with mathematical rationality (*Technique*,
328–30). See Greenman et al., *Understanding Jacques Ellul*, 31–34, who offer the case
study of the automobile; Van Vleet, *Dialectical Theology and Jacques Ellul*, 89–97, citing
the example of Wal-Mart; Goddard, *Living the Word*, 142–45.

66. Goddard suggests that these classical ethical problems are for Ellul "mere epi-
phenomena of Technique" (*Living the Word*, 316).

67. See Lyon, *Electronic Eye*, for a seminal treatment of surveillance explicitly
rooted in Ellul.

of society and the decline of conversation,[68] and the challenges of "multiple partial attention" and "internet addiction," especially in the field of education. In the near distance loom questions about the ethical questions raised by rapid advances in artificial intelligence, as well as the discourses of post-humanism, its exponents and their motives.[69]

It is perhaps then no surprise that the past few years have seen a rise in interest in engaging and applying Ellul's thought. The year 2012 marked the one hundredth anniversary of his birth, and either side of it a number of conferences and colloquia were convened.[70] With the centenary marked by the reprinting of many of Ellul's texts in French, after decades on the margins, Ellul's voice is being heard again in France, perhaps most forcefully among radical ecological groups but also in academic theology. From an American perspective, David Gill attests to a particular concern with Ellul's dialectic of sociology and theology, taken forward by the *International Jacques Ellul Society*.[71]

The number of books published on Ellul in the past five years has far outstripped those produced in the previous ten years, all seeking to explore and expand his critique.[72] It has, in this regard, been a good time to be reading Ellul in the company of others. However, whereas much English-language Ellul scholarship works from translations, I have tried as much as possible to work from original French texts as well as rarer and unexplored parts of the corpus which have not yet been translated. Moreover, I make a particular effort to draw on the insights of French-language Ellul scholarship, especially the breakthrough work of Frédéric Rognon.[73] While there are already good relationships between Ellul's interpreters across the world,

68. E.g., Turkle, *Alone Together*.

69. The late James Martin, a well-known technological apologist, founded and funded his own institute, the Oxford Martin School, at the University of Oxford. In *The Meaning of the Twenty-First Century*, Martin offers a seemingly uncritical celebration of the prospects of "trans-humanism" offered by genetic modification, a "nanodeluge," and "automated evolution" (see part 2, "Technologies of Sorcery," 149–221).

70. Ellul's legacy is the central concern of *Générations Ellul*, released for the Bordeaux centenary conference. Rognon charts the ebb and flow of his influence through a series of profiles of and interviews with "Ellulians."

71. See the interview with Gill in Rognon, *Générations Ellul*, 153–59. Wipf & Stock Publishers has also undertaken to republish many of Ellul's better known texts in a recent series.

72. Recent texts of note have been cited above. See also Dunham, *Jesus and the City*.

73. The definite sociological interpreter, Patrick Chastenet; a leading theological voice, Antoine Nouis; and even the polemical journalist, Jean-Luc Porquet, have all made important contributions to shaping my reading.

I have in this task attempted to offer a number of insights into the significance of interpreting Ellul in French.[74]

In all this, of course, I owe a deep debt of gratitude to the original faith and insight of Jacques Ellul. However, I do not seek to follow Ellul slavishly but to suggest a "faithful betrayal,"[75] to offer theological perspectives on technology through Ellul but moving markedly beyond his work at points. Indeed, given the theological concern and training I bring to this enterprise, while I display an awareness of other sociological writings on technology, my primary focus is on the theological frameworks for understanding technology Ellul provides, and how we might nuance and develop them today.[76]

Here I argue that Ellul offers a theology of Technique, contrasting the work of our hands with the Word of God. As he would put it most starkly in *La parole humiliée*, a key work which will help us unpack Ellul's understanding of the divine word, "We must realize that the word is absolutely and in every way incompatible with Technique."[77]

Ellul's naming of Technique as a power capable of numbing our senses to God is an essentially theological, prophetic judgment, and one which motivates his entire project, both in its form and its content. When I argue that this project has a theological underpinning, I mean to say that his work merits consideration as prophetic. I accept that this is a bald assertion that cannot be proven but which I will now seek to probe.

74. At key points I offer discussion of the theological range for Ellul of the crucial French terms "technique" (13–16, 15n52, 113, 215–19), "rupture" (57n18, 68–69, 104–08), and "puissance" (69–70, 131–34, 177–81). This range is more clearly visible when surveyed across the original texts. Moreover, the translations I offer are generally curter than the paraphrased or overly redacted translations sometimes attested, to capture something of Ellul's punchy style. Pourquet notes that one of the reasons for Ellul's relative obscurity from the intellectual ferment of Paris is his blunt and unpretentious style (Porquet, *Jacques Ellul*, 20). Moreover, I make a case below for the importance of a late text, as yet untranslated, *Théologie et technique* (2014).

75. The term belongs to Rognon, and I will explore it in my first chapter. A significant dialogue partner in my critical appraisal of Ellul's ethics will be Brian Brock, who sets up at numerous points an implicit contrast between the divine Word and technology (see especially chapter 4, "Advent and the Renewal of the Senses," which calls for an "ethos of listening for God's Word"). Indeed, at the outset, his focus on the language or "grammar" of technology assessment seems close to Ellul's concern with the language used to justify Technique. Yet in the final analysis, Martin Heidegger is a greater influence on Brock's formative discussion of "Technology as a Form of Life" and Ellul is notable by his absence from much of the fine-grained biblical-theological material, although there are echoes and implicit critiques of Ellul at points.

76. Entire sociological careers have been and continue to be devoted to the social significance of technology (e.g., A. Borgmann, M. Castells, A. Feenberg, A. Pacey, M. Kranzberg) but this is not a literature which I have privileged in this account of Ellul.

77. *Parole*, 177.

I

Not by Sociology Alone

The Asymmetry of Theology and Sociology in the Work of Jacques Ellul

IN MY INTRODUCTION, I explored why I believe Jacques Ellul to be a valuable guide for the mission of the church today. To restate my basic reading of Ellul in negative terms: his work is misunderstood if we think of his theology and sociology as separate categories each with their own integrity. I will argue that Ellul's life work is an integrated whole born of what he himself would call a biblical dialectic.

I do not claim that approaching Ellul's thought in this way is entirely new; it has been broached in various forms during the past thirty years of reading Ellul.[1] Indeed, Simon Charbonneau, the son of Ellul's early soul mate Bernard Charbonneau, and an avowed agnostic like his father, states clearly that Ellul's technology criticism stems from his faith:

> This book announces all that his life and work was to be, with its two strands of theology and sociology, each inseparable from the other, despite what people often say. His entire critical stance towards modern society stems from his Christian faith.[2]

As Charbonneau notes, within the fiercely positivist context of French academic life, *separation has been the habitual model*, but to the detriment of retrieving Ellul's legacy today.

To make my case, in this chapter, I will draw on two types of evidence, each in a separate section. In the first section, I will navigate the Ellul's own statements about the relationship between his theology and his sociology, and their reception by others.

1. In chronological order, Fasching (1981), Dawn (1992), Goddard (2002), Landgraf (2003), and Rognon (2007) have been the main exponents of this view, and I will explore their contributions below.

2. In Chastenet, *Être Ellulien au XXIe Siècle*, 419. This article is a development of his address at the conference marking the centenary of Ellul's birth in Bordeaux in 2012.

In the second section, I shall explore Frédéric Rognon's argument for
the key influence of Kierkegaard on Ellul and what he calls the *asymmetry*
between theology and sociology in Ellul's work. In an original reconstruction, I will bring together a number of texts defying easy categorization,
which I shall term programmatic, exhibiting *an internal dialectic between
theology and sociology.* They are, in order of publication, *Présence au monde
moderne* (1948); *Les nouveaux possédés* (1973); *La parole humiliée* (1981);
and *Changer de révolution* (1982); and the posthumous collection, *Théologie et technique: pour une éthique de la non-puissance* (2014). Within the
standard classification of Ellul's work, the first is commonly classed as theological, the next three as sociological. Bringing my arguments together in
chapter six, I contend that the last and most recently published, *Théologie
et technique*, demonstrates that Ellul's technology criticism is founded on a
dialectical "theology of Technique."[3]

Theology as the Key to Jacques Ellul?

Ellul's reflections upon his work have been a happy hunting ground for his
interpreters over the years. American philosopher Jacob Van Vleet has been
the latest to offer an outline of what he terms Ellul's "dialectical Theology."
Based on a careful study of Ellul's writings, with particular attention to Ellul's own statements of method, Van Vleet argues that "Theology is the key
to Jacques Ellul."[4]

Noting that reading Ellul's sociology alone should perhaps come with
a health warning, he begins by attending to the infamous misreading of
Ellul identified with the American Unabomber Ted Kaczynski. Kaczynski, who possessed only a number of Ellul's sociological texts, penned a
sentence which should bring a chill to all readers of Ellul: "When I read
Technological Society for the first time, I was delighted because I thought:
here is someone who is saying what I have already been thinking."[5] Taking
this book as his "bible," Kaczynski's Ellul was a paranoid "neo-Luddite calling for a complete overthrow of the system," Van Vleet claims.[6] Outlining
Ellul's thought in a clear, integrated and complete way, Van Vleet seeks to

3. There is a long history behind Ellul's preparation of this work, which dates from
the late 1970s, and its final publication (outlined in Frédéric Rognon's introduction in
Théologie et Technique, 9–25).

4. Van Vleet, *Dialectical Theology*, 4.

5. Van Vleet, *Dialectical Theology*, 1, citing Chase, *Harvard and the Unabomber*. See
also Rognon, *Générations Ellul*, 151–52.

6. Van Vleet, *Dialectical Theology*, 2.

dispel the myth of Ellul's work as "fatalistic" or "deterministic"[7] current in popular rejections of his work.

It is of course possible to isolate Ellul's technology criticism from his theology without such extreme consequences. The 2007 book *L'Homme qui avait (presque) tout prévu*, by the French journalist Jean-Luc Porquet, re-popularized Ellul's work in France after years of neglect but essentially dispenses with his faith. Porquet makes a lively case for Ellul as a twentieth-century seer whose work should be required reading today. In encapsulating twenty of Ellul's "great ideas," Porquet mines neglected Ellulian analyses from varied works and highlights how they have been validated by events, using an eclectic mix of media clichés, government announcements and purported scientific studies. In closing, he offers a brief chapter on Ellul's theology, conceding that Ellul's theology predetermined his iconoclasm, but defending the independence of Ellul's sociological methods and the prescience of his conclusions.

Porquet's book is an engaging attempt to apply Ellul's technology criticism to the present moment, a task Ellul would no doubt have commended. However, its inevitable weakness is its lack of detailed engagement with the theology. To clarify at this point, my purpose here is not to deny interpreters disinterested in theology the freedom to apply Ellul's work, and to arrive at similar conclusions about certain technologies. Indeed, any who share Ellul's Marxian account of Technique as the key driver of our age may be enriched by his critique of technological power. Moreover, it is quite possible to note the theological drivers behind Ellul's work, while not sharing his faith. In Simon Charbonneau's contribution to the centenary conference, he admits that although, like his father, he does not share Ellul's faith, as "a Post-Christian and unbelieving agnostic," he can admire "an incarnational way of thinking . . . directly concerned with what is becoming of the contemporary world."[8] One of the enduring legacies of Ellul's work is its continuing ability to engage those who do not share his Christian faith but who share aspects of his modernity criticism. It is in this sense that, in the words of David Gill, Ellul was a "prophet to the intellectuals."[9] Moreover, any application of Ellul's work which corrals it only for the theological academy will have done him a grave disservice.

7. Feenberg, *Questioning Technology*.

8. Chastenet, *Etre Ellulien Au XXIe Siècle*, 422.

9. This was related to me in a personal conversation in July 2014. It is interesting to note in this connection that William Vanderberg states that in organizing a symposium to mark Ellul's death in 1994, he found that all but one of the French University professors he had invited to speak had become Christians through reading Ellul's work. See Ellul, *On Freedom, Love, and Power*, 5.

At the same time, Ellul's theology cannot be short-changed. For example, to cash out the Incarnation merely to mean something like the "the importance of the material world" or "the principle of human embodiment" is to lose its value.[10] Most seriously, while re-interpretations of Ellul's sociology may offer an interesting and prescient analysis of the overreach of technological power, they will often trade in despair about the future. This is, as I shall argue, to misunderstand the purpose of biblical prophecy.[11] More significantly, what solely sociological accounts lack is the living hope that Ellul brought to his enterprise—a hope rooted in the apocalypse of Jesus Christ. Confronting technology without this hope, as Van Vleet rightly points out, is not only mistaken, it is indeed dangerous. Having begun by crediting Van Vleet for this suggestive starting point, we will now move to a more nuanced response to his breakthrough work.

Ellul: The Marxist Theologian?

Van Vleet has rendered a great service by exploring Ellul's intellectual influences, and I share much common ground with him. However, it is somewhat problematic to approach Ellul theoretically, primarily through his own rather abstract apologia, such as *Ce que je crois* (1987), a late text Van Vleet draws upon heavily. Basing much of his analysis on this and an earlier essay on dialectic, Van Vleet argues that Ellul's work "forms a coherent whole, united by his dialectical outlook."[12]

This outlook is what, for Van Vleet, makes Ellul a philosopher first and foremost. Dialectic is on his account a philosophical worldview first and secondarily a methodology, inherited by Ellul from Marx, Kierkegaard and Barth, but ultimately rooted in the work of Hegel. As he notes, "It is impossible to have a worldview without it affecting one's methodology."[13] As if to support Van Vleet's perspective, in an interview published in *A temps* in 1981, Ellul points us in this philosophical direction to understand his dialectical reading of scripture:

> Of course, my reading of the Bible has been influenced by a number of elements in our society. For example, it is not because

10. See, e.g., Cérézuelle in Chastenet, *Sur Jacques Ellul*. Indeed, Ellul devoted an entire book to tackling misapplications of his notion of Incarnation in *Fausse!*

11. Ellul never wished to be credited as a seer or to be proven right in his predictions but rather thought of himself as a lucid realist. See *A temps*, 193–94; Rognon, *Pensée*, 164–65.

12. Van Vleet, *Dialectical Theology*, 5.

13. Van Vleet, *Dialectical Theology*, 5.

I am a genius that I undertook a dialectical reading of the Bible,
but because the dialectic of Hegel and Marx was brought to
light, and because Barth himself was a dialectical theologian.[14]

However, I contend that Van Vleet overplays the influence upon Ellul
of Hegel. Granted, Van Vleet notes Kierkegaard's central influence on Ellul,
which lends Ellul some distance from Hegel, as we shall explore.[15] However,
at the same time he proposes that Ellul is more influenced by Hegel than
he admits,[16] and that at moments (his better moments, Van Vleet implies),
Ellul is more Hegelian than not.[17]

Central to Van Vleet's concern is to reinstate especially Marx as a key
influence upon Ellul's social thought, noting that this has been downplayed
by "evangelical Protestants," nervous of "touchy subjects" such as "politics
and economics," and more comfortable with the legacy of the supposedly
apolitical Kierkegaard, who, Van Vleet argues, informs Ellul's "theological" hermeneutics.[18] Although he concedes that Ellul did not call himself a
Marxist, Van Vleet argues persuasively that Ellul's critique of capitalism, his
concept of alienation in a technological society and his understanding of
Technique as ideology are developments of Marx's thought.

Van Vleet is of course right that Ellul does receive a hostile reception in
some evangelical circles. In a lacerating article by the conservative evangelical Michael Bauman, former Tutor at the Centre for Medieval and Renaissance Studies in Oxford, we find the charge that Ellul is a barely disguised
Marxist theologian.[19] Although Bauman is most concerned to refute Ellul's

14. *A temps*, 56.

15. Noting that David Lovekin sees Hegel as Ellul's primary influence, he writes: "It
would be more accurate to state that Ellul was influenced primarily by Kierkegaard's
dialectical method" (Van Vleet, *Dialectical Theology*, 28).

16. Van Vleet, *Dialectical Theology*, 30.

17. Van Vleet, *Dialectical Theology*, 30. Van Vleet comments tellingly that "Hegel's
approach seems more coherent than Ellul's."

18. Van Vleet, *Dialectical Theology*, 16–17. The strange claim that Kierkegaard has
"relatively little to say about economics and politics" is refuted by Stephen Backhouse,
who provides an engaging account of Kierkegaard's dialectic, and much else in his
approach, in *Kierkegaard*. "I am drawn to those places where Kierkegaard's theology
abuts against social and political factors. Fortunately for me, Kierkegaard's oft-stated
aim to 'to reintroduce Christianity into Christendom' provides plenty of those places"
(Backhouse, *Kierkegaard*, 210) Indeed, Rognon notes that Ellul's legacy in the US is
most alive among Christian radicals, such as Shane Claiborne, who are rejecting the
theological ethics of "Christian America" and seeking to reach out to those turning
away from mainstream denominations. See Rognon, *Générations Ellul*, 151; http://
www.jesusradicals.com.

19. Bauman, "Jesus, Anarchy, and Marx," 199–216. The claim here is that while this
is a marginal text, this view of Ellul is well established.

political theology, he concludes by arguing for the "nefarious influence" of Marxist thinking throughout Ellul's work: "Jacques Ellul . . . it seems to me, has made an imperfect and insufficient break from his own Marxist past and from the ideology that necessarily attaches to it."[20]

For Bauman, Ellul's Marxist ideology furnishes his hidden presuppositions about power, money, production, freedom, revolution and indeed dialectical method itself, concluding, "Time and space would fail were I to identify the full range of Ellul's Marxisms."[21]

The charge that Ellul can be reduced to a "crypto-Marxist" theologian was one he faced from the earliest years of his public career. Indeed, as Goddard's autobiographical account shows, Ellul, led by his non-Christian friend Charbonneau, saw Marx's work as crucial for understanding the modern world.[22] One simply cannot understand the ambitious scope of Ellul's thought without acknowledging his reading of Hegel and Marx. Van Vleet, and even Bauman, renders us a service in acknowledging the shaping of Ellul's social thought, whether we consider that for good or for ill.

Ellul, the Biblical Dialectician

There is undoubted value in seeking to assess Ellul's dialectic from a philosophical perspective. However, I will now seek to nuance this account by arguing that Ellul's dialectic is more a practical methodology than a philosophical worldview. I advance three overlapping pieces of evidence: Ellul's ultimate rejection of Hegel, his defense of dialectic as a lived methodology and his concern to allow the Bible to define his dialectical method.

20. Bauman, "Jesus, Anarchy, and Marx," 212.

21. Bauman, "Jesus, Anarchy, and Marx," 215.

22. This became a problem within Personalist circles, and Goddard offers an illuminating account of the early parting of the ways between the Paris-based Catholic Personalist movement *Esprit*, under the influence of Emmanuel Mounier, and Charbonneau and Ellul's Bordeaux-based and largely Protestant group. He outlines how their "theoretical" convictions, a combination of theological and sociological differences, were mutually self-reinforcing. On the one hand, Mounier's metropolitan Thomism, operating close to the seat of power, led perhaps inevitably to an optimistic natural theology with man as "demiurge" or co-creator, acting for the common good. On the other hand, Ellul's provincial pessimism, a heady Marxian-Protestant cocktail, saw this as an all too convenient legitimation of the powers-that-be. Mounier, for his part, was unable to understand Ellul's "active pessimism" about technical autonomy, just as Ellul, for his part, dissented from Mounier's "tragic optimism." See Goddard, *Living the Word*, 21–30.

The Rejection of Hegel

Ellul's own statements dissent from the contention that he is best assessed as a Hegelian philosopher. For one thing, Ellul always emphatically rejected the title of philosopher.[23] Van Vleet's claim that Ellul is more influenced by Hegel than he admits follows a dominant philosophical interpretation of Ellul in North America established by John Wilkinson's preface to *The Technological Society*,[24] and supported in David Lovekin's work.[25]

If we look closer at his own account in *Ce que je crois*, we see that although Ellul acknowledges his philosophical debts (though with an eerie silence about Kierkegaard),[26] he is at pains to trace his dialectic to the Bible:

> In my view, I believe that long before these intellectual formula-
> tions, dialectic appeared from the eighth century BC in Hebrew
> thought. . . . I do not mean there is an explicit theory of dialec-
> tic . . . but that we are in the presence of an original process of
> thought, bearing the marks of what will later be called dialectic.[27]

According to Ellul, where the Bible and the "intellectual formulations" of Socrates and Plato agree is on this: dialectic is not merely a rhetorical technique, but *an ontological account of reality*. That is to say, dialectic de-scribes how things actually move and change through time, not only how ideas are expressed. Whereas sociologists may call this "revolution," Ellul describes this as the spiritual dynamic of "conversion."[28] The ancient He-brews expressed their experience of the revelation of God as other to, even in contradiction with, the very world in which they were living. Yet this revelation of God's otherness did not lead them away from this world, but to an open-ended adventure whereby they, and the world itself, change, not simply once, but over and over again through the constant process Ellul happily describes as "creative synthesis."

Yet where Hebrew thought especially differs from a philosophical view of dialectic, developed in the modern world by Hegel and Marx, is

23. *Ce que je crois*, 43.

24. The translator of *La Technique et l'enjeu du siècle*, John Wilkinson, in his preface compares it to Hegel's *Phenomenology of Spirit*, arguing that "Ellul can echo the dictum of Hegel's phenomenology that the only imaginable departure of philosophy is experi-ence" (*Technological Society*, xv).

25. Lovekin, *Technique, Discourse, and Consciousness*.

26. In *Ce que je crois*, as elsewhere, Ellul almost seems keen to maintain Kierkeg-aard's elusive pseudonymity by making numerous unaccredited Kierkegaardian state-ments, as we shall explore below.

27. *Ce que je crois*, 51.

28. *Ce que je crois*, 50.

on the question of human responsibility to God. Ellul debunks the all too easy assumption that if reality is dialectically constituted, it must have its own *intrinsic* process of thesis—antithesis—synthesis, leading to *inexorable* progress over time. What matters for Ellul is our active engagement in the adventure of responding to God, for he rejects the idea that history moves by itself, directed by an indwelling dialectical spirit.[29] As he puts it: "Dialectic is not a machine which automatically produces results. It implies undeniable human responsibility and hence a freedom of choice and decision."[30]

Indeed, what bothers Ellul perhaps most of all is the *theological appropriation* of Hegelian synthesis to underwrite the ideologies of historical and technological progress, for he contends these lead all too easily, as we shall explore, to the renunciation of human responsibility and the closure of history.[31] It is worth citing at length from the closing chapter of *Parole*, a programmatic text for my reading, to which we shall return:

> Thus the certainty of the great reconciliation at the time of the New Creation, but only then, situates us in a perspective different from the perspective traditionally adopted in theological research. Two theological concepts contradict each other: the concept of a synthesis *hic et nunc* and the concept of the final reconciliation lived now in hope. I might say that the concept of synthesis is characteristic of all philosophical theologies, usually Catholic or Orthodox. The concept of contradiction is specifically a biblical concept. . . . The Bible shows us the reconciliation between image and word, between reality and truth, as the end point and the metahistorical moment reached *after the historical process of contradiction.*[32]

I thus acknowledge that Ellul's dialectic is ontological, in the sense of truly concerned with changing reality, and not merely a technique of debate. And yet this does not imply that reality rolls upwards inexorably through a series of syntheses. For Ellul, all things *end* in reconciliation, but

29. *Ce que je crois,* 49.

30. *Ce que je crois,* 51.

31. Backhouse well expresses what Ellul is rejecting in Hegel: "One of Hegel's Big Ideas was that the historical development of art, religion, and philosophy told us something true about the development of the Divine Mind in the universe. The revelation of God was to be found not in a person or a holy text but in the development of a culture's history. . . . Both the liberal myth of progress and the conservative myth of the Golden Age owe a debt of gratitude to Hegel. Wherever one finds a commitment to one's culture and history as itself a vehicle for truth, one finds Hegel's fingerprints" (Backhouse, *Kierkegaard,* 66).

32. *Parole,* 281 (my italics).

that end exists only *beyond* history. The anticipation of the final reconciliation can break into this time but only as transcendent truth constantly
challenges reality, for no situation *here and now* can remain unchallenged
given the full horizon of hope.[33]

Despite this, Van Vleet insists that Ellul's theology of reconciliation
must be placed alongside Hegel's notion of synthesis and be assessed on
these philosophical grounds, even to be made more coherently Hegelian.
Yet Ellul intends to critique Hegel, a critique inspired by Kierkegaard.

Practical Theological Methodology: "Christian Realism"

My second piece of evidence is found in the way Ellul puts biblical dialectic
into practice in his reading of culture and society; we shall consider this
at greater length in section 2 when we turn to a number of programmatic
texts. And here, the influence of Kierkegaard comes to the fore. In the opening chapter of *Parole* Ellul makes explicit reference to Kierkegaard's lived
dialectic in refuting Hegel's dialectic:

> Kierkegaard's dialectic is a qualitative dialectic (as contrasted
> with Hegel's dialectic, which Kierkegaard terms "quantitative"),
> and a dialectic of life rather than a system of concepts. For the
> word is dialectical in itself and at the same time integrated into
> the whole of existence. By this I mean that the word is intended
> to be lived.[34]

In the light of this compressed statement, we can read Ellul's entire life
work as an attempt to live out the hope of God's final reconciliation. Ellul's
concern with all of life, with its social and political dimensions, was an outworking of his biblical dialectical methodology, as his earliest writings show.
Here Ellul articulated his way of reading the world as a kind of "Christian
realism," over and against on the one hand offering philosophical accounts
of existence and on the other hand simply attending to current affairs.[35]

Ellul often described this approach using the metaphor of an ocean,
perhaps the epitome of perpetual change. The superficial level of the waves
was the flotsam of everyday events, while sounding the depths was the
domain of the philosopher.[36] Where Ellul wished to operate was at the
intermediate level of the currents, what Ellul termed the "structures" of

33. For a longer discussion, see 91–94; chapter 4.

34. *Parole*, 45.

35. See the article "Political Realism" (1947), made available in English translation
in Ellul, *Sources and Trajectories*. See in particular on realism and the Incarnation, 53.

36. In various texts but restated in *Bluff*, 14.

society. Taken together, the lack of a detailed philosophical underpinning (the depths) allied with his polemical disengagement from mathematical and statistical analysis (the waves) account for the difficulty of considering Ellul a sociologist in any recognized modern sense. Put otherwise, it is fair to say, as Goddard surmises, that "Ellul nowhere explicitly elaborates the method he used to get behind the superficial level of events [and] discern the fundamental structures." Yet Goddard argues that what Ellul attempts in discerning these structures might be termed a "global sociology . . . qualitatively different from social scientific studies."[37] Indeed, when we actually read Ellul's texts (as we shall), we do gain insight into his method: attention to lived experience alongside an immersion in the thought patterns, habits, behaviors and language of wider society. Numerous interpreters have rightly drawn attention to Ellul's early statement of this Christian realism in *Présence*:

> The first duty of a Christian intellectual today is the duty of awareness. It is the refusal of appearances, and news for the sake of news, the refusal of the abstract phenomenon. . . . We must not think of Man, but of my neighbor Mario. . . . It is in concrete life of this man that I see the repercussions of the machine, the media, political discourse and bureaucracy.[38]

Van Vleet helpfully casts Ellul's social thought as phenomenological since in his writings, Ellul deliberately eschews a quantitative approach in favor of the qualitative. "He simply describes reality as it presents itself to consciousness."[39] In short, Ellul is more a Christian phenomenologist than a social scientist.

The Dialectics of Creation, Incarnation, and New Creation

Thirdly, and finally, there is another significant implication of Ellul's rejection of philosophical synthesis we must consider now, for it expresses another distinction between my work and Van Vleet's. As a lived practice, Ellul's theology cannot be isolated and systematized in terms of a theory which then has certain social implications. Van Vleet offers a neat and cogent summary of Ellul's doctrine of God in terms of God as wholly other, living, Trinity and love. All of these statements can be demonstrated from key passages in Ellul's "theological" writings. However, Ellul himself

37. Goddard, *Living the Word*, 119.

38. *Présence* in *Défi*, 93–94, in Goddard, *Living the Word*, 120–21; Greenman et al., *Understanding Jacques Ellul*, 17.

39. Van Vleet, *Dialectical Theology*, 30.

is skeptical about the value of offering a systematic theology, and he does not even do this in *Ce que je crois*, which clearly lends itself to such an approach. In a passing but significant comment about his doctrine of God in chapter 13, he writes:

> The first order of reflection revolves around the conviction that
> I cannot have a single coherent image of God. At no time can
> I say that God is for me this or that. He is but He is something
> else at the same time and possibly the opposite. I cannot attempt
> to synthesize or reconcile the various elements of what I under-
> stand about God. I hereby renounce all intellectual coherence.[40]

Statements like this make for a rather unsystematic theology, not only because Ellul's work is vast but because God is not an object to be fixed. The only coherence Ellul will allow for his work is a basic coherence with the dialectical methodology he finds in the Bible. "The basis of my thought is biblical revelation; the content of my thought is biblical revelation; the starting point is given to me by the biblical revelation."[41]

Faced with introducing a dialectical worldview to the Bible, or allow-ing the Bible to shape his dialectical methodology, Ellul opts clearly for the latter, although Van Vleet (and Bauman!) is not wrong to suggest that Ellul does bring Marxist freight with him.[42]

Therefore, what I offer here is not an account of Ellul as a coherent dialectical theologian but an engagement with Ellul as a reader of the Bible and human culture. Moreover, as Van Vleet begins to explore, the shape of Ellul's biblical dialectical methodology is clearly visible in *Ce que je crois* where Ellul highlights three biblical dialectics which arise in the OT and which the NT deploys in the light of Christ.[43]

---

40. *Ce que je crois*, 226 (cited by Van Vleet, by way of concession).

41. *Théologie*, 18.

42. Indeed, as Ellul would often argue, Marx's revolutionary dialectic was itself a secularization of biblical dialectic. For an exploration of Ellul's theological reading of Marx, see Marva Dawn's translation of Ellul's iconic 1947 article, "Needed: A New Karl Marx!" in Ellul, *Sources and Trajectories*, 29–49. In short, whereas in Marx, the processes of history are understood in purely materialist terms, "for Ellul, alienation and submission to ideology can only be overcome by submitting to the Spirit," from the outside (Van Vleet, *Dialectical Theology*, 16). "Because of what Ellul found so penetrat-ing and admirable about Marx's critique, he set a similarly ambitious agenda for his own work. . . . This is in part attributable to his preoccupations with totalitarianism and technique, against which he levelled a critique so grand as to encompass all of the main political economic systems of his time" (Greenman et al., *Understanding Jacques Ellul*, 83; see also 155–57).

43. Van Vleet, *Dialectical Theology*, 31.

I. The first dialectic is between *the Creator and the creation*. The revelation to the people of Israel was that the transcendent God can dwell with his people. He enters history and bears with human suffering and sin. Although, as Creator, God is wholly other to us, he "enters into relation with us," and his purpose in so doing is to reconcile all things to himself, but only through a process of judgment and response. This reconciliation is none other than *"the incredible revelation of the freedom of God."*[44]

II. The second dialectic is between the *promise and its fulfillment*, a process we see clearly in the OT. For Ellul, the promise of Jesus Christ is entirely consistent with OT dialectic, though Jesus is the unique paradox of God immanent and transcendent in a person. However, although God once became incarnate, this promise is not yet fully fulfilled: Christ is *"already* the LORD of the world, but *not yet*, for he will be so at his *parousia,"* and we must not attempt a hasty reconciliation. The individual Christian lives in the present "with the contradiction of what is fully accomplished but obviously not yet accomplished."[45]

III. The third dialectic is *between the whole and the remnant.* In historical development, the Bible witnesses to a constant process of *judgment and election* (paradigmatically the election of Israel). And yet as Ellul argues, because the part is linked to the whole, what happens to the part is destined for the whole: as the remnant is reduced historically—ultimately it is reduced to Jesus alone, he says—so election is extended to all.[46] For Ellul therefore, there is a universal election in Jesus, which begins the process leading to the "recapitulation of all history, nature and all human works" in a new creation.

Following Ellul, this threefold, biblical-dialectically conceived narrative of Creation, Incarnation and New Creation is the schema I will apply in my following chapters, but in reverse order, for reasons I shall explain. But we pause first to reflect on an interesting question. Although Ellul did not attempt anything as systematic as the *Church Dogmatics*, Ellul's biblical dialectic can be seen to map onto the tripartite theological schema associated with the dialectical theology of Karl Barth. Does this imply the contrary charge that, far from being a Marxist theologian, Ellul was, in effect,

---

44. *Ce que je crois,* 52 (my italics).

45. *Ce que je crois,* 53–54 (my italics). Here, he credits Moltmann's *Theology of Hope.*

46. *Ce que je crois,* 55–56.

a Barthian sociologist? It is important to pause briefly here to tease out the relationship between the two authors.[47]

Ellul: The Barthian Sociologist?

Ellul called Barth the greatest theologian of the twentieth century.[48] For Ellul, Barth gave full force to biblical dialectic, poised between the "No" of divine transcendence and the "Yes" of election in Christ. "Karl Barth's theology is prodigiously balanced, and I believe it to be true insofar as it reflects the extraordinary dialectic that is revealed throughout the Bible."[49] Ellul liked to claim that the implications of Barth's work had not been adequately explored, and despite the fact that people were keen to declare themselves post-Barth, he quipped post-Barthians were in reality fifty years behind him![50]

Indeed, when asked to express his precise debt to Barth, he chooses to single out Barth's contribution to anthropology: "Barth gave a renewed place to humanity in his theology . . . given the fact that a theology of grace had contrived (not in the work of Calvin but in that of Calvinists) to dispose of humanity. For a theology of grace that totally denies human works leads to total pessimism."[51]

Despite the common impression that Barth focused too much on the transcendence of God, Ellul credits Barth with recovering anthropology, recovering a place for humanity within the Reformed tradition.

Moreover, this gave Ellul an agenda to pursue: he considered that Barth had blazed a trail, without marking the track particularly well. Ellul's desire was therefore to construct an ethics through but *beyond* Barth's theology: "I had the impression that the ethical consequences of Barth's theology had never been elicited. I was not satisfied with his volumes of ethics and politics, which seemed to be based on an insufficient knowledge of the world and of politics."[52]

This is why comparing Ellul with Barth is indeed not comparing like with like: Ellul's anthropology is far less rigorously "theological," that is to say "conceptual" than Barth's, and far more interested in concrete social

47. See Rognon, *Pensée*, 235–71; Gill, *Word of God*, 30–31.

48. *Conférence*, 23.

49. *Fausse*, 13.

50. Rognon, *Pensée*, 239. In the same breath, Ellul declared that he was not an "unconditional Barthian."

51. *A temps*, 73–74.

52. Greenman et al., *Understanding Jacques Ellul*, 12, citing Ellul, *Technological Society*. Wilkinson's preface to *City* refers to Barth being "nonplussed" by technology unless it could be "politicized" (*City*, xiii).

realities, far more "phenomenological." For example, Ellul skates on the surface of the depths of Barth's christological anthropology, as we shall explore in chapter 4.

Much more can be said about their interrelationship, and as we go along, I will turn at points to the constant shadow of Barth over Ellul's work. However, in summary, it is perhaps best to see Ellul as building upon Barth's recovery of theological anthropology in developing an easily accessible genre of theological ethics. He believed that Barth's forays into ethics were at the same time too theologically abstract and too sociologically naive: Bromiley notes that Ellul feels "comfortable sidelining Barth on sociology"[53] and likewise, Rognon suggests that Ellul keeps a "critical distance" from Barth's ethics, because of the latter's "naivety" about technology, work and the state.[54]

And here perhaps we glimpse why Ellul fiercely defended the independence of his sociological methods, for he did not wish others to see his sociology as the unprofessional attempt of a theological naïf. We glimpse this ambivalence when he is asked whether his sociology does not inevitably work from a theological framework: "That's a question I asked myself early on. I do not think I have used a theological basis in this way. . . . And it is for this reason that I have clearly dissociated two lines of research."[55]

Yet, of course, when pushed to explain how theology funds his sociology, Ellul alludes to the way in which he seeks to overcome social-scientific reductionism, the illusion that sociology is a science in which the human being can be considered in isolation from ethical, spiritual and moral questions, precisely, for example, in relation to productive activity alone. Ellul offered instead a method which considered "the human phenomenon in its entirety."[56] In justifying this, he explains that his approach is based quite simply upon a theological conviction about our creatureliness and our broken relationship to a transcendent God: "Man is an indivisible whole . . . he has been 'created' . . . he remains in relation with the transcendent . . . he is created in right relationship with God, and at the same time free to break that relationship. And despite that break, God maintains a relationship."[57]

Basing myself upon this suggestive statement, I argue that Ellul develops a theology of Technique which enriches rather than impoverishes his

53. Bromiley in Christians and Van Hook, *Jacques Ellul*, 35.

54. *Théologie et Technique*, 19. See also Rognon, *Pensée*, 252–56. Greenman et al. comment that Ellul builds on a foundation of Marxist analytical inclinations and Barthian theology (*Understanding Jacques Ellul*, 11).

55. *A temps*, 159.

56. *A temps*, 160.

57. *A temps*, 161.

sociology. Phenomenological reflection upon lived experience and historical engagement with contemporary sources both have a dialectical theological basis, and the account of humanity in a technological society which thus
emerges is all the richer for that basis. Ellul's first training as a historian
is particularly significant for understanding his interdisciplinary inclinations: "My own theological method had to involve a certain philosophical
confrontation, a sociological method; a means of observing facts . . . it may
be that my training as a historian came to hand here because the historian
paints on various canvasses."[58]

None of this should be taken to imply that Ellul's sociology is simply
crypto-Barthianism. Only a neglect of Ellul's sociology or an excessive suspicion would suggest that Ellul's technology criticism is "the barely camou-
flaged judgment of a Huguenot prophet."[59]

Given that this is primarily a theological study, it is important perhaps
to clarify that I am not arguing for a neglect of Ellul's sociology. A recent
work, which tends in this direction, by way of example, is Trey Dunham's *Jesus and the City: A Theology of Technique in Jacques Ellul.*[60] Dunham starts
well: "The majority of analyses tend heavily towards either the examination
of Ellul's Biblical criticisms or method or, on the other hand, his sociological
analyses, and woefully neglect the explicit connections between the two."[61]

In highlighting the important principle that sociological works are
held in tension with theological counterpoints, Dunham is arguing along
the lines that Ellul himself lay down. Moreover, his central conclusion is an
insight which will emerge in what I shall go on to argue:

> Technique, in its modern form, is more than simply a material,
> physical project that attends only to the corporeal needs of hu-
> manity. . . . Technique, it can be concluded, is first and foremost
> a spiritual project, which corresponds to that described by the
> city in the Biblical text. Technique seeks to exclude, eliminate,
> and replace God.[62]

58. *A temps*, 158. It is worth perhaps comparing this argument with Michael Banner's contention that moral theology needs to gain distance from philosophy and enter
into dialogue with social anthropology. See Banner, *Ethics of Everyday Life.*

59. Goddard, *Living the Word*, 154, citing Margolis. In this kind of criticism, Ellul's
own rejection of Calvinism is barely taken in hand.

60. The quotations below are sourced from the thesis on which the book is based,
entitled "The Meaning of Technology: A Theology of Technique in Jacques Ellul"
(2002). It is essentially a study of *Technique* and *Sans feu* in dialogue.

61. Dunham, "Meaning of Technology," 4.

62. Dunham, "Meaning of Technology," 96.

However, along the way, Dunham make some unnecessary moves. For example, he argues that Ellul's sevenfold sociological description of Technique bears an "uncanny correspondence" to his reading of the narratives of Cain, Nimrod, Babel, Babylon and Jerusalem, implying that Ellul's account of the independent rigor of his sociological methods is disingenuous; or by way of *reductio ad absurdum*, that all we need to understand technology is the Bible.[63] And when Dunham argues that "A major implication of this study is that the numerous connections between the technological society and the Biblical text serve to validate and authenticate the veracity of the Biblical text," he seems to suggest that Ellul's purpose is to produce an ingenious apologetic for the Bible.[64]

Dunham does make a helpful contribution but we must be careful here. For Ellul explicitly declares that it was not theology that led him to analyze Technique; rather, as we have noted, he situates the origins of his concern autobiographically in his friendship with Charbonneau and his reading of Marx. Moreover, he stated often enough that his theology did not predetermine his sociological concerns and conclusions.

We may surmise that over the course of his career, Ellul adopted a pragmatic, tactical position, trained as he was within a context which suspected theology.[65] It was that very suspicion which had led to Ellul's marginal status in his native France, in stark contrast to the significance of Ellul in North American Protestantism. For decades, the only serious theological engagement in French with Ellul was from his fellow Reformed theologian, Gabriel Vahanian. A former colleague of Ellul in the "Fédération" of the French Reformed Church and an early supporter, Vahanian used his influence in the United States to assist in the translation into English of Ellul's first major work *Technique*. However, having taught outside France for a significant period of time, he developed a far more critical stance towards Ellul's work. He acknowledges Ellul's prescience in his concern with modern technology but suggests two fatal problems with Ellul's reading of Technique, rooted in theological presuppositions:

---

63. "For example, in *The Technological Society* and *The Meaning of the City*, the task will be to show how the specific characteristics of Technique, its growth, and its implications in society correspond to the Biblical stories of Cain, Nimrod, Babel, Babylon and Jerusalem" (Dunham, "Meaning of Technology," 20).

64. Dunham, "Meaning of Technology," 200.

65. John Howard Yoder, influenced by Ellul but also notably distanced from him at times, argues that "the dialectic of creatureliess and rebellion" is "the key to Ellul's entire thought, although because of his desire to keep his social thought from being set aside . . . as confessionally biased, Ellul made little of this connection" (Yoder, *Politics of Jesus*, 160).

Firstly, Vahanian disputes Ellul's definition of Technique as the pursuit of absolute efficiency. He offers a positive definition of Technique as rooted in creation: "The human vocation to humanize all that is foreign to us, beginning with ourselves."[66] On this definition, all human culture is technical, and indeed, language is a technique par excellence. Attacking what he sees as the naivety of Ellul's Barthian separation of revelation from reason, he argues both that Ellul was "too theological," narrowly opposed to contemporary thought; and yet at the same time, "not properly theological enough" because his hermeneutical method was too simplistic, "paraphrasing" biblical texts for his own purposes, rejecting out of hand historical-critical methods which would strengthen rather than enfeeble his theological reflection.[67]

Secondly, he states that Ellul's criticism of technical progress is bound up with an understanding of apocalypse as catastrophic end, and in this, Vahanian states, he is "Barthian to his fingertips." For Vahanian, this leads Ellul to emphasize the discontinuity between the present and the end time, between human work and God's work. Ellul's notion of Technique as an autonomous power over and against humanity is said to be rooted in his theology of crisis, which then underwrites a misreading of sociological facts to bolster it.

In summing up their parting of the ways, Vahanian proposes instead that technological power can be understood within the category of gift. After all, God's grace is a model of perfect efficiency. Unsurprisingly, this starting point leads Vahanian to a very different reading of Technique today. Ellul's post-war fears of the "megamachine" have proven unfounded, he states, as what we have actually seen is a growth in a movement towards miniaturization, technologies on a human scale.[68]

There are valid points here to which we shall return. Vahanian rightly points out a feature of Ellul's hermeneutics, and I will not in the chapters to come shy away from the flaws of Ellul's poorly supported readings of important biblical texts. And yet, in the final analysis, this will be found to be unjust to Ellul's understanding of the human vocation in creation, an understanding he seeks to develop, precisely, through a dialogue between social anthropology and theology. Moreover, it must be said that what counted most for Ellul was not being Barthian but being biblical. As

66. Rognon, *Générations Ellul*, 308.
67. Rognon, *Générations Ellul*, 309.
68. Rognon, *Générations Ellul*, 309.

Geoffrey Bromiley, a translator of both Ellul and Barth, well puts it: "Ellul is a highly original thinker who goes his own way without obvious dependence on anyone else. Above all, Ellul has also studied the biblical text and drawn conclusions for himself."[69]

The Bible as the Key: Speaking a Living Word

The Bible is thus the key to Jacques Ellul. Neither "Barthian sociologist" nor "Marxist theologian," Ellul strove for a *both-and* dialectical relationship of constant confrontation between the Bible and culture, between God and the world.

Indeed, a hugely influential figure in the reception of Ellul's work, his friend and close collaborator, Patrick Chastenet, who has worked hard to defend the independence of Ellul's sociology, argues that Ellul did not operate a one-way street, but was rather open to social experience in his interpretation of the Bible.[70] As Ellul related to him in a testimonial book, although the Incarnation provided the theological rationale for Christian realism, it did not provide the experience or the methods of social analysis, the academic tools of the trade: "If you take into account only the theological dimension, you will miss the element of Incarnation. If you are only interested in the socio-political dimension, you will constantly come up against a lack of response or openness."[71]

And when we draw back from this dense discussion, we remember the momentous significance Ellul attached to Technique in the first place. It posed an unprecedented challenge to the reception of the Word of God, and therefore, to engage theologically in a technological society was to seek to speak a living rather than a dead word: "Sociology was to be the instrument which enabled me to distinguish, within theology, what could prove 'useful,' so that I might speak a living word today."[72]

This methodology was no mere theory for Ellul: it was a prophetic protest against the abstraction and ineffectiveness of much existing theological writing and training. He expressed this concern within his own French Reformed Church and from the early 1970s, as a member of the governing *Fédération*, he became responsible for the reform of its

69. See Bromiley's chapter, "The Influence of Barth," in Christians and Van Hook, *Jacques Ellul*, 33–40.

70. Patrick Chastenet commented at a conference in June 2012 marking the centenary of Ellul's birth that Ellul was wont to observe that few critics took as much interest in the influence of his sociology on his theology as vice versa.

71. Chastenet in *Théologie et Technique*, 10.

72. *A temps*, 157.

structures of theological education creating what we might now call pro-grams of "contextual theology."[73]

In *A temps*, he explains how he advocated models of theological educa-tion open to all, beyond a clerical cadre, operating within an interdisciplin-ary framework: "We cannot evade today the relationship between theology and psychology, sociology, political economy, political science." Above all, Ellul hoped his programme would enable "a confrontation between life and thought,"[74] by which the problems associated with a mass society undergo-ing technological change, such as poor urban living and working conditions, could be addressed through experiencing them first-hand, often through in-context training, or *stages*. In short, Ellul's model of theological forma-tion sought to enable the church to speak a living word. Lived experience could even show up those aspects of the theological tradition which for Ellul needed recasting or even rejecting as irrelevant speculation.

However, sociology could never supplant theology. Goddard summa-rizes well the relationship between theology and sociology when he distin-guishes the macro and micro-levels of Ellul's work. He suggests that at the macro-level, Ellul works "from above," from theology to sociology.[75] In this sense, "The lack of communion between God and the world can be seen as the *foundation* for Ellul's dialectic of theology and sociology because God and his world are now ruptured from one another."[76] However, as Goddard goes on to argue, at the micro-level of Ellul's consideration of particular social issues, the situation is reversed, and Ellul usually works "from below." More-over, the levels interrelate for "the independently reached *conclusions* of [his] sociological reflection can be given a theological interpretation."[77] Indeed, in Ellul's model, such conclusions can even enrich our interpretation of Scrip-ture for today, as insights drawn from social analysis of the modern context bring fresh illumination to their counterparts in the ancient texts.

This model of confrontation between the ancient text and the modern context is what Ellul offers us but crucially he was not the first to do so. We now turn to consider the critical influence upon Ellul of the Danish thinker Søren Kierkegaard.

---

73. See, e.g., Moynagh and Harrold, *Church for Every Context*.

74. *A temps*, 101.

75. Goddard, *Living the Word*, 163.

76. Goddard, *Living the Word*, 161. On the importance to Ellul of the concept of "the rupture" as denoting what the theological tradition has called "the Fall," see God-dard, *Living the Word*, chapter 2.

77. Goddard, *Living the Word*, 156.

A "Faithful Betrayal"

For many years, Vahanian was the leading interpreter of Ellul's theology in France, though he was, at the most, a critical friend. However, a renewed interest in Ellul's dialectical theology has been pioneered by a successor to Vahanian at Strasbourg University, Frédéric Rognon. In his 2007 book *Jacques Ellul: Une pensée en dialogue*, Rognon offered a case for a renewal of Ellul's theological method in our day. Writing of "l'héritage impossible" of Ellul's thought, Rognon eschews a restatement of Ellul's intentions, offering instead a subtle re-reading which he calls a "faithful betrayal."[78] Citing Didier Nordon, he argues that Ellul wanted more than anything else not a repetition of his judgments or an Ellulian project: rather to engage readers in the same dialectical patterns of thought.[79] Before I outline such a "faithful betrayal" of my own, I will briefly consider Rognon's reading, as it helpfully prepares the ground.

Ellul: A Twentieth-Century Kierkegaard?

Rognon argues cogently that the form and content of Ellul's entire oeuvre only makes sense when we look not primarily to Marx or Barth, but to Kierkegaard as his "basic source."[80] What does he mean by this? Firstly, he notes that in significant autobiographical statements, Ellul confesses an almost unconditional allegiance to Kierkegaard. Secondly, as he points out, Ellul's entire project of writing two sets of books mirrors the division of Kierkegaard's works into the aesthetic and religious.[81] Thirdly, Rognon argues that like Kierkegaard's dialectic, Ellul's dialectic is polemically opposed to Hegel's.[82] As a result, Rognon contends that Ellul constantly seeks confrontation between the word of God and human culture, resisting a hasty reconciliation. Stephen Backhouse's comment on Kierkegaard's portrayal of Socrates provides an excellent summary of the dialectic Ellul inherits from Kierkegaard:

> In *The Concept of Irony* Socrates represents a position of infinite negativity: always demolishing but not able to build. In his longing for universal Truth Socrates rejected all the temporary

78. See Rognon, *Pensée*, 351.
79. Rognon, *Pensée*, 369.
80. Rognon, *Pensée*, 169.
81. Rognon, *Pensée*, 173.
82. Rognon, *Pensée*, 176.

truths of his society. This might be negative but at least it does not topple one lesser god only to put another up in its place.[83]

Kierkegaard's influence is implicit in Ellul's use of dialectics such as truth and reality, freedom and necessity, end and means, Christianity and Christendom, individual and crowd, Word and Technique.[84] Each expresses the basic contradiction in our present existence, between God and the world. For Rognon, Ellul's sociology is just as Kierkegaardian as his theology: and he notes that in his "technological trilogy" Ellul deploys these dialectics, often unacknowledged.[85]

Indeed, in the preface to a collection of varied published articles as well as previously unpublished writings, issued under the telling rubric, *Théologie et technique*, Rognon argues forcefully for a reading of Ellul which does not separate out theology and sociology. Surveying the classic division of the corpus into these two categories, he highlights the numerous exceptions which do not quite fit. It is worth citing him at length:

> However, there are exceptions to the rule. Most importantly, we need to flag up several published works which seem to have been able, within Ellul's lifetime, to articulate theology and sociology within a single text . . . bringing into play a kind of internal dialectic. *Présence au monde moderne . . . Les Nouveaux Possédés . . . La Parole Humiliée . . . Changer de révolution*. It should be added that all the books in the theological strand contain within themselves a dialectical orientation, which is not the case for the sociological strand. One might best express this

83. Backhouse, *Kierkegaard*, 217. "In this way, Kierkegaard means to undermine the idea that human cultures can generate eternal Truth. This is also a central concern of *Either/Or*" (218).

84. Rognon comments that the truth-reality dialectic is a golden thread in Ellul's biblical commentaries (Rognon, *Pensée*, 83). Different theological studies of Ellul make different dialectics central; see Goddard, *Living the Word*, 60–61 for a helpful survey. Van Vleet argues that "many of the distinctions Kierkegaard makes, Ellul revises and updates" (*Dialectical Theology*, 17n.31). He has in mind especially the dialectic within human existence of freedom and necessity, which is a corollary, he claims, of the fact that human beings are both spirit and matter (18). In summary, he notes that "many of Kierkegaard's tenets continue to play central roles in Ellul's work" (19).

85. There is a single reference to Kierkegaard in *Technique*, arguing that "he demonstrated a truly prophetic lucidity . . . at a time when the dominance of technological means had not yet become blinglingly obvious" (Rognon, *Pensée*, 197; *Technique*, 51). *Technique* speaks of the loss of true ends, which is developed into a chapter-length treatment on the problem of teleology in *Système*. *Bluff* is concerned with the word and Technique; he alludes to Kierkegaard's category of the "Interesting" in his discussion of television as an audiovisual technology which "fascinates" us and draws us away from the Word.

clear asymmetry by saying that the sociological pole is always despairing, and in this respect calls for the other pole, while the theological pole is always fundamentally incarnate, by virtue of the presence of the other pole within it.[86]

Rognon calls our attention to these "exceptional" texts within the corpus, texts I shall consider to be *programmatic*. He argues moreover, for an "asymmetry" between Ellul's theology and sociology: all of Ellul's theological work is itself dialectical, *incarnational* in his terms, because it contains within itself a dialogue with the world Scripture addresses. However, what is lacking in the "technological trilogy" is explicit attention to the Word incarnate in the world.

To find an early example of this "asymmetry" one need only turn to two of Ellul's best known texts, *The Meaning of the City* and *Technique*. *City* is perhaps Ellul's "most important theological work," and although it was first published in English, followed by the French version, *Sans feu ni lieu: la signification biblique de la grande ville* (1975), Ellul had written much of the text as early as the late 1940s, during the very period in which his most sustained and definitive sociological work on Technique, *La Technique ou l'enjeu du siècle* was taking shape.[87] It has been a commonplace of Ellul scholarship to read Ellul's biblical theology of the city alongside this formative sociological study of Technique. Indeed, in a significant article first published in English in *The Christian Century*, Ellul tells us to do so:

> The writing I had undertaken in a tentative frame of mind assumed a progressively better structure. The whole of it is a composition in counterpoint. . . . To my book on technology corresponds my theologically based study of the great city as the supreme achievement of man's technology.[88]

However, what can be neglected in reading *City* as merely *theological* (i.e., non-sociological) is the *incarnational methodology of the text itself*, the restless back-and-forth movement between on the one hand, theological interpretation and on the other, urban experience and urban theory that strikes the attentive reader. Here, one might suggest, Ellul explicates and demonstrates his understanding of the relationship between theology and social theory: "Revelation illuminates, synthesizes and explains what

---

86. *Théologie*, 12–14 (my italics).

87. See Goddard, *Living the Word*, 76n58, for an account of the early composition of *Sans feu*. The earliest published articles on the theme—"La Bible et la ville" and "Urbanisme et théologie biblique"—both date from 1950.

88. Ellul in Gill, *Word of God*, 90.

is discovered by our reason, as well as by our experience and our sense of the world we live in."[89]

For this reason Greenman, et al., rightly describe *City* as "meta-methodological": "Of all of Ellul's books, *The Meaning of the City* contains some of the most explicit statements of his agenda for relating faith and reason, supernatural revelation and the natural and social sciences."[90] Because of its length and importance, I will devote my entire next chapter to it, for it outlines the methodology at the heart of all Ellul's theological works.

But first, what of the texts that Rognon considers "exceptions to the rule," *Présence, Possédés, Parole* and *Changer de révolution*? For it was through sustained engagement with these texts that I arrived at the conclusion that Ellul's life work should not be bifurcated.

Internal Dialectics and Revolutionary Texts

Ellul was neither professional theologian nor professional sociologist. On the one hand, his global sociology broke all the rules, exceeding his first training as a "jurist," an expert in Roman law, although his second training as an expositor of Marx was more pertinent. On the other hand, he was not a formally trained pastor or theologian, a point his theological detractors would often make. In short, he cannot be easily pigeon-holed.

Granted, Ellul's global sociology was an intellectually ambitious project. And yet he insisted from the first that it was never a clever intellectual game, but a call to revolution. As Ellul put it in a letter written as early as 1936, he pursued "the dialectic between the observation of sociological reality and the theological challenge to that observation, in the certainty that it is in the play of these factors that humanity can find a way out."[91] Only revelation could open up a future beyond the limited horizon of technological progress.

I therefore move beyond methodological discussion and offer my own faithful betrayal of Ellul. As someone who has wrestled with his writings over a number of years, I can testify that, given the vastness of the corpus, and, it must be said, his occasionally verbose and repetitive style, reading Ellul is a necessarily selective business. Moreover, corroborating Rognon's approach, Ellul was himself reluctant to offer a definitive interpretation,

---

89. *Sans feu*, 275.

90. Greenman et al., *Understanding Jacques Ellul*, 67.

91. Ellul cited by an important voice within the French Reformed Church today, Stéphane Lavignotte, in the special issue of *Réforme* dedicated to Ellul, on the 100th anniversary of his birth (Lavignotte, "Inclassable et iconoclaste," 4).

preferring to leave it to the readers themselves to find a way to engage with his work.[92] This is why I do not want to become caught in "intentionality traps," as if Ellul's account of his intentions were definitive for his readers. This study is biased by the concerns that I bring to Ellul, and the concerns his work has elicited in me as reader. If I am open to the charge that I have reduced the vast complexity of Ellul to a "canon within the canon," that is perhaps the price of betrayal.

La Présence au monde moderne

First translated into English as *The Presence of the Kingdom* (1951), and recently retranslated more literally as *Presence in the Modern World* (2016), this is perhaps Ellul's best known and most quotable work.[93] Answering his own call for a new Karl Marx, Ellul argues for a revolution to liberate humanity from powers ranged against it. Yet this revolution, Ellul claims in a cascading argument, is only possible by bringing biblical *truth* to confront social *reality* (chapter 2); tackling the problem of *the end* and *the means* (chapter 3) and communicating the *Word of God* in a world of *Technique* (chapter 4).

Taking a familiar biblical metaphor about Christian presence in the world, that of "salt and light," Ellul states that "the Christian is in the world and must remain in the world."[94] Ellul is concerned to assert the need for the Incarnation to be lived out today, and he puts us on guard against two ways in which we deny the Incarnation, denying the vitality of Christian presence. "God did not become incarnate only for us to undo that work."[95]

Firstly, caught in the inextricably woven complexity of a technological society, the Christian flees from the material realm, cultivating a pure interior life.[96] For those who retreat in this way, the Incarnation is considered a material means to a hidden spiritual end. Instead, Ellul argues that the Word must always be expressed in concrete, social reality, for the Word of God became flesh both as the means *and* the end of the new creation. Yet by being present in the material world, Ellul does not at all mean *embracing* it as it is; rather in many respects, he means *resisting* it as it is. Indeed, the problem for the

---

92. *A temps*, 69. Ellul even encourages readers to find connections between his sociological and theological works that he himself did not intend (*A temps*, 162).

93. See also the recent English translation by Lisa Richmond, *Presence in the Modern World*.

94. *Présence* in *Défi*, 19.

95. *Présence* in *Défi*, 24.

96. *Présence* in *Défi*, 24.

spiritualizing tendency is precisely that in its naivety it does not resist, for if our material situation is seen as neutral, it is all too easy to assume that any technical means can be "put to use" for a spiritual end.[97]

Secondly, and more subtly, the Incarnation is denied by assuming that the end is already here, without remainder. On this account, the material world can easily be Christened and Christianized by the presence of the church, and the simple course of world history is seen as inexorable progress towards the kingdom of God.[98] This is, for Ellul, to capitulate to "the facts" of politics, economics and technology, to abolish the essential distinction between reality and truth. In his second chapter on *Revolutionary Christianity*, we see that for Ellul true revolution depends not on existing political realities, but future truth. "Now this the revolutionary situation: to be revolutionary is to pass judgment on what is, on the current facts, in the name of a truth which is not yet (but which is coming), holding that truth to be more authentic, more real than the reality that surrounds us."[99]

This second politicizing tendency becomes the greater concern for Ellul, since at face value, Christian political activism seems to share precisely his concern for changing the world.[100] What Ellul seeks is a deeper diagnosis of the theological truth behind sociological reality. Ellul writes of the power structures of the world, Technique, the State and Money, which condition our actions now; lurking in the background here are the "exouisai" which exercise sway in the world.[101] Moreover, in his closing chapter on the problem of communication, Ellul argues that the characteristic work today of the Christian intellectual is to discover a new language,[102] to make a breach into a closed world. Ellul is really talking about evangelization, a door for the Word of God in the world of Technique. This will enable "a new attentiveness to reality," to "the neighbor," and to what Ellul calls "the event," a rediscovery of the meaning of all history in the light of the Incarnation.

This brief reading highlights that the hope for revolution in *Presence* stems from Ellul's "apocalyptic exousiology," his theology of the powers and

---

97. *Presence* in *Défi*, 23.

98. *Présence* in *Défi*, 14.

99. *Présence* in *Défi*, 48.

100. Ellul later added a counterpart to *Présence,* in which his apocalyptic mode is even clearer. Published in 1963 and entitled *Fausse présence au monde moderne*, it could not be clearer. "Giving the world a value is to deny the incarnation," for as Ellul puts it, the world is still the world (*Fausse*, 36).

101. Ellul cites Ephesians 6:10–20, which speaks of *exousias, kosmocratas,* and *pneumatika*.

102. *Présence* in *Défi*, 123–27, 150, in Tomlin, *Provocative Church*, 22.

their eventual defeat.[103] Having outlined an apocalyptic hermeneutic in chapter two, in chapter three entitled *Apocalypse Then*, I will explore in detail what that defeat signifies by engaging Ellul's reading of the eponymously apocalyptic book of Revelation.

Les Nouveaux possédés

In his 1973 book *Les Nouveaux Possédés* (the reference is to Dostoevsky, hence the English translation, *The New Demons*), Ellul picks up the agenda he laid down in *Présence*. Writing a form of social history, he reviews the history of the West in the light of the Incarnation. Usually categorized as a sociological text, here Ellul offers his particular treatment of the secularization thesis.

Drawing on an eclectic mix of scholarship, Ellul puts forward his own theory of the "sacred." At its most basic, the sacred is the order of the world, for it gives reference points, sacred places and sacred times, meaning and orientation in a disordered world. Human beings love the sacred, for it is a means of interpreting and stabilizing the inner and outer worlds, holding conflicting forces in tension. Furthermore, the sacred creates the group, although this order must be incarnated in a single person who stands for the group.[104]

The sacred order is, however, based on a fundamental lie: it is a human order masquerading as divine. Moreover, this order requires violence to police it.[105] This is because it is never without contestation, and various threats will either be defeated or victorious over the existing order. However, paradoxically, for Ellul, that which threatens the sacred, if it eventually conquers, is always liable to become the new sacred. Indeed, Ellul puts forward this essential sociological axiom which we will have reason to explore below: that which "desacralizes" will then in turn be "sacralized."

However, for Ellul, biblical Revelation is unique at just this point: it requires no sacred, but makes the world wholly secular. The God of Israel is not tied to the world but is holy, wholly other: "A Creator as well as Liberator God, Jesus Christ LORD of history and incarnation of the love of God: from this point on, a sacred organization of the world is no longer necessary."[106]

---

103. Goddard, *Living the Word*, 156, credits Marva Dawn with reading *Présence* in this way.

104. *Nouveaux possédés*, 79–93.

105. As we shall see, the sacred is a sociological approximation of the theological concept of the powers.

106. *Nouveaux possédés*, 93.

Revelation therefore leads to *incessant desacralization* for the world can now live without the sacred. Jesus has revealed the high and holy God within history. The Incarnation was a radically new story, the story of divine strength incarnate in weakness, a first great moment of desacralization, sweeping away the myths of the Greco-Roman world.[107] Ellul unfurls the same essential argument as *Présence*: that the Incarnation demands an incarnation in mundane, secular reality, for the truth of God has now been translated into the historical reality of the world. Indeed, Ellul claims that our very notions of truth and reality are a legacy of the Incarnation, drawing on the well known work *Mimesis* by Eric Auerbach. "The Incarnation ushered in a particular collective mode of being, a particular way of representing reality funded by Christianity."[108]

On Ellul's account here, Christendom was, *ab initio*, an attempt to replace pagan myths with this new story. Yet Ellul argues that over time Christendom came to sacralize the new orders which it had created, justifying its power over culture and nature.[109] For Ellul, it was this process of "resacralization" that gave rise to a second moment: the Reformation. This was, again, inspired by the Bible. Indeed, he claims that in successfully desacralizing the medieval church, the Reformation laid the foundation for the Enlightenment, and the modern secular order of science and Technique. The modern secular society has theological roots.

However, although Technique and Reformation are related, writing from a French perspective, it is the era of Enlightenment and Revolution that is decisive, destroying the remnants of the old order in two further desecrations. Firstly, of culture, as the king and his sacred office, is executed, and the nation state established. Secondly, of nature, as Technique disenchants and exploits the natural world. Although in Ellul's brief historical sketches, there are often few clear markers laid down, in *Nouveaux Possédés* Ellul points the finger at a fascination with technical efficiency in the key transitional period of the eighteenth century. "And from the perspective of the efficiency that had just taken humanity over, it was clear that religion displayed a remarkable level of inefficiency."[110]

---

107. *Nouveaux possédés*, 34.

108. *Nouveaux possédés*, 32.

109. See *Nouveaux possédés*, chapter 2. As an ancient and medieval historian, Ellul debunks the popular myth that the Constantinian church simply took flight from this world in the hope of heaven; rather, it became all too worldly, all too powerful (34).

110. *Nouveaux possédés*, 95–96. On Ellul's historical account, this pragmatic confluence of politics and Technique, rather than a philosophical project, is what constitutes the deeper secularisation of the Enlightenment.

This is an extremely brief summary of a complex book we shall return to explore. What clearly corroborates my argument here is the entirely theological basis upon which Ellul takes his stand. In *Nouveaux*, Ellul intends to dissent from the idea that the modern world is inevitably secularizing. Christians have no problem with the secular, but they are not to christen any particular order, for they are called to a constant reformation, to exorcise the old demons (Religion), but also the new demons (Science and Technique).[111]

This does not mean the rejection of Science and Technique, but their chastening. In conclusion Ellul clearly reveals his hand. "It is not Technique that enslaves us but the sacred power attributed to Technique, which stops us exercising our critical faculties."[112] The presenting task is not to attack Technique, but to reduce it to a mere set of methods and means, useful but no more: "A set of methods, which must be put through the mill of truth; utilitarian processes, interesting of course, but not life-enriching."[113]

Ellul will not say how this might be done in the main body of the text, but leaves the question hanging. It is only in a closing theological *Coda for Christians* that, reflecting on the thirty years of his theological career, Ellul takes aim at theologians who are taking Christians in entirely the wrong direction. Even his own writings had been misunderstood: "When I advanced the need for desacralization . . . I had in mind desacralizing the realities of the world with the truth of the Gospel."[114] What is needed is not the demythologization of the Bible and "secular theology" but the shattering our technological idols.[115]

It was Ellul scholar Darrell Fasching who first considered *Nouveaux* to be the "Rosetta Stone" of Ellul's work, unifying its two strands of theology and sociology: "The sociology of the sacred is the critical link in the dialectical relationship between Ellul's sociology . . . and his Apocalyptic theology of revolution."[116] Indeed, *Nouveaux* lays down an agenda which I shall explore in my fourth chapter on *Apocalypse Now* and in my sixth chapter on going beyond Ellul. However, I contend that *La Parole humiliée*

---

111. With reference to Jesus' parable of the seven demons, Ellul mocks Cox's notion of the "scientific exorcism" of past knowledge, noting that seven new demons have now taken up residence (*Nouveaux possédés*, 324).

112. *Nouveaux possédés*, 316.

113. *Nouveaux possédés*, 341.

114. *Nouveaux possédés*, 339.

115. *Nouveaux possédés*, 348.

116. Fasching, *Thought of Jacques Ellul*, 116. See also Rognon, *Pensée*, 205, noting that the argument of *Subversion*, a "theological" text, runs along similar lines.

(1981) takes us even further by offering a fully integrated *programmatic, revolutionary* text.[117]

La Parole humiliée

In *Parole*, we find Ellul interweaving chapters of theology and sociology, with internal dialectics within the body of a single text. In form, the chapters seem to operate in dialectical relationship, from the phenomenology of word and Technique (chapter 1 on hearing and seeing, chapters 3, 4, 6) to the theology of the Word and Technique (chapter 2 on creation and rupture, chapter 5 on the Incarnation and the church, and chapter 7 on eschatology).

Notably, here we find Ellul's clearest attempt at a theology of creation, positing from OT exegesis the dialectic of the word and the image, arguing that there is an order of truth pertaining to the word, the inner realm of spiritual and ethical discourse and deliberation, and an order of reality, which pertains to the image, the outer realm of action and actualization in the world. Both are essential, and yet what we see now, Ellul argues, is the total victory of reality over truth, the image over the humiliated word, in an age of *Technique*. Yet, in the light of the NT, Ellul gestures towards their promised reconciliation at the new creation, in the final chapter, entitled "Reconciliation."

For many years, *Parole* did not receive the attention it deserves, although this has recently been addressed.[118] Given his preoccupation with structuralism, some have concluded that Ellul is out of his depth. But we have already noted Ellul's early concern with the problem of communication, and in a prominent chapter on the Word in *Ce que je crois* Ellul himself makes clear that his concern with language dates "from a much earlier date" than the contemporary interest in linguistics.[119]

It must be admitted that *Parole* is a demanding text, requiring of interpreters more than a simple re-appropriation of its arguments today. For on the one hand, its sociological topics are inevitably dated, deeply immersed in the questions raised by earlier "means of mass communication," for example, debating the use of radio communication during the 1968 student protests in Paris, the ubiquity of advertising billboards at the roadside, the

---

117. Published the year after Ellul's retirement from his teaching post at the University of Bordeaux, *Parole* was reprinted in 2014.

118. David Lovekin's work *Technique, Discourse, and Consciousness* was first of note. His recent contributions to *The Ellul Forum* have drawn upon *Parole* and *Empire du non-sens*. On this theme, see also Dawn, *Tabernacling of God*; Porquet, *Jacques Ellul*; Marlin, *Propaganda and the Ethics of Persuasion*; Rollison, *Revolution of Necessity*.

119. *Ce que je crois*, 35.

rising effect of television news on public perception, and the implications for language of the microcomputer. And on the other hand, Ellul's theological approach in *Parole* is provocative in the extreme, bringing to the fore the iconoclasm that drives his whole life's work. It is not therefore surprising that it lends itself to journalistic treatment in Porquet's engaging application of *Parole* to contemporary mass media.[120]

Theological interpreters may be deterred by the fact that Ellul appears to lump together much of ancient Orthodox iconography and medieval Catholic art, as well as the embrace of structuralist analyses in modern theology and the enthusiasm for mass media communication and audiovisual techniques in modern evangelism, under a single banner: idolatry. There is much here that is off-putting, crossing "thresholds of radicality:"[121] our modern obsession with evidence is evil;[122] language has been technicized;[123] the conversation with a computer has become the model for all conversation;[124] modern art has no meaning;[125] audiovisual systems are an "anti-human war machine."[126]

Ruptured from the spiritual truth of the word, ironically, Ellul contends, we also lose our hold on material reality, the domain where we are meant to be grounded:

> Such is our situation today.... We have restricted "truth" to "reality"; we have banished the shy and fleeting expression of truth. Yet the strangest thing is not the identifying of truth with reality, as we already find in science, but the identifying of truth with a fake reality, literally a "pretend," that is to say, painted reality.[127]

For Ellul, this is an intolerable situation, and a person cannot survive situated in a fiction of technologically produced images.[128] The "multiplication of images" leads to two types of "technical apocalypse"—the hope we can have it all now, or the despair that the world will end *soon*:

---

120. See Porquet, *Jacques Ellul*, chapter 16.

121. Rognon helpfully puts forward the concept of "thresholds of radicality" in describing how Ellul goads his readers into a confrontation. See Rognon, *Pensée*, 365–66.

122. Evidence also implies obviousness in French, so Ellul's polemic is against seeking absolute proof of our positions (*Parole*, 108–9). Ellul here blames Descartes.

123. *Parole*, 177.

124. *Parole*, 178.

125. *Parole*, 245.

126. *Parole*, 285.

127. *Parole*, 252.

128. *Parole*, 252.

> These two trends: the demand for everything all at once, and terror about the end of the world, result from the infinite multiplication of images and combine to produce all around us apocalyptic and messianic currents.[129]

In his own terms, this is in effect Ellul's account of hyper-reality, the term coined by the far more prominent French sociologist Jean Baudrillard in *Simulacra and Simulation,* published the same year as *Parole.*[130] In this construal, Technique has made a world dangerous not only because of its abandonment of truth, but equally because of its loss of creaturely reality. *Parole* ends with a clarion call for a genuine revolution, the freedom of the word. Language must be freed first of all, for that is how humanity can be freed: "If you want to save humanity today, start by saving the word."[131]

Parole is clearly an exceptional text in the corpus, serving as a bridge between Ellul's sociology and theology.[132] Indeed, an early American commentator on Ellul, Marva Dawn had already noted that *Parole* is "a notable and helpful exception" in his work.[133] Moreover, the English translator of *Parole,* Joyce Main Hanks considers *Parole* to be a new development: "Ellul could have chosen to write a sociological treatise on language and paired it with a later theological work, as he has previously done. . . . But in *The Humiliation of the Word* the author has preferred to integrate sociology and theology into a single whole, for reasons he has not yet explained in print."[134]

There is no account of Ellul's intentions I know of, but on my reading, *Parole* unveils in condensed form Ellul's project from the first, which was to interrogate whether in a world of Technique, and its "one best way," it becomes harder for us hear the Word of God.

Conclusion

I have put forward a thesis that the existence of key programmatic texts in the Ellul corpus belies the categorization of his work into separate tracks of theology and sociology. This is not to deny the obvious fact that Ellul's

---

129. *Parole,* 231. Ellul claims the television news bulletin best expresses and exemplifies this situation.

130. Baudrillard shares some of Ellul's concerns in *Parole.* For a treatment of the potential theological applications of Baudrillard's work, see Walters, *Baudrillard and Theology.*

131. *Parole,* 281.

132. Rognon, *Pensée,* 79.

133. Dawn, *Tabernacling of God,* 26.

134. See Hanks's preface in *Humiliation,* xii–xiii.

writing on Technique was nurtured within the cradle of French Personalism. Under the influence of Marx and more directly, Bernard Charbonneau, Ellul's sociology was to stand up to scrutiny within the positivistic and at best agnostic academic environment of post-Second World War France.[135] But I have argued for a fundamental asymmetry between Ellul's sociology and theology. Whereas Ellul's sociology is one side of a dialogue, his theology always contains an internal dialectic, exemplified by *Sans feu*, to which I will turn in my next chapter. Moreover, the counter-point of sociology and theology was to mean *revolutionary* confrontation, rather than *methodological* separation, and in these texts, this confrontation comes to the fore and becomes the main subject, with Ellul's theology of Technique laid bare.

These texts, and their "internal dialectics," are at the heart of my "faithful betrayal" of Ellul. They have become the Ellulian lens through which I look at the world and attempt to speak a living word today. This does not mean I neglect Ellul's "sociology." For to assume that the legacy of Ellul's technology criticism lies in trying to restate and reapply the seven characteristics of Ellulian Technique as stated in the introduction is, on my account, to miss the point. In the argument I offer here, Ellul's central bequest to us is the dialectical methodology he pioneered in his work: a simultaneous reading of the Bible and of social experience, enriched by social analysis. Ellul warns us against naively assuming technologies are simply a divine gift and against the illusion that "things can only get better." For Ellul, accounts both of creation and of eschatology need to be apocalyptic.

---

135. On the relationship between Ellul and Charbonneau, see Goddard, *Living the Word*, 21–30.

Rupture

The Bible, the City, and Technique

IN THE PRECEDING CHAPTER, I suggested that without the theological horizon, Ellul's technology criticism is a dangerous dead end, devoid of hope. In contrast, in the preface to *Sans feu*, Ellul could go as far as to state: "This book is a complete and utter affirmation of the most radical hope."[1]

This is not to say that it is brimming with optimism about the city. Indeed, in the statement quoted above, Ellul was responding here to Harvey Cox's criticism that *Sans feu* had nothing positive to say about human culture! *Sans feu* soon became a notorious and divisive text, and from then on, there was no shortage of critics lined up to label it "pessimistic," "contrarian," "dualist," or "Manichean." A reader of *Sans feu* commentating in the popular Sojourner magazine spoke for many when he despaired, "In vain I searched for any indications of a doctrine of creation."[2] Even a generally favorable interpreter, David Gill, who still commends *The Meaning of the City* today,[3] critiques Ellul for eclipsing creation: "Ellul's work on the city and technique is a great stride forward for Christians. Nevertheless it can be improved. The greatest difficulty is Ellul's failure to see any survival of God's creation after the fall."[4]

Erasing Cain

What was the reason for this reception? It does not take long to discover, for to readers looking for a basis for a "cultural mandate" for technology in Genesis 1 and 2,[5] Ellul brings an unwelcome challenge: as his lapidary first

1. *Sans feu*, 23. Ellul here adds that he has held this conviction for thirty years.

2. Goddard, *Living the Word*, 67.

3. Gill provided the foreword for the 2011 republication of *City* by Wipf & Stock.

4. Gill, *Word of God*, 178. He suggests that Ellul's argument against creation "erects a straw man."

5. E.g., Gen 1:28; 2:15.

53

sentence puts it, "The first city-builder was Cain."[6] Clearly locating Technique within an often neglected biblical narrative, the narrative of Cain and Abel in Genesis 4, Ellul makes Cain the prototypical urban-technologist.[7]

Greenman, et al., in the book *Understanding Jacques Ellul*, attempt to revive an interest in Ellul's work but concede that this starting point is a real barrier to his reception today, pitching him against Protestant and Catholic tradition alike. Ellul's original critique was largely directed against what he polemically called the "Thomist heresy" of man as co-creator, as he baldly states in the concluding chapter of *Sans feu*.[8] As we have noted, Ellul's polemic against Thomism originates within the context of differing parties within the French Personalist movements of the 1930s. And throughout his later works, Ellul essentially extends the same critique of what he understands by Thomism.

Greenman, et al., offer a treatment pitched more towards North American Protestants, and this explains their concern in exploring the theology of the cultural mandate. Ellul, they contend, refuses to see the city as "one expression of human sociality, which originates in the social order described by Genesis 1 and 2," but argues that "the story of the city begins after the account of the Fall and the curse with Gen 4:1–17: the story of Cain."[9] In a brief survey of the avalanche of criticism the book received, they conclude that, "To this date, the majority sentiment seems to be that *The Meaning of the City* should have been titled, *Demeaning the City*."[10] What first strikes the reader looking for hope for the city is Ellul's "active pessimism," which can initially present as "bleak and static."[11] Indeed, as early as his introduction to the 1965 English translation, *The Meaning of the City*, John Wilkinson had aptly written: "The major problem in writing an introduction . . . is to persuade sensible people not to throw it down before . . . the first ten pages."[12]

A Cainite reading of the urban life does not seem to provide a very promising starting point for an exploration of a technological society. The authors of *Why Cities Matter* are quite candid in this respect:

6. *Sans feu*, 22.

7. *Sans feu*, 25.

8. *Sans feu*, 322.

9. Greenman et al., *Understanding Jacques Ellul*, 68.

10. Greenman et al., *Understanding Jacques Ellul*, 64.

11. Murray, *City Vision*, 8, noting that "active pessimism" was Ellul's own term. However, Murray argues that "there is much that is useful," and his biblical hermeneutic, especially his reading of Cain, appears indebted to Ellul.

12. *City*, xii. Despite this, it was hailed by *Time Magazine* as "perhaps the most important theological book of the year."

Because Cain is cast as a shadowy character throughout the scriptural narrative, many have assumed that his shadow falls on the city. However, the city is not to be regarded as an evil invention of fallen man. . . . *The ultimate goal set before humanity at the very beginning was that human culture should take city-form.* . . . There should be an urban structuring of human historical existence. . . . The cultural mandate given at creation was a mandate to build the city. Now, after the fall, the city is still a benefit, serving humankind as refuge from the howling wilderness condition into which the fallen human race, exiled from paradise, has been driven. . . . The "common grace" city has remedial benefits even in a fallen world.[13]

However, at the same time, can Cain be so summarily erased from the biblical account of the city? Indeed, one might wonder, is this predominantly first-world debate about urban-technological society in need, precisely, of Ellul's reading of Cain in order to refine and sharpen it? From the outset, as with *Technique, Sans feu* was a confrontational text, intended precisely to challenge what he saw as optimistic and decidedly undialectical readings of the urban-technological world resulting from the "30 glorious years" of post-WWII economic expansion.[14]

For Ellul, starting with the biblical account of Cain was axiomatic, in dialogue with his own experience and sociological reflection upon it.[15] In this sense, he himself was the "man in the crowd," the "everyman" for whom he wrote.[16] One could even contend that what Ellul found in Marxism, a description of the experience of the urban alienation he knew, he found also in the Bible's account of the city built by Cain and his descendents, the archetypical account of enslaved work. However, Ellul's concern is to trace Marx's concept of urban alienation to its roots in alienation from God, a break between us and our Creator. "Marx of course observes all this for the capitalist and modern city, based on his sociological analysis, but in fact he cannot help generalizing. The whole city, every city, and the judgment upon it is organized around this implicit spiritual perspective (as very often in Marx!)"[17]

As we have begun to see in the first chapter, Ellul tends to speak not of the fall, but rather of "la rupture" from God, a "break" which has cosmic

13. Um and Buzzard, *Why Cities Matter*, 54 (my italics), following Meredith Kline's biblical scholarship.

14. See, for example, Ellul, "Cain."

15. Greenman et al., *Understanding Jacques Ellul*, 2.

16. *Sans feu*, 231; *Présence* in *Défi*, 93–94.

17. *Sans feu*, 79.

knock-on effects. Goddard therefore rightly summarizes the theological task as Ellul conceived it in these terms: "to understand our present world our primary task is . . . not to study the world that God created in communion with him, but the world which resulted from man's rupture with God and God's new relationship with that world."[18] In other words, Ellul was determined to read Genesis 1 and 2 in tension with Genesis 3 and 4, and indeed in tension with the entire biblical revelation. Yet to have any idea of Ellul's hermeneutic of scripture and culture, one must begin with Cain.

Cain, the Primordial Technologist?

After expulsion from the Garden, east of Eden, Adam and Eve bear two sons, Cain and Abel. In a dispute over cultic offering, the precise meaning of which is opaque, Cain murders Abel, an act for which he comes under further divine judgment. Cain's condemnation gives the book its title, *Sans feu ni lieu*, for Cain is now without hearth or home, for henceforth "he will have neither place nor friends to call his own."[19] Cain now knows a broken relationship with place, and a broken relationship with others. Yet judgment is immediately tempered with grace, for Cain receives from God "the mark of Cain" as a promise of life. "He is under God's protection and that's what allows him to live."[20]

However, Cain's refusal to believe in this promise and his rejection of God's protection results in a further break, a definitive *rupture from God*. It is hence that instead of accepting God's protection, Cain creates the city, a place where he can protect himself. Despite the significance for the NT of Genesis 3, Ellul arguably gives to Genesis 4 an unprecedented significance, for it offers to him a concrete account, as it were, of the consequences of human rejection of God.[21] "The world might have been difficult after the fall of Adam, but it was not yet marked by murder. Now it

18. Goddard, *Living the Word*, 75. Where the word is used instead of the fall, I have stuck with the English "rupture." Where verbal forms are used, I have turned at times to the language of breaking. There is at times an ambivalence in the term "rupture," for it can also imply a "breach" in the sense of a "way in," a "route through" (and of course the French "route" comes from the same base).

19. *Sans feu*, 26.

20. *Sans feu*, 28.

21. Ellul of course does not neglect the massive significance of the Adam and Eve narrative for Christian theology. It is at the starting point of his 1964 work of ethics, *Le Vouloir et le Faire*.

is. The city is the direct consequence of Cain's murderous act and Cain's refusal to accept God's protection."[22]

This new world, built in rejection of God's creation, is what Ellul calls "a counter-creation." This, for Ellul, is the meaning of the Hebrew *Enoch* which he takes to be the name of Cain's city, its etymology signifying "initiation and beginning of utilization." Cain begins again with Enoch, and this represents a solid departure point for all civilization.[23] Whatever creation was is now unknown.[24] Only with *homo faber* do we begin:

> Cain takes possession of the world and uses it as he wishes. . . .
> Cain creates technique. Cain cuts stones and thereby renders
> them impure, unfit to build an altar for God (Exod 20:20). Cain
> bends all creation to his will. He knows well that he is the head
> of creation by divine order, and he seizes on that too. He com-
> pels creation to follow his destiny, and his destiny is the slavery
> of sin, of rebelling to escape creation. From this seizure, this
> upheaval, the city is born.[25]

This godless order, founded on an original act of violence, is the order we now take for granted. And this is also the order of Technique, for the city and Technique are directly related in Ellul's interpretation of Cain. As the founder of the city, Cain becomes the founder of Technique.

At this stage, having begun to outline the meaning of the city for Ellul, we must pause and reflect briefly on the presuppositions of Ellul's interpretation. For once again we need to feel the vast implications of what Ellul is suggesting. Does Ellul really mean to suggest that Cain was the primordial technologist, and that all technology—from the wheel, to the mill, to the atom bomb, to the Smartphone—has its roots in Cain? The English translation stops short of rendering "technique" as "technology" here, preferring instead the translation: "the art of craftsmanship," undoubtedly as a concession to the obvious problem of anachronism.[26] For to read Ellul's biblical theology of the city in parallel with social anthropology, even Ellul's own "sociologie," is far from unproblematic. As we have seen, Ellul argued that we live in an unprecedented technological civilization, incommensurate

22. *Sans feu,* 29.

23. *Sans feu,* 31.

24. "Cain begins a new world . . . though it's not a beginning in Cain's eyes. God's creation is held for nothing. God has done nothing, and certainly nothing was completed." (*Sans feu,* 30).

25. *San feu,* 36. Ellul has in mind the prohibition in Exod 20:25 upon hewing stones for an altar.

26. *City,* 6.

with the past.[27] Therefore, three questions immediately press upon us. Firstly, why should we read biblical texts emerging from the context of these past milieux as at all relevant to today's entirely novel modern "technical phenomenon"? Secondly, how can the particular biblical story of Cain as a city-founder generate an enduring account of Technique that makes any kind of sense today? And thirdly, how can the Bible help us to interpret, engage and name the powers of the increasingly changeable and mobile urban-technological world of the early twenty-first century?

Having "scandalized" his readers by starting with Cain,[28] Ellul then proceeds to articulate three powerful and programmatic responses to these three questions. These are not summary answers, but *a priori* starting points without which it is impossible to understand the kinds of answers Ellul offers in his life's work. These commitments are firstly to the *canon of scripture*, secondly to the *category of myth*, and thirdly to the *apocalyptic mode*.

Ellul's Theological Hermeneutic: Canon, Myth, and Apocalypse

Canon

In *Sans feu*, Ellul avows his commitment to a consistent and coherent biblical message about the city, from Genesis to Revelation, a message so all-encompassing that he claims it is the key to unlocking the entire biblical witness. Addressing the skeptical interlocutor, he writes:

> *Perhaps* there is a single teaching throughout Scripture: *perhaps* from the first book to the last book of the Bible, there is the same judgment, the same word said about the city. And what if that is the case, if we find this judgment carried at all times over seven or eight centuries, and in all forms? If we discover a complete, coherent doctrine of the city, with an undeniable bearing on man's life, his destiny, his relationship with God, and ultimately his salvation, if we discover a history of the city, encompassed in the Lordship of Jesus Christ?[29]

Before he attends to what the Bible as a whole says about the city, Ellul tries to convince the reader of his underlying hermeneutical strategy in his foreword, mounting a direct challenge to the dominance of historical

---

27. See my introduction, 12n36; Goddard, *Living the Word*, 146.

28. *Sans feu*, 38.

29. *Sans feu*, 38.

criticism, a challenge understood in terms of the truth-reality dialectic we have encountered. As we have seen, this hermeneutic derives from Kierkegaard and as with Kierkegaard, Ellul's theological work in *Sans feu* is essentially an extended biblical meditation, in which the Bible interrogates the reader.[30] Standing by Kierkegaard's reading of the narrative of Abraham and Isaac in *Fear and Trembling*, Ellul claims that interpretations which subject the text to extra-textual questions of source, form and historicity "tell us nothing abou the truth," whereas Kierkegaard's "spiritual meditation," though not buttressed by science, "puts me in the presence of something I cannot deny without denying myself."[31]

It is on account of this characteristic approach that Greenman, et al., surmise that Ellul was "an unmistakable proponent of what is being called "theological interpretation" of Scripture."[32] Certainly there are aspects of Ellul's approach which fit well with this approach, notably his respect for the canon of Scripture. Ellul vigorously defends himself against both the charge of undisciplined exegesis and "conservative literalism," by displaying a remarkable fidelity and attentiveness to the final canonical form of the texts, while being aware of the history of their compilation. And in this, he acknowledges the influence upon him of Barth's and von Rad's biblical theology: "Through the diversity of sources and origins (moreover, which are never hidden), is it not the whole that contains the truth of the message, is it not the text transmitted in its final construction that is meaningful?"[33]

For Ellul, as for Barth and von Rad, it is the interplay between particular texts and their placing within the overall canon as a product of the history of the people of God that is significant: "I therefore firmly retain in this study the globalizing view that each text is explained by the whole and is part of an overall trajectory (the very history of the chosen people) that has its own internal coherence, which we can uncover only by reading the texts in their relationships with one another."[34]

30. Rognon, *Pensée*, 83. Rognon suggests that the entire method of *Sans Feu* is a tribute to Kierkegaard (*Pensée*, 178).

31. *Sans feu*, 17. See Backhouse's account and his contention that Kierkegaard later distances himself from *Fear and Trembling* (*Kierkegaard*, 226–27).

32. See Greenman et al., *Understanding Jacques Ellul*, 117.

33. *Sans feu*, 13. Ellul was clearly a reader not only of Barth but also of von Rad, as we shall see.

34. *Sans feu*, 14. Canonical criticism is a term now associated with the later biblical scholar Brevard Childs. Yet, the shadow of Karl Barth is cast long on the very different work of first von Rad, then Ellul, and later, Childs. As Brian Brock notes, Childs could state in his later work that Barth's analysis "had not been superseded in its basic insight" (Brock, *Singing the Ethos of God*, 54). Brock later comments on the formative influence on Barth of Kierkegaard's "exegetical theologizing" (71).

The dialogue and allusions between texts within the canon, that is, biblical intertextuality and the added significance it gives to texts over time, is, for Ellul, intrinsic to the self-revelation of the incarnate God:

> But if it is a theological truth that the God of Israel and of Jesus Christ is a God who reveals himself in history, do we take this revelation seriously by fixing a revealed word to a moment of history, like a butterfly nailed to the wall, so that, nicely framed by cultural data, it can no longer move from that spot to signify something else? Is there not a contradiction between such a hermeneutical attitude and the very truth of God incarnate?[35]

This does not mean that this "something else" that a text can come to signify is at the whim of the later reader. Ellul's concern with interpreting any particular text is marked by attention to that text's logical flow, its literary structures and features.[36] To those who claim this approach is at best "naïve," Ellul, once again enthusiastic about etymology, claims that he seeks above all to allow Scripture to interpret Scripture, which may thus speak for itself. This is what he calls a "native" reading.[37]

When we attend to its own language, Ellul claims that the Bible speaks over its entire sweep with a united voice about the city, and indeed Technique. Within the vast expanse of different cultural contexts, Ellul declares he finds "a Revelation about the city," which is itself a "decoding" of the city in every age.[38] The sometimes cryptic and lengthy argument of *Sans feu* is bluntly stated in *Théologie et Technique*. "I believe that one can apply to Technique in general everything I have tried . . . to demonstrate from the Bible to be the theological meaning of the City. What the Bible tells us about the City must be taken and interpreted for Technique."[39]

Reading the Bible's account of early civilization as pertinent to contemporary Technique may seem impossibly anachronistic, but for Ellul, the Holy Spirit inspires Scripture to reveal for all time what is only implicit at the

---

35. *Sans feu*, 17.

36. "For his work on both Ecclesiastes and Revelation, the decisive interpretive moves are prompted by nuanced observations about the literary structure of those books. It would be unfair to suggest that Ellul's approach to Scripture is undisciplined by the text itself or arbitrary in its interpretive decisions." See Greenman et al., *Understanding Jacques Ellul*, 118.

37. *Sans feu*, 15. Greenman et al. say of Theological Interpretation that "this movement insists that its approach to interpretation is best suited to the Bible's own account of its nature and purpose" (*Understanding Jacques Ellul*, 98).

38. "The Bible is perhaps the first language about the City which is also a decoding of the City's own language" (*Sans feu*, 18 [my italics]).

39. *Théologie et Technique*, 161.

origins of civilization: "What is remarkable is the very fact that Scripture tells us about this entity [the city], whose full figure we know today. In this way the teaching of Scripture is truly prophetic. . . . The Holy Spirit reveals to humanity the depths of his own work and God's judgment upon it. He does that from the very first and in the face of man's inability yet to understand it."[40]

Granted, the ziggurat is not the Burj-Khalifa Tower but Ellul claims that the biblical *myth* of the city (the term is carefully chosen), rippling out from Genesis 4, speaks a living word for every age. Ellul's use of the term *myth*, while potentially misleading today, situates him against the backdrop of the hermeneutical debates of his day. Let us then consider his use of the term, at the same time briefly bringing him into dialogue with perhaps surprising contemporary parallels.

Myth

The very word "myth" is opposed, in popular usage, to historical truth.[41] To call the narrative of Cain a "myth" could be taken in our day, as in Ellul's, to invite the modern reader either to consign it to fiction, or perhaps to pursue some etiological meaning. Ellul indulges his polemical taste for irony by referring to the story of Cain as a myth—"everyone agrees today in saying that this story is a myth and it does not tell us the reality of the situation"[42]—before calling on the skeptical reader to look further:

> What appears to us remarkable in this brief and rich hint from Scripture is that it is true whatever position one takes toward the Bible. If it is God's revelation, then we have what God thinks of the matter. . . . If Scripture is only a historical text, dependent on earlier documents, themselves dependent on myths created at the beginning of the dawn of consciousness, our texts are also significant because they tell us what man wanted to do when he built the city, what he claimed to conquer, what he thought he could establish.[43]

Surfing a rising tide of interest in myth, Ellul argues in *Sans feu* that the early chapters of Genesis are not naively etiological conceits, embroidered with "anecdotal details" for the sake of verisimilitude.[44] Rather, they

40. *Sans feu*, 94.

41. Vanhoozer, *Remythologizing Theology*, 3.

42. *Sans feu*, 25.

43. *Sans feu*, 36 (my italics).

44. Ellul engages Roland Barthes in the preface to *Sans feu*. Barthes's famous *Mythologies* was first published as a set of magazine articles in the early 1950s.

are dense and loaded accounts of the meaning of human origins, revealing something profoundly true about what our ancestors desired, and what they established.[45] And in this argument, Ellul seeks to align himself more with social anthropologists than with theologians concerned with "myth," notably Rudolf Bultmann.

Indeed, even excluding a theological horizon, the narrative of Cain would still be a significant cultural-historical text, Ellul claims. As we see in his later exhaustive *sociological* treatment in *Nouveaux*, in three cumulative chapters on the sacred, myth, and religion, Ellul contends that myths convey "something permanent about humanity, in our relationship with the universe, and in the very structure of our souls."[46] For the ancients, these were the only means by which such profound and enduring human apprehensions could be expressed: "Humanity had discovered a singular language, suited to express our very depths, to express what is otherwise inexpressible."[47] Myths seek to encapsulate what other means cannot express: *how the world came to be this way and how we relate to it.* Indeed, throughout *Nouveaux*, Ellul is perhaps above all concerned to argue that the modern world has its legitimating myths, just as much as did the ancient world.

In Ellul's later and most important *theological* treatment of myth, in *Parole*, we see how he understands biblical texts which appear to be in the form of myth. For Ellul, the expression of myth we find in the Bible is born of hearing God's Word, and it is therefore particular, both related to and distinct from extra-biblical myth:

> God speaks. Myth is born from this word. . . . Myth is the analogy that enables us to grasp the meaning of what God has said. . . . As discourse constructed to paraphrase the revelation, it is a metaphor that should lead the listener beyond what he has heard. Myth is born of the revealed Word of God, but because it is figurative, it has no visible image. As the highest expression of the word. . . . Myth is the living word that soon will become a text.[48]

Through biblical myths God speaks a living word, a word in the same form as, yet polemically opposed to, the myths of the world. In this way, the Hebrew Scriptures shout back defiantly at the Ancient Near East's myths:

45. For Ellul's use of the word "myth" in *Sans feu*, see 22, 31–32, 36–37, 42–45.

46. *Nouveaux possédés*, 140 (my italics). Ellul's main dialogue partners are Karl Marx, Emile Durkheim, Max Weber, Roland Barthes, René Girard, Jean Baudrillard, Mircea Eliade, and Claude Lévi-Strauss.

47. *Nouveaux possédés*, 141 (my italics).

48. *Parole*, 118–19.

whereas the pagan myths picture nature and culture as the playground of the gods, biblical myth and metaphor are given to lift our eyes, to carry us beyond this world, to the Transcendent God who is outside it but who speaks into it, creating history.[49]

In short, in his polemical use of the term "myth" in *Sans feu*, later expanded in *Parole*, Ellul was attempting to argue that the genre of myth adds significance to the biblical texts rather than taking significance away. In stark contrast with Karl Barth who eschewed the term to avoid confusion, Ellul takes on the demythologizers who stripped texts to their purported historical bones. Yet such is the influence of Barth upon him that Ellul addresses in a long footnote Barth's reluctance to use the term:

> It is with apprehension that I use the term Myth. . . . And yet, one feels behind this term something fitting and maybe even true about human beings. . . . When I use this word here, I mean by it the adding of theological meaning to a fact which, by itself, as a historical fact or supposedly such, or as a psychological or human fact, has no such obvious significance. It is thus a matter of making a fact "significant," showing it to be the bearer of God's revelation, whereas in its materiality it is neither significant nor revelatory. This is how myth works, and *it in no way destroys the historical reality of the event, but rather gives it its full dimension.*[50]

The historical reality behind the texts is not Ellul's primary concern, rather their theological meaning in the light of revelation as a whole. Indeed, in his preface to *City*, the translator John Wilkinson alludes to this precise passage, noting that Ellul "regards 'myth' as the 'addition of theological significance' to some fact that as such does not obviously have any. Dialectically speaking, myth as the addition of significance . . . reaches out to the concrete-universal of revelation that bears up and is borne up in the biblical texts."[51] A text does not have to be myth *or* history: for Ellul, the genre of myth serves to show the full significance of events whose meaning we would not otherwise know.

49. Ellul refers several times to Ricoeur's opposition between proclamation and manifestation, claiming that in the Bible a theology of history takes the place of a "hierophany," a theology of nature (*Parole*, 78).

50. *Sans feu*, 53 (my italics). Geoffrey Bromiley, the translator of Barth and Ellul, notes that the category of myth marks a significant area of disagreement between them. In reference to the early chapters of the Bible, Barth preferred to use the term "saga" over and against myth. See, e.g., Barth, *CD* 3/1:41, 51.

51. *City*, viii–ix. Wilkinson claims Ellul works implicitly with Barth's concept of *Geschichte*, that is, the meaning of history.

In the case of Genesis 4, therefore, Ellul's concern is not to reduce it to debates about the historical Kenites, but to allow the text to speak a word about the city, and Technique, today. Indeed, Ellul contends that to interpret our contemporary civilization, we need the apparent naivety of the story of Cain and Abel, precisely because it tells the hidden truth about civilization: "the prodigious complexity of our world conceals humanity's simple aim, which remains the same."[52]

In all this, therefore, Ellul has constantly in mind the way readers can still hear God in Scripture and challenge our contemporary myths. Hermeneutics itself is implicated here. At the outset the theological hermeneut must be aware that the dominant myth of our era is scientism, the desire to reduce everything to a scientific and technological paradigm.[53] It is thus most ironic that texts which reveal our desire to control and order the world, are betrayed by interpreters who seek to limit these texts, either by relying on a "plain meaning" or by the rigid application of a quasi-scientific method of interpretation:

> The text that encloses the truth of the Word of God is never so exact that it only bears repeating. This text invites me to retell the myth, to recreate it. And the recreated myth calls me to listen to the ultimate, absolute Word. *The Word forces me to speak* . . . the text should never be fixed, reduced to structures, enclosed within itself or understood as if it were an exact and precise mathematical formula. No valid semiotic diagram exists that can exhaust the text that is a metaphor for the Word of God.[54]

For Ellul, the very form of the text as myth and metaphor means it cannot be captured, but must be embodied, conveyed only by the weak and dependent word of the witness.

---

52. *Sans feu*, 32. See Angel and Wright, *Playing with Dragons*, 1–36, for a contemporary discussion of biblical use of the genre of myth, although in the final analysis the authors prefer to speak of "story."

53. Rognon well describes Ellul's challenge to historical critics to give themselves over to the text: "The hermeneut must be released from seeing previous scientific knowledge as untouchable" (*Pensée*, 303).

54. *Parole*, 119 (my italics). As ever, Ellul pushes things to the extreme. See, in contrast, N. T. Wright's enthusiastic use of Greimas's diagrams in Wright, *New Testament*, 70–77. However, Wright sounds rather Ellulian when he defends the language of myth as "foundational story," over and against Bultmann, when applied to the New Testament: "The Gospels then are *myth* in the sense that they are foundational stories . . . the only language in which Israel can appropriately describe her history is language which, while it does indeed refer to actual events in the space-time universe, simultaneously invests those events with . . . trans-historical significance" (426).

To sum up, the category of myth allows Ellul to evade the question of the "hermeneutical gap" between ancient biblical settlements and the urban-technological world of his sociological studies.[55] His concern is more with the textual than the ancient city, and the Bible presents, he claims, a coherent picture. The myth of Cain is soon complemented by the myths of Nimrod (Gen 6) and Babel (Gen 11).[56] Historically speaking, Babel is Babylon, and yet Ellul does not look to reconstruct the historical Babylonia; rather he interprets Babylon and every city through the lens of Genesis 11.[57] That is to say that for Ellul, biblical Babel/Babylon is not simply a city, it is *the* city, and every city is a Babylon, even in present history. And above all, Babylon is a site of power: "Babylon (and for Babylon, read all cities) is at the center of civilization. Commerce works for the city's sake. Industry develops within the city. This is where power arises."[58]

Writing at a time when many theologians were demythologizing the Bible, just as sociologists were turning to myth, Ellul claims that the biblical myths speak a truer word than the demytholizers could imagine.[59] Above

---

55. See Clark's insightful article, "The Mythic Meaning of the City," in Christians and Van Hook, *Jacques Ellul*, 275. In contrast, much recent "urban theology" evades the Bible by pointing out the incongruity between the ancient city and the present city. See, e.g., Davey, *Urban Christianity and Global Order*. Davey, formerly Church of England Adviser on Urban Mission, privileges contemporary sociological analyses instead, e.g., Manuel Castells on informational capitalism and Leonie Sandercock on *Cosmopolis*. Ellul is granted a single mention in a dismissive aside: "The texts of our previous generations of urban theologians may be of little value, be they Jacques Elull [*sic*], Harvey Cox, David Shepherd, or the Church of England's *Faith in the City* report" (10).

56. Alluding to Nimrod, Ellul briefly explores the relationship between the city, warfare, and Technique, noting that all our social, economic, and political life still revolves around this complex (*Sans feu*, 39).

57. *Sans feu*, 48. This is a process Ellul refers to in terms of the "progressive enriching of the myth without contradicting it for it remains the expression of revelation."

58. *Sans feu*, 50.

59. An extended explanatory note is in order. By and large, the debate around the terms "myth" and "metaphor" is no longer raging. However, it is hard to say whether that is because the once opposed factions of historical criticism and biblical theology have entered into a fruitful coalition, or because opposing sides have retreated to their base camps. If we are to understand Ellul as a hermeneut and to seek to read the Bible in a fruitfully Ellulian way, we will need not to revisit the detail of the debates of the 1960s (although the texts we have considered and his accessible 1968 article, "Innocent Notes on the Hermeneutical Question," in Ellul, *Sources and Trajectories*, 184–203, bear re-reading), but to find how Ellul can help us to hear God's voice and speak a living word today. Three recent works to assist in this task are Brock, *Singing the Ethos of God*; Vanhoozer, *Remythologizing Theology*; Radner, *Time and the Word*. Brock contends the centrality of metaphor in Western society is a reflection of the historic importance of biblical interpretation in the West. Metaphor reveals God's world, and on this account, "is not a substitute for realistic language but the only realistic language adequate to

all, this was a word about the hidden but "permanent desire" of humanity for rupture from God, for autonomous power. "The *Meaning of the City* is not just about urbanism, any more than *The Technological Society* is just about technology . . . both studies concern the supreme achievements of human creativity which vary in each historical period, but which ironically acquire powers over man and dehumanize him."[60]

That this world is a contest of powers is no revelation. But how is it that what we have ourselves created so frequently overpowers us?

Apocalypse

The history of the past century has seen an exponential growth in the power of cities, and theological treatments of the city commonly begin with a sociological sketch of the various powers driving the world, often celebrating the essential contribution of technology.[61] However, whereas such accounts are rigidly materialist, Ellul's concern is to reveal the spiritual "power dynamics" at work. I contend that this concern marks him out as an *apocalyptic theologian*.

A keen reader of the Hebrew text, Ellul attaches ominous significance to the first word the Bible uses to describe a settlement, the word `iyr, claiming this connotes an alarming association of ideas: "It is not only the city, but it is also perhaps the watching angel, Vengeance, Terror."[62] The central significance of religion in ancient settlements and city-states is of course a

---

the reality it describes." Exploring the pre-modern exegesis of the Psalms in Augustine and Luther, he argues that Scripture-as-metaphor conveys God's very presence to us. "Song is the basic form of Israel's theologising because it is concomitant to a theology of advent" (Brock, *Singing the Ethos of God*, 272). Vanhoozer takes up the term "myth," though preferring "mythos," and explores Von Balthasar's model of Scripture as a Theo-drama, the dialogue between God and the world. Radner bases himself on Auerbach (a key influence upon Ellul's understanding of myth in *Nouveaux*) in arguing that scripture presents us with "figures" which connect one moment in time with another, investing them with a greater significance and connecting time and eternity. Scriptural figuralism suggests that past events in scripture may stand as significant and historical in their own right, while only having full meaning as they point beyond to Christ's life and through Him, to God's redemptive activity in the present. Seen in this light, Ellul's reading of Christ and the city appears to be a revival of the patristic allegorical interpretation of scripture, what Radner refers to as "figuralism." Moreover, Ellul clearly sees Babylon as a figure of the city in every age, especially the age of Technique, just as clearly as he sees Jerusalem as a figure of the eternal Incarnation.

60. Clark in Christians and Van Hook, *Jacques Ellul*, 275–76.

61. See for example, the use of Harvard economist Edward Glaeser's book, *Triumph of the City*, in Um and Buzzard, *Why Cities Matter*.

62. *Sans feu*, 39.

relatively commonplace observation[63] but Ellul intends to push this a little further. Does he mean that each city corresponds to an angelic counterpart, a being? Ellul does not intend to scandalize the reader further and this he does not say. But he is clear that the city is more than the sum of its physical parts, for it expresses a spiritual power:

> And without wanting to go too far, we must recognize that the city is not only this conglomeration and this rampart, but it is also a spiritual power. I do not say a being. But as Angel, as power, as what appears portentous, it functions on a spiritual level. The city has a spiritual significance, and is capable of directing and changing the spiritual life of a human being, exercising power over him and changing his life, his entire life and not only where he lives. And it appears a frightening mystery. . . . But how could this purely material fact . . . ? Because Cain sites his entire rebellion here. Humanity sites its entire power here, and powers rush in to reinforce human power.[64]

In this passage, Ellul outlines in incipient form the "apocalyptic exousiology" that comes to mark his work. Human rebellion is a "power grab" from God. Hence Cain puts his "power" into his rebellion, and this extends a range of "powers" which at first empower Cain. But because these powers stem from Cain's autonomy from God, they are more than just the material product of his own power. They have this original spiritual aspect embodied within them. This spiritual aspect—this "surplus"—is what Ellul denotes by the slippery term "l'esprit de puissance," the spirit of power. Humanity is never more creative than when acting in defiance of the divine curse, although this curse is in fact intended as a gracious barrier to further harm: "Humanity creates the arts and the sciences, they own chariots, build cities. The spirit of power is their response to the divine curse, and one might almost say that there would be no spirit of power if there was not at first a curse."[65]

And yet, as he goes on to show, this spirit of power always meets its answer in the judgment and grace of God. This is for Ellul what the myth of Babel decisively adds to the myths of Cain and Nimrod. In Babel, the city signifies the pursuit of a name, understood by Ellul as the pursuit

---

63. See Um and Buzzard, *Why Cities Matter*, 33, citing Mumford.

64. *Sans feu*, 35 (my italics). Ellul references in a footnote Daniel 4 and the account of the "watchers" in Enoch. Dismissing a traditional interpretation that these are literal "guardian angels," he argues that they denote a spiritual "surplus of power" beyond materialist explanation. On the "watchers," see Boyd, *God at War*, 262–87.

65. *Sans feu*, 37.

of the spiritual power inherent in naming and being named, renowned. However, the biblical myth portrays the way in which language itself becomes the means of God's gracious judgment, as the confusion of tongues scatters the builders.

Indeed, contrary to the popular reception of *Sans feu*, Ellul is concerned to show that the Creator God continually and graciously breaks into a world which wanted to break relationship with Him:

> God moves in response to our move. The Creator's desire for order responds to the creature's desire for spiritual conquest. For the Creator knows that in this spiritual conquest we only head towards one goal: death, material and spiritual death, because all separation from God is death . . . and if all relationship is broken between us and God . . . then we die. And because God wants His creature to live, He prevents this rupture. And we can do absolutely nothing to get rid of God because we cannot prevent the subject of all things from being the subject.[66]

The world's rupture from God is never complete: God remains the sovereign Subject, and he breaks in on the side of life.

There has been a marked interest in the genre of *apocalyptic* in modern theology. For Ellul, apocalyptic has no generalized definition; it only has the meaning that it has in particular biblical texts, principally in the Apocalypse of John, commonly known as the Book of Revelation.[67] This text, as well as preceding Hebrew texts within the canon and key texts of the Apostle Paul, are concerned to show the Creator God's ultimate power and sovereignty over all other powers, and the necessary break or discontinuity between the order of the world established by human action, the world as we know it, and God's final action in Jesus Christ.[68]

A simple scan of Bible references in *Sans feu* shows that Ellul is particularly concerned with biblical writings usually categorized as apocalyptic, often passages concerned directly with cities. Indeed, *Sans feu* ends with an extended meditation upon the New Jerusalem in the Book of Revelation.[69]

66. *Sans feu*, 45.

67. See Ellul's engagement with this wider trend in the introduction to *Apocalypse*. See also 86–91 below.

68. For a careful account of apocalyptic theology, see Harink, *Paul among the Postliberals*. For Harink, the language of apocalyptic "captures several elements in this claim [the claim that Jesus is at the center of history] that . . . the language of revelation and eschatology do not. First and foremost is a strong emphasis on *God's action* in the history of Jesus Christ, rather than human action or response" (68). Harink describes Hauerwas and, before him, Karl Barth as apocalyptic theologians.

69. Isaiah, Revelation, Ezekiel, Jeremiah, Daniel, and Zechariah are particularly

Ellul's theological interpretation is resolutely christological: centered on the work of Jesus in direct contrast to the human work of the city, as we will explore below. His entire way of reading history and culture is indebted to this Christ-centered theology, as we shall explore in the next chapter. Indeed, Ellul's dialectic of truth and reality, though it is undoubtedly shaped by his immersion in the writings of Kierkegaard, is essentially a biblical, apocalyptic dialectic. Among Ellul's interpreters, it is Marva Dawn who has most clearly argued for this position. Sociology alone, Dawn contends in a number of texts we shall explore as we proceed, cannot get at the true meaning of power, for within Ellul's characteristic terminology, sociology deals with reality and biblical revelation deals with truth.[70]

Ellul himself outlines his essentially apocalyptic approach in *Sans feu* in an important preface to the 1975 French edition, where he offers a response to the critique of the influential American Baptist theologian Harvey Cox, author of the celebrated work, *The Secular City* (1965). Cox had criticized Ellul for offering no positive account of power or powers rooted in either their creation or redemption. Ellul's response is illuminating for he first affirms that his use of "puissances" is intended to translate the Greek *exousiai*. The powers have for Ellul been defeated in Christ, but they are categorically not redeemed, and remain rebellious: "They always remain harmful and rebellious, defeated, chained etc., but never positive."[71]

However, Ellul argues that he does not thereby consider power to be intrinsically bad. Leaning on the semantic distinction in French between "pouvoirs" and "esprit de puissance," he argues that:

> [Cox] confuses *power* [pouvoir] and the *spirit of power* [esprit de puissance]. He makes me say that human powers [pouvoirs] derive from our rebellion against God: which is absurd. I know well that in creation, God has given us power [pouvoir]. But it is the spirit of power which is referred to in my text. He confuses a curse on the power of the City (the work of this spirit of power) with a general curse on humanity, of which I have not spoken.[72]

---

significant for Ellul (in that order of priority). In my next chapter, I will explore Dawn's writings on the powers, as I deal with Ellul's writings on the Book of Revelation, where we see the interrelationship between the terms eschatology, prophecy, and apocalyptic in Ellul's understanding.

70. See Dawn, "Principalities and Powers." In a popular form, see Dawn's short commentaries on the early Ellul's texts she brought to light and translated in *Sources and Trajectories*.

71. *Sans feu*, 22.

72. *Sans feu*, 23.

Ellul does not mean that *everything we can do* originates in our rupture from God. He sees that we have "pouvoirs" in a positive sense, capacities grounded in a creation order, unrevoked, although *Sans feu* will tell us little about them.[73] However, the point for Ellul is that our collective projects are subject to the "spirit of power." The city is "a phenomenon absolutely outside of human power, that fundamentally, we can do nothing about."[74]

Does Ellul Go Too Far?

We must pause at this point and ask: granted Ellul necessarily highlights the negative side of the city and Technique, but does he not go much too far? It is one thing to understand the coherence of Ellul's interpretation and the importance of his challenge, and quite another to swallow it wholesale. Indeed, as Greenman, et al., rightly comment, "It is possible, even after giving Ellul's analysis a fair shake, to find significant faults."[75] Put baldly, to make Cain the murderer the prototypical "urban-technologist" appears at first sight to suggest that the city and technology are in themselves sinful. For this reason, American theologian Martin Marty spoke for many in his strident rejection of Ellul's work, suggesting he comes close to heresy in implying that all history is "a fall into time," and that "Technique and its development are 'The Fall' for moderns."[76]

Whilst Ellul emphatically denies this charge, he does intend to offer a fundamental theological paradigm-shift. Undoubtedly that shift goes too far at times, and yet that must not deter us from feeling the force of his argument and finding corroborating evidence for it. Before moving on to engage the overall theology of *Sans feu*, let us pause briefly to consider whether Ellul's recovery of Cain can be supported in recent biblical scholarship, social anthropology and theology, corresponding more or less to my categories of canon, myth and apocalypse.

---

73. Genesis 1 and 2 are sparsely alluded to within the main text of *Sans feu*. Ellul states that *God's creation was complete*, a finished work within which God offered to humanity *a given purpose*. Humanity was created to be a *delegated and dependent master* of creation, e.g., *Sans feu*, 36. In his later writings—most obviously in his published talks on Genesis, to be considered in chapter 5—"Ellul developed an elaborate doctrine of creation . . . expressed in terms of a relationship of communion between God and the world" (Goddard, *Living the Word*, 67).

74. *Sans feu*, 85.

75. Greenman et al., *Understanding Jacques Ellul*, 74.

76. Marty in Christians and Van Hook, *Jacques Ellul*, 9–11.

The Canonical Cain

This first task of finding evidence for Ellul's reading of Genesis 4 in biblical scholarship is hampered by the fact that Ellul rarely cites the specialist sources he draws upon in his own biblical interpretation. In *Sans feu*, Ellul cites only the work of Gerhard von Rad, who seems to be a significant ally in reading Genesis 4. Indeed, von Rad does suggest straightforwardly that for the biblical narrator, the "primeval history" of Cain "shows the cultural history of man," and he perceives here the narrator's concern to highlight "the other side of that advance . . . the change in human attitude that goes with higher development . . . by which the human community is more and more profoundly ruptured."[77]

However, Ellul is not without support in readings of the narrative of Cain in later biblical studies. Jon Levenson can go as far as to say that "it is possible that the story of Cain and Abel itself once served as an account of the primal sin and the expulsion from paradise," noting that the text is clear that the most important cultural institution, the proper worship of God, emerges not from Cain's line, but from Seth's.[78] In Gordon Wenham's ambivalent reading, he argues that the writer of Genesis 4 is seeking to mark a contrast from other Ancient Near Eastern myths by demonstrating that "technology was a human achievement, not the gift of the gods."[79] Echoing Ellul's account, he considers these narratives to be "protohistorical," concerning real individuals, whose stories moreover have "paradigmatic" significance for all.[80] He concurs markedly with Ellul that "by linking urbanization and nomadism, music and metalworking to the genealogy of Cain, the biblical writer seems to be suggesting that all aspects of human culture are in some way tainted by Cain's sin."[81] John Goldingay argues that Genesis 4 does indeed offer an account of "technology," but without "value judgments" at first. It is at one and the same time the "fulfillment of God's creation purpose" but also deeply ambiguous, as the story develops.[82]

77. Rad and Marks, *Genesis*, 107. Ellul casts a shadow over the work of the French Evangelical biblical scholar Henri Blocher. Blocher evinces some agreement with Ellul by affirming that Genesis 4 does indeed locate the biblical origins of civilization, although he argues against a possible Manicheism in considering civilization to be the "fruit of sin." Yet, he agrees (in explicit dialogue with Ellul) that "the means are not neutral," and that where power increases, sin increases (*In the Beginning*, 200).

78. Levenson in Berlin et al., *Jewish Study Bible*, 19.

79. Wenham, *Genesis*, 111.

80. Wenham, *Genesis*, 117.

81. Wenham, *Genesis*, 117.

82. Goldingay, *Genesis for Everyone*, 79.

Walter Brueggemann argues that these arts are a "legitimate enterprise," yet with a reference to Freud, he asserts that the narrative presciently shows up the link between culture and desire. "Cain's mastery leading to culture is never an untainted one: it brings together desire and control."[83]

The Mythological Cain

This last reference to Freud leads us to our second task of finding support for Ellul in social anthropology. We have already alluded above to Franco-American Roman Catholic scholar, René Girard, whose reputation far outstrips that of Ellul, but who exerted an early influence on Ellul's understanding of myth. Space does not allow here for a detailed account of Girard's thought or its connections with Ellul, and my concern here is only briefly to outline the perhaps surprising correspondence between Ellul's account of civilization and technology and the implications of Girard's landmark mimetic theory for his account of those same phenomena.[84]

Andrew Goddard notes that a dialogue between Girard and Ellul would be illuminating[85] and Marva Dawn also notes the resonance between their respective works.[86] Such a fruitful rapprochement is attempted in a number of articles by Anabaptist writer Matthew Pattillo which I draw upon below. David Gill devoted an entire edition of *The Ellul Forum* to a dialogue between the two, which involved an interview with Girard himself.[87] Moreover, as Rognon notes, the two authors even shared the same editor for a while.[88]

First and foremost a literary and critical theorist, and as a result, a theorist of myth and the sacred, Girard attaches a crucial significance to the biblical account of Cain and Abel, the myth of the founding sacrificial murder. This is a myth common to all ancient, and modern, civilizations, he contends, but in the Bible's definitive treatment of the myth, however, sacrificial violence is demythologized and thereby condemned, for Abel is justified. Like Ellul,

83. Brueggemann, *Genesis*, 65.

84. Chapter 5 on creation will make a number of explicit connections between Girard and Ellul. On his election to l'Académie Française in 2005, Girard was praised as "the Darwin of the human sciences." Girard's theory and its theological implications are brilliantly introduced in Alison, *Living in the End Times,* 18–32. This is updated in *Raising Abel.*

85. Goddard, *Living the Word*, 186.

86. Dawn, *Tabernacling of God*, 125n3.

87. Gill, "Conversation with René Girard."

88. Jean-Claude Guillebaud, who is interviewed as an "inheritor" of Ellul's thought, in Rognon, *Générations Ellul*, 60–62.

> Girard sees that the sciences and arts, and every form of human
> communication have their origins in ritual violence. . . . The de-
> nial of sacrificial origins for the arts and sciences is an indication
> of the veiled and veiling character of ritual violence. Suppression
> of the knowledge of its origins enables human culture to flourish.
> The Biblical revelation . . . by unveiling the sacred violence at the
> heart of religion, poses a threat to human society.[89]

For Girard as for Ellul, Genesis 4 has a demythologizing power,
unveiling that what we call civilization depends on resolving the instinc-
tive competition between humans over the same goods, which Girard fa-
mously frames in terms of "mimetic desire." This unveiling creates a crisis,
however, for if a single victim or scapegoat cannot resolve the problem of
competitiveness, the risk is of the violence of all against all. In a reading
strikingly similar to Ellul's, Girard argues that the Bible's account of Cain
reveals the illegitimacy of the Cainite solution to the problem of "negative
mimesis." But on what basis can a civilization exist and flourish if not
under the sign of Cain?

In a late and more concertedly theological work, *I see Satan Fall like
Lightning*, Girard argues that the apocalypse of Jesus Christ decisively reveals the lie at the heart of human culture, but crucially moreover offers a
resolution. The death of Jesus, voluntarily accepted, and vindicated by his
resurrection unveils the violent sacred. Jesus' victory enables a new "positive mimesis" or unselfish imitation, a relationship modeled for us in the
relationship between the human Jesus and the God he called Father, a God
of grace, who demands no redemptive violence. Yet, for Girard, at the same
time Christ's victory ushers in a time of final "apocalyptic danger," by calling for an ultimate decision.[90] The parallels with Ellul are striking, and will
become more evident as we proceed.

It will not work however to make Ellul a Girardian theologian *avant
la lettre*, and despite hints, there is no clear articulation of a theory of mimetic desire in Ellul. However, it is significant that Ellul offers a brief but
basically Girardian account of the significance of "desire" in his account

---

89. As Pattillo notes: "For Girard, Cain represents the chaotic mob in the grip of
a violent frenzy, uniting against a single victim, a scapegoat. This unity achieves a real
peace and allows for the development of all that is collectively termed civilization" (Pattillo, "Christianity, Violence & Anarchy," 6).

90. Girard, *I See Satan Fall*, 184. For the early Girard, it is the Incarnation, by desacralizing a primitive order, which opens the door to modernity. Later in his career,
Girard became more critical of the sacred violence implicit in modernity, especially in
its technology (See Rognon's preface in *Théologie et Technique*, 21).

of Cain and Abel[91] as well as of the role of sacrifice in the foundation of cities.[92] Ellul himself shows a growing awareness in the trajectory of his thought of the parallels with Girard, although the insights of *Sans feu* clearly predate the work of Girard.[93]

The Apocalyptic Cain

Girard has been a major influence upon a number of later theologians, among them Rowan Williams and James Alison, who, from the margins of Roman Catholic theology, has argued against the dominant Thomist account of the orders of creation. This accounts for the perhaps surprising agreement between Alison and Ellul, which I will return to in my fifth chapter on creation. However, within his own Protestant tradition, Ellul has had a more direct influence on a number of theological voices who are decidedly not part of the Ellul guild.

In a fascinating theological account of place, *Where Mortals Dwell: A Christian View of Place Today*, the South African-born OT scholar and theologian Craig Bartholomew, an invaluable source for Um and Buzzard's urban theology, begins with the Bible's account of Cain. Engaging explicitly with Ellul, Bartholomew sets out to offer a dialectical treatment of the city, although in the final analysis his theology of place leans more towards the positive than the negative pole.

On the one hand, citing Ellul, Bartholomew clearly acknowledges the important connection between place and the fall, concluding that "In Genesis 1–11, then, cities do not appear favorably, to put it mildly."[94] However, on the other, he explicitly disagrees with Ellul's assessment that "scripture is hostile to cities," arguing that "the spiritual influence of cities . . . is not always negative." Yet, he adds that "Ellul's dialectical approach makes it hard to assess him."[95] Assessing Ellul's dialectical approach to the city must take account of the positive pole—Ellul's christological reading of the city, which we will consider below. Yet, as Bartholomew recognizes in constructing his own dialectical account, we cannot simply jettison Genesis 4.

91. *Sans feu*, 25.

92. *Sans feu*, 60–61.

93. "Grace excludes sacrifice. Girard is quite right when he shows how basic sacrifice is to humanity. There can be no accepted life or social relation without sacrifice. But gracious grace rejects the validity of all human sacrifice. It ruins a basic element in human psychology" (Ellul, *Subversion*, 159).

94. Bartholomew, *Where Mortals Dwell*, 38.

95. Bartholomew, *Where Mortals Dwell*, 47n29.

A similar dialectic is employed by the British theologian and Barth scholar Timothy Gorringe in his 2002 book on the city, *A Theology of the Built Environment: Justice, Empowerment, Redemption*. Over and against "undialectical" treatments of God's activity in human history, he praises Ellul's "radically dialectical theology" of God's judgment and grace in *Sans feu*. However, Gorringe too observes that "most theologies of the city tend to fall on one side or the other of this dialectic." On the one hand, he agrees entirely with Ellul's critique of the "secular city theology of the 1960s."[96] Yet on the other, Gorringe notes that Ellul is overly influenced by an anti-urban and reactionary romanticism.[97]

However, in the final analysis, Gorringe notes that to judge Ellul on the basis of his reading of Cain alone is misguided. In a very perceptive comment which in a sense frames all that I will argue in the rest of this chapter, he contends that "Whilst rejecting the Thomist doctrine of grace, Ellul replaces it by a doctrine of pardon and acceptance which concretely amount to the very same thing."[98] What Gorringe perceives is that Ellul is concerned, as Barth was, to provide an account of God's grace breaking into history. Moreover, in his attention to the city, he was concerned to demonstrate that this grace reaches not only individuals but the works of human history also, an anticipation of God's final gracing of all history in the New Jerusalem. Reading *Sans feu* apocalyptically means reading it back to front, and several times, for as Ellul himself puts it in his response to Harvey Cox: "The eschatological reality comes from the end of time towards the present time."[99]

It is this apocalyptic, back-to-front reading that the following chapters will explore, but first we will outline the two movements that Ellul explores, in classic canonical fashion, in *Sans feu*: the movement from Cain's City to Christ, and the movement from Christ to the New Jerusalem. As we explore the movement of this text, we will sow seeds which will mature into fruitful treatment in my later chapters.

96. Gorringe, *Theology of the Built Environment*, 142–43.

97. "The idea that God intended human beings to live in the country is, as we have seen, quite new, a product of the cult of nature of the seventeenth and eighteenth centuries" (Gorringe, *Theology of the Built Environment*, 120).

98. Gorringe, *Theology of the Built Environment*, 20.

99. *Sans feu*, 22. See, for example, his defense to Cox: "Obviously, Cox has not noticed the dialectical movement of my work overall" (*Sans feu*, 23).

From Cain to Christ: Judgment and Desacralization

The central chapter of *Sans feu* is simply titled *Jésus-Christ* and Ellul sets up an opposition between this power of the city and the power of Jesus Christ:

> Now from all this, it is apparent that the city is humanity's great work. It is here that all these efforts come together, where all these powers are born. No other work, whether our techniques or our philosophy, is equivalent to the city, which is not the creation of another instrument but is the very environment in which such instruments can appear. . . . So all these works are secondary to the city. As it has been said that Jesus Christ is the great work of God, so we can truly say . . . that the city is the great work of humanity.[100]

In this respect, he surveys the terrain for his final, explicitly apocalyptic chapter on the "myth of the New Jerusalem," entitled *Yahvé Chamma* ("The LORD is here" Ezek 48:35).[101] Ellul claims that from Genesis to Revelation the Bible contains a decisive *language about the city* that reveals both the city's present rupture from God, but also its eschatological redemption within what he calls the recapitulation of all things. This is the full extent of Ellul's apocalyptic hope.

As we have noted in chapter 2, this recovery of hope was rooted in Ellul's reading of scripture, through the lens of Karl Barth. This has often led to the judgment that Ellul copies Barth in a rather slavish and amateur fashion. Yet, as Bromiley notes, "Ellul creates a Christian theology of the city for which there are no counterparts at all in Barth."[102] At one level, this is because, as we have already noted, Ellul's personal experience of the city led him to this enquiry. Moreover, the significance Ellul attaches to myth is certainly not Barthian, but stems from his social and historical studies.

For all that, *Sans feu* is clearly indebted to the work of Karl Barth, most especially in the apocalyptic mode of Ellul's theology. For Ellul, Christ is both the apocalypse, or revelation, of history and the true end of all history. This becomes explicit in chapter 5 where Ellul states that there is no history of the city apart from the true history of Jesus Christ. This is why Ellul does not offer a "historical history" of the city but rather "a true history." There is Jesus Christ, who, as Karl Barth says, 'makes history because he is

---

100. *Sans feu*, 275–76.

101. The relatively brief (32-page) account Ellul gives of the Book of Revelation in the final chapter of *Sans feu* emerges from his central chapter on Jesus Christ.

102. Bromiley in Christians and Van Hook, *Jacques Ellul*, 47.

history."[103] He then sketches out two trajectories, firstly the trajectory from Cain to Jerusalem, the trajectory of discontinuity, in which Christ breaks the significance of Cain's act of rebellion. And secondly the trajectory of continuity, from Eden to the New Jerusalem, in which Jesus Christ brings about the reconciliation and recapitulation of all things.

Desacralizing Jerusalem

Indeed, if one grants *Sans feu* a second reading, one can already clearly see this in-breaking grace in its early chapters. The tone of judgment dominates in Ellul's second chapter, entitled "Thunder over the City," and yet it is here that Ellul opens up a decisive avenue of grace. He argues that in the early narratives of Sodom and Nineveh, we find a "consoling word," a word of hope for the city.[104] This word is first heard clearly in the "myth of Jonah," a narrative to which Ellul devoted an entire commentary and to which he gives a decisively christological interpretation.[105]

However, grace most decisively breaks in through the election of Jerusalem. Liberated from forced city-building in captivity, after their release, and the conquest of Canaan, Israel is mandated to take over existing cities, not to build but rather to occupy. Most significantly, they occupy the Jebusite city which becomes known as Jerusalem. Ellul writes of Jerusalem as a city chosen by God, an election most evident in the adoption of the city as David's capital, the king who, in a pregnant expression, "knew what the city represents," and whose choice of Jerusalem as his capital coincides with God's gracious choice.[106] David begins to undo the work of Cain.[107]

The building of the Temple is for Ellul a divine concession to David, for he takes the account in 2 Samuel 7 to imply that the Temple is a mere sign, a mirror of God's promise to build a house for David. Therefore Solomon's Temple is ambivalent from the start, placed under the LORD's promise, "I will build a house for you."[108] This is why Ellul takes the later urban developments of Solomon and his son, Rehoboam, viewed through the eyes of the

---

103. *Sans feu,* 266.

104. Gill argues that Ellul notes only the experience of Abraham at Sodom, whereas the narrative of Abraham at Salem (Gen 14) "pushes the gracing of the city of Jerusalem back further" (*Word of God,* 112).

105. "This story can't be real, but it is true" (*Sans feu,* 112). Ellul calls it "a mythic story" which has a prophetic and christological meaning (242–43).

106. *Sans feu,* 179.

107. *Sans feu,* 190.

108. *Sans feu,* 180.

Chronicler, to be a sinful overreach of their limited mandate, the misguided attempt to build up Jerusalem as an earthly power.[109]

Nevertheless, just as the Temple is a mirror of God's covenant, so Jerusalem is, for Ellul, "an image of the Incarnation."[110] In a formula which recalls the patristic doctrine of kenosis, in loving humility, God meets us on our own territory, within our counter-creation, by choosing Jerusalem. Moreover, this election does not just hold for this one city, it is intended to imply God's future adoption of all cities, for Jerusalem is the "first fruits" of the cities. Citing the whole of Psalm 87, Ellul concludes that Jerusalem will forever have a universal significance as the city chosen for others.[111] God fully adopts both humanity, and indeed our works, in his election of Jerusalem. Indeed, the Creator brings life even to dead works done in rebellion. "In reality, when humanity takes the titanic path of counter-creation . . . when we build with dead matter, stone, tarmac, asphalt, cement, cast iron, steel, glass, aluminium . . . still there is life. The LORD of all Creation . . . is within."[112]

And yet the story of the OT is of the constant dialectical movement between grace and judgment. Jerusalem is chosen *as a city* and condemned *as a city*, a bloody city like all the others. This is for Ellul the significance of exile: Israel breaks covenant with God and brings rupture within itself and rupture from God. However, grace triumphs after judgment and Ellul takes the unnuanced post-exilic divine commands to rebuild the city as God's final adoption of city-building. For Ellul, the LORD now definitively takes the side of the builders: even God becomes a builder.[113]

It is within this framework of judgment and grace that Ellul describes the encounter of Jesus with Jerusalem. Here Ellul draws almost exclusively upon Matthew's Gospel, although in line with his hermeneutical method, he is conspicuously disinterested in debates conducted within historical-critical scholarship.[114] Instead, Ellul develops an original and somewhat idiosyncratic reading of the significance of Jesus for an urban-technological world. Ellul marks three particular emphases, two of which denote judgment, and one, finally and decisively, grace: Jesus' homelessness in the city, Jesus' approach to the crowds, and Jesus' act of adoption and substitution.

---

109. *Sans feu*, 181–83. He regards the latter as breaking with God, and therefore creating a break, a rupture within God's people (*Sans feu*, 65, see also 79 on rupture).

110. *Sans feu*, 190, in Gorringe, *Theology of the Built Environment*, 145.

111. *Sans feu*, 206.

112. *Sans feu*, 191.

113. *Sans feu*, 193.

114. *Sans feu*, 212.

Jesus: Homeless in the City

First of all, considering Jesus' words to the towns of Judea in Matthew 23, Ellul says *Jesus does not participate in the work of building the city*:

> Thus Jesus . . . declares himself a stranger to the world of the city. He does not participate in this human work, he who in other respects participated in the whole of human life. Now it is precisely because he took the whole of human life upon himself that he refused this false remedy, this fake grandeur. He rejected . . . this human counter-creation.[115]

For Ellul, Jesus takes on the fullness of the human condition and yet he refuses to participate in this work. Moreover, he argues that Jesus never proclaims grace for the city as a work of human power, although he has words of grace for people within it.[116] Rather, Jesus is Ellul's eponymous hero, a "homeless" wanderer with "neither hearth nor home."[117] Entering into the curse that Cain had tried to escape, Jesus wanders and builds no city, instead accepting God's protection, and in this confidence, an alternative kingdom is built for humanity.[118] In death too, Jesus rejects the city, and as a scapegoat, he is sacrificed outside the city of Jerusalem. Yet by that very action the city, and its powers, are desacralized.

We will allow for now the power of Ellul's portrayal to be felt, although we must note for later an evident problem he does not address, the neglect here of Jesus' settled lifestyle in Capernaum and his work as a *tekton*, or construction worker.[119]

Jesus' Approach to the "Mass Society"

Secondly, elaborating on this initial position, Ellul marks *an important distinction between the city as a collective power and the city as a crowd of persons.* Drawing on Matthew's account of the Sermon on the Mount and a number of healing miracles, Ellul contends that Jesus speaks to the crowd, and then to the city, with a clear distinction between them. Jesus judges

115. *Sans feu*, 226.

116. *Sans feu*, 209.

117. *Sans feu*, 219. "Sans feu ni lieu" means "neither hearth nor home."

118. "He knows nothing of the capital and the progress of civilization. He knows that the only legitimate resting place is found in resting in God and he knows that in his acceptance of a wandering life, the kingdom is being built" (*Sans feu*, 223).

119. As recorded in Mark 6:3. Ellul's denuded understanding of work will be considered in chapter 6.

the power of the city but sees in the crowd not power, but indecision (he explores this in the story of Jairus, noting that by gathering they were merely obeying a "sociological reflex"). For Ellul, Jesus consistently has compassion for the crowd, and for this reason, he *resists* becoming its shepherd or leader.[120] Rather it is to a person in the crowd he speaks, or to the few surrounded by the many. In this way, Ellul reads Jesus' very mode of address as a challenge to the power of the masses, bringing into sharp relief the encounter with the person, in this encounter with Jesus, the individual is personalized from within the crowd.[121]

Characteristically, Ellul suggests this interpretation holds good for Jesus' encounter with the mass urban society of modernity, the subject of utopian movements within modern theology as far ranging as Mounier's *Esprit* movement and Cox's lyrical *Secular City*.[122] Gorringe picks up that Ellul clearly intends a challenge to such urban utopianism, as he notes that for Ellul, "building [the city] is an attempt to prolong a temporary gift," a misguided attempt to "build Jerusalem."[123] Whilst such a project might spring from good motives, in practice it serves to veil the spirit of power, in direct challenge to the gift. For Ellul, the Incarnation was a unique gift, the temporary invasion of divine truth within temporal reality.

We see here the stark contrast between Ellul's theology and other, more positive theological accounts of human progress as a continuation of the Incarnation. The treatment of the Incarnation in Ellul's early work *Présence au monde moderne* seems to tilt in this direction at times, although he applied a corrective in his later *Fausse*. In *Sans feu*, he is insistent that the Incarnation does not establish the kingdom here and now, a view which Ellul calls in numerous places a "huge error."[124] Rather it leads to a time of apocalyptic crisis. "Nothing is more decisive. . . . The work of Jesus Christ is the very work of Truth. He is the Truth, he has come into this world of reality, though reality has not received it but rejected it. But it does not prevent his Incarnation being the entrance of the truth into the world of the real."[125]

Drawing on Oscar Cullman's famous analogy of the ending Second World War, Ellul notes that after the defeats of 1943, the Nazi spirit of war redoubled until eventual capitulation in 1945. Just so, after the Incarnation,

120. This is how Ellul interprets the phrase, "Sheep without a shepherd" (*Sans feu*, 232). Thus by seeing the crowd with compassion, Jesus diffuses the crowd and resists becoming a false Messiah.

121. *Sans feu*, 235.

122. *Sans feu*, 228.

123. Gorringe, *Theology of the Built Environment*, 19.

124. See Goddard's complete discussion of this point in *Living the Word*, 101.

125. *Sans feu*, 295.

the spirit of power has redoubled its rebellion in the world. "Thus the powers defeated by Christ are still at work, unwilling to acknowledge their defeat, and even struggle with increasing violence."[126] We will explore this notion of apocalyptic escalation in chapter 3.

Incarnation as Desacralization, Adoption, and Substitution

The incarnation is understood by Ellul in terms of a *double action of adoption and substitution*. What does Ellul mean by these terms? First, Ellul argues that "in Jesus Christ, it is not a disembodied, workless human being that God adopts but . . . this person here, inseparable from what he does, from where he is embodied."[127] By this Ellul means us to understand that the Incarnation embraces and transforms not an abstract human nature (which has no meaning, Ellul says) but the entirety of human history. Jesus takes humanity and all human works upon himself. This leads secondly to the logic of substitution, and here Ellul considers the relationship between Jesus and the Jerusalem Temple to be paradigmatic.[128] In Jesus' assertion concerning the Temple, "Destroy it and in three days, I will raise it up," Jesus' body is substituted for the Temple, which stands for the whole of Jerusalem, understood as the universal city, holding meaning for all civilization. The word addressed to every city is the word of the cross.[129]

Moreover, by this substitution, Jesus takes on Jerusalem's universal role. "Jesus completely substitutes himself for Jerusalem, fulfilling the history of the nations and the history of the city. He will henceforth play Jerusalem's role, fulfil its function."[130] The earthly Jerusalem is profaned, becoming a city like all the rest: in Ellul's language it is "desacralized" by Jesus' holy presence: "It is precisely the incarnation that sanctifies profane things and consequently the whole nature of things is made profane, including, in this nature of things, Jerusalem."[131]

Historically, this desacralization is finally enacted by the Temple's fall in AD 70, which implies for Ellul that Jerusalem is henceforth a city like all others. Therefore, Ellul argues this "double action" of Jesus' adoption and

---

126. *Sans feu*, 296.
127. *Sans feu*, 247.
128. *Sans feu*, 249.
129. *Sans feu*, 130.
130. *Sans feu*, 250.
131. *Sans feu*, 250.

substitution leads away from the temporal Jerusalem, towards the heavenly Jerusalem, a movement prophesied in the canonical apocalyptic literature.[132]

From Christ to New Jerusalem: Recapitulation and Reconciliation

In chapter 5 on "True Horizons," Ellul turns to what he calls the "Hebrew myth" of the heavenly city in the OT's apocalyptic writings, which for him signifies the acceptance of humanity's urban history, and not a return to nature.[133] In his definitive closing section "From Eden to Jerusalem," he notes that as a result of the work of Christ, truth and reality, once ruptured, will one day be reunited:

> Then, in the creation of the heavenly Jerusalem, the victory of Christ is inscribed definitively in reality. At the end of time, Truth joins and informs Reality, but not by taking again the path of the humble Incarnation . . . but by a new creation of reality . . . this is realized precisely in the creation of a city.[134]

What marked the Incarnation was its humility, but what will mark the new creation will be its glory. By referring to the *myth* of the New Jerusalem, Ellul intends to draw our attention away from a literal reading of the material parts of the New Jerusalem, towards a consideration of their possible symbolism. To puzzle over the materiality of the city is for Ellul to miss the truth of the myth, which is to teach a universal salvation: "affirming that God chooses the city as the place of encounter between us and him."[135] At the end of history, God makes all things new, states Ellul: "And if God accepts this new form, it is simply because humanity has chosen it."[136]

Ellul thus argues that God's adoption of the city implies a kenosis, a self-emptying, as if God must reconcile Godself to the decision of humanity to build the city. However, in perhaps one of the most poetic passages of *Sans feu*, Ellul writes of God's freedom and God's love (two sides of the same coin). God takes into account human desires, and acts because humanity

132. Ellul is at pains however to assert that Jerusalem has not been abandoned, but rather its task fulfilled. Yet Jerusalem is still Jerusalem, and its name contains the promise that a new Jerusalem is coming (*Sans feu*, 261). We see hints here and there of a theology of Israel which will preoccupy Ellul in his later work. See his *An Unjust God?*

133. *Sans feu*, 290 (alluding to Ezekiel), in Gorringe, *Theology of the Built Environment*, 8.

134. *Sans feu*, 308.

135. *Sans feu*, 310.

136. *Sans feu*, 310.

has acted.[137] "It is only our human decision that somehow causes God to act, which causes him to accept what humanity desires and seeks, making Him transform his creation."[138]

Ellul never loses sight of the particular, for God wants to save not an abstract humanity but each individual, "those unfortunates weighed down and wandering with the crowds."[139] The term Ellul reaches for to describe this salvation is the term, *assumption*. "[God] himself assumes our terrible rebellion. And so God assumes progressively the entire work of humanity."[140]

The term "progressively" might suggest the influence of Hegel, and point in the direction of process theology. Yet we have already noted Ellul's rejection of Hegel at this point, and it is clear that assumption is used with patristic rather than modern echoes.[141] Moreover, in order to mark that creation does not simply evolve into new creation, Ellul clearly asserts the need for discontinuity, for the crowning act of history is a break with history. We will not build Jerusalem on earth, but this is good news, as Christians are now free to do good work without having to bear the full weight of history, for only God will bring completion.

In case there should be any doubt of the patristic inspiration behind this theology, Ellul turns finally to the language of *recapitulation*,[142] alluding to its scriptural source in Ephesians 1: God unites "all things, things in heaven and earth," uniquely in Christ the Head and not outside of him. Recapitulation is the meaning of the entire symbol of the New Jerusalem in the book of Revelation but its significance is perhaps best expressed in two particular images.

Firstly, the opening of the books (Rev 20:11–15), and secondly, the glory of the nations entering the city (Rev 21:24–26).[143] Together, these denote not the judgment of the deeds of individuals but God's record-keeping of the turns of history and the corporate works of the nations. For Ellul,

137. *Sans feu*, 312. God's account-keeping is not of sins and works, for "that has all been settled in advance in the forgiveness of the Cross."

138. *Sans feu*, 310–11.

139. *Sans feu*, 311.

140. Clark argues that this notion makes him a "radical optimist" about God's response to human history in Christians and Van Hook, *Jacques Ellul*, 283.

141. The term "assumption" is associated with Gregory of Nazianzus, although Ellul does not acknowledge this source. Goddard contends that Ellul often omits to "dialogue with Christian tradition" (*Living the Word*, 315), yet perhaps it would be more accurate to say that Ellul rarely enters into explicit dialogue with the tradition.

142. Ellul is clearly reworking Irenaeus of Lyons's concept of *anakephalaiosis*, and we will explore this in the next chapter. For a brief summary, see Clement, *Roots of Christian Mysticism*, 344–45.

143. *Sans feu*, 314.

assumption and recapitulation in Christ is the meaning of the heavenly city. As he puts it in the closing words of *Sans feu*, nothing will be lost for the jumble, mud, mess and dirt of the earthly city will find itself transfigured in the heavenly city, as the supreme act of God's grace: "All that has been involved in human life is retrieved by the LORD's grace and goodness, as he too joins in the chosen city."[144]

Conclusion

It would not be too much to argue that in both form and content *Sans feu* could be interpreted as a modern apocalypse. In form, as Clark rightly argues, deploying "considerable mythopoetic talent," Ellul creates a text which functions as a "great poem or play," with a "creative power beyond the intent of the author."[145] In content, as Greenman, et al., note, *Sans feu* is a bold attempt to unveil what they call the "soteriological mythology of the city," and therefore, by extension of Technique. Moreover, by attempting to unveil the spiritual dynamics at the heart of the modern technopolis, Ellul left himself open to ridicule. "Reading Ellul required reckoning with an approach that was entirely foreign, one that challenged and interrogated predominant approaches to studying the city. For this, Ellul was regarded as a fool, and perhaps with good reason."[146]

And yet, if the reader understands, this is a fundamentally hopeful book, offering true hope beyond the false dawn of technological progress. Cain's order is not the Creator's order, but nonetheless being open to judgment it is open to God's final recapitulation. Against a Thomist account of grace perfecting nature, Ellul glorifies instead God's apocalyptic grace breaking in from the future, desacralizing human works and even reconciling them to God. In short, as Gill argues, "Ellul takes everything away from us. . . . Both through his sociological criticism and through biblical exposition . . . he leaves us with no hope. But wait! Ellul gives it all back with what can only be described as an inspiring vision of hope and freedom."[147]

Sans feu set Ellul a lifelong theological agenda and he would often refer to it as the basic framework of his thought throughout his corpus. In particular, it begs three questions which I intend to explore in the three chapters to come.

144. *Sans feu*, 369. "The awful mixture made by man is rearranged by grace . . . and by the LORD's act of accepting and gracing the chosen city with his presence."

145. Clark in Christians and Van Hook, *Jacques Ellul*, 287–89.

146. Greenman et al., *Understanding Jacques Ellul*, 78.

147. Gill, *Word of God*, 184.

Firstly, if the New Jerusalem promises a future reconciliation, what can be known now about the shape of that reconciliation? In the following chapter on *Apocalypse Then*, I will engage with Ellul's writing on the book of Revelation, arguing that Ellul makes crucial distinctions between the powers of history (such as Technique), human works and humans themselves. In short, I will outline what I will call his "apocalyptic exousiology" and what it means for the future of the powers, human works and us humans ourselves at the new creation.

Secondly, how can this future hope fund an understanding of how to engage the powers of the technological society today? In common theological parlance, *Sans feu* outlines an "inaugurated" eschatology: "apocalyptic grace" breaking into the present. Indeed, Ellul's concern in *Sans feu* is primarily that the promise of the New Jerusalem gives meaning to our present task: "The glorious vision of the city . . . pertains only to this work assigned to us by God, as human beings fully responsible and fully alive on this earth, with our fellow human beings."[148]

In this sense, Ellul clearly argues for *Apocalypse Now*. How he understands that task is what I will explore in chapter 4, through his writings on the Incarnation.

Thirdly, in a more critical mode, I will tackle at length the question with which this chapter began: what kind of doctrine of creation, if any, does Ellul allow? In the closing theological chapter 6 on the *Apocalypse of Creation*, engaging with often neglected writings, I will argue that Ellul opens up what we might call an *apocalyptic doctrine of creation*, by outlining how creation is won over and against the threat of chaos.

---

148. *Sans feu*, 332.

3

Apocalypse Then

The Destruction of the Powers and the Recapitulation of All Things

The Architecture of Revelation

ELLUL'S STUDY OF THE final book in the biblical canon is one of the defining characteristics of his work. Below we will consider Ellul's innovative and fine-grained commentary, *L'Apocalypse: Architecture en movement* (1975, published in English in 1977), hereafter *Apocalypse*; and *La conférence sur l'Apocalypse de Jean*, a transcript of three public lectures (1985, untranslated), hereafter *Conférence*. It is not my aim in what follows to give a full account Ellul's interpretation in the light of other scholarship.[1] However, it is important to sketch briefly at the outset its basic shape and concerns, before turning to our central focus in this chapter, Ellul's account of the judgment of the powers, human works and human beings at the Eschaton.

In *Apocalypse* Ellul intends to challenge head on the misguided reading of *Revelation* as a historical book, unfurling worsening catastrophes in a progression towards the future end of the world. Such an interpretation is so deeply embedded in its reception that it has become a cultural commonplace: "in popular speech, apocalypse means catastophe, doesn't it?"[2] Pointing out that the original meaning of the word "*apokalypsis*" is "revelation" and noting moreover that only 98 verses out of over 400 verses in the text

---

1. Ellul scholars such as Darrell Fasching, David Gill, and Marva Dawn have engaged with this key area of Ellul's theology. However it is fair to say that once again there is somewhat limited awareness of Ellul's work in this area outside the confines of Ellul scholarship. Notable exceptions outside the Ellul guild are the "theological commentary" by Canadian biblical scholar Joseph Mangina, *Revelation*, and the political reading of American Anabaptist scholars Howard-Brook and Gwyther in *Unveiling Empire*. The latter recognize Ellul's work on Revelation as "incisive" (xiii).

2. *Conférence*, 13, 20. In this respect, Ellul engages with the widespread popular fascination with the prospect of apocalyptic catastrophe, an interest which has only intensified in the past 40 years since his commentary was written.

speak of judgment, he argues that Revelation is not an esoteric corruption of true prophecy, as significant movements in modern theology had argued, but rather an inspired summation of prophecy.

What is decisive for Ellul is reading the whole text in its structural integrity—its architecture, as he denotes it. Defending this "structuralist" approach, Ellul's reading starts, characteristically as we have seen, from the end, for this book demands especially to be read back to front:

> The end is the heavenly Jerusalem . . . and it is from that point that everything else must be read, understood and interpreted, in terms of the end . . . the eschatological event is that which comes from the final reality, where, if you like, God is waiting for us, coming towards us, rather than us moving towards it.[3]

When read in this way, Revelation is an ultimately perspicuous book, Ellul claims, with a relentless focus on the person of Jesus (Rev 1:1). Indeed, the entire opening chapter, clearly attributing divine transcendence to Jesus Christ, the "one like the Son of Man" (1:14) demonstrates that John the Divine is, above all, a "theologian of the Incarnation."[4] Moreover, Ellul's christological reading takes the central chapters 9–14 to be precisely the center of Revelation.[5] The apocalyptic symbolism of the sounding trumpets, which has often confused interpreters, is a way of rendering the heavenly significance of the events of Jesus' earthly life. "What is the heart of what he has to say? It is, of course, Jesus Christ. The heart of this entire revelation is the Incarnation, Death and Resurrection of Jesus Christ."[6]

This is why for Ellul, John's vision does not detract from but rather complements and completes the revelation given in the Gospels. The Gospels characteristically tell of Jesus' history on earth: truth entering reality. It is the particular concern of the "apocalypses" of the New Testament, the visions of Revelation but also the so-called "little apocalypses" embedded in the Synoptics, as well as key passages in the Gospel of John[7] and Paul's writings, to reveal the full, heavenly implications of the Incarnation: "The

3. *Conférence*, 18.

4. Ellul notes that this is prior to a "dogmatic trinitarian theology." For discussion of Revelation's inchoate Trinitarian theology, see Bauckham, *Theology of the Book of Revelation*, 23–25, and chapters 2–5. Ellul is clear, however, that John the Divine must be seen as both theologian *and* seer.

5. Rognon argues Ellul here follows St. Augustine, and his "christocentric reading" of the book (see Rognon's preface in *Apocalypse*, 10).

6. *Conférence*, 49–50.

7. Ellul refers to parallels between the two books (*Conférence*, 49; *Apocalypse*, 25, 34), but is not interested in the question of the relationship between the purported Johannine community and Revelation.

Incarnation has two sides, two histories. What happens on earth, and what happens in heaven."[8]

The Revelation of the Powers and of Divine Non-Power

Another way of putting this is to say that heaven touches earth in two decisive ways, revealing on the one hand the character of God's power and on the other hand the character of the hostile powers. Let us briefly explore these two revelations.

Firstly, what Ellul calls the "adventure of Jesus" on earth reveals the character of the Father in heaven: on his account, the *very doctrine of God* is fully defined by the Incarnation. For Ellul, Revelation undercuts the metaphysical formulations of the philosophical theological tradition, offering instead a theology entirely shaped by the Jesus Christ of history. If the Father and the Son share "this earthly adventure," the Creator God is not impassable, immutable, or totally omniscient. Indeed, any theology which does not begin with the Incarnation in time chases instead "insoluble mysteries" in eternity:

> What happens in the divine world is defined, determined, provoked by the adventure of Jesus on earth. We are not told that according to an arbitrary decree, taken from all eternity by God the Father . . . the crucifixion and resurrection occurs on earth. We are not told that the Incarnation itself is the result of a sort of intra-divine deliberation. Is the Son the Son from all eternity? But even if we answer yes, does this mean that the man Jesus was this Son from all eternity?[9]

The central position of the crucifixion within Revelation (Rev 11) underlines the central significance of the crucifixion to its theology. Quite simply, we see in Jesus a God who dies and rises: who risks everything, who empties himself of power, control and foreknowledge and reveals himself thereby as love. This challenge to other doctrines of God is what is expressed by Ellul's coinage of "non-puissance," or non-power, a concept to which we shall return.[10] The Revelation of John insists that the sovereign God conquers not through power but through weakness.[11]

8. *Conférence*, 50.

9. *Apocalypse*, 61. Ellul's talk of the "divine adventure" anticipates to some degree the development of "open theism." For a defense of pre-existence, see Gathercole, *Pre-existent Son*.

10. E.g., *Apocalypse*, 145, 298.

11. As Bauckham notes, the book of Revelation is often wrongly criticized for presenting an overbearingly transcendent God (*Theology of Revelation*, 43).

Moreover, Revelation tells us that with the Incarnation, in an important sense, the victory has already been won. For Ellul, this book functions then not as an historical progression into the unknown future, but rather through a chiastic structure, around the architectural "keystone" of the Incarnation, as below.[12]

Incarnation
(Rev 9–14)

History (Rev 5–8)		Judgment (Rev 15–19)

The Church
and Her
LORD
(Rev 1–4)

New Creation
(Rev 20–22)

Read in this way, Revelation is not a forward-moving historical book. Rather, drawing again upon the dialectic of reality and truth, Ellul argues it reveals "the permanent depth of the historical," the presence of the eschatological moment in time:

> The Apocalypse is not a historical book. Quite literally the Apocalypse tells us at every moment: the end is here. . . . It reveals to us . . . the permanent depth of the historical, that is to say it helps us discern the Eternal in the present and the End at work in the present. . . . There is in the Apocalypse a certain relationship between reality and truth, it does give an interpretation of reality but it does this by showing us the mystery latent in reality.[13]

We now turn, secondly, from divine non-power to the powers or *exousiai*. If God's presence in Christ on earth touches heaven, it also touches the *heavenly powers* which are the evident concern of apocalyptic: "the world of the powers, the world of evil, the world of angels and demons."[14] We have already devoted some attention to Ellul's concern with these powers in *Présence, Nouveaux,* and *Sans feu* and we will explore further below.

---

12. *Apocalypse,* 65.

13. *Conférence,* 26 (my italics). Similarly: "Reality provides Truth with the means to express itself; Truth transfigures Reality by giving it a meaning that it does not have in itself" (*Apocalypse,* 26).

14. *Conférence,* 51–53. Ellul points significantly to Colossians 2:10, a text we will return to below.

What is revealed in Revelation 15 to 19, often considered its most complex chapters, is God's war and judgment against these hostile powers. For Ellul, history is in fact the arena of these powers, which have no eternal future and against which Jesus has won a decisive victory. Elaborating upon this structure, Ellul contends that what contrasts the first two blocks, Church (Rev 1–4) and History (Rev 5–8), from the last two is their theological relationship to the keystone: Incarnation (Rev 9–14). Placed after the central section, the blocks on the Judgment of the powers (Rev 15–19) and New Creation (Rev 20–22) denote respectively the consequence of the Incarnation for the powers within history—the angels and the plagues—and then for the powers at the end of all things—the Beasts and the Dragons. Moreover, the fact this end will involve a definitive rupture between Creation and New Creation is for Ellul the particular insight of the genre of apocalyptic, as first developed in the OT writings.[15]

Drawing back from this necessarily brief account of the architecture of Revelation, we surmise that Ellul sees in his construction a polemic against a progressivist view of history, a polemic which then funds both his critique of the ideology of progress and his own dialectical methodology. For this is a polemic against the assumption that the powers drive history and that social-scientific reasoning gives a sufficient accounting of their sway: against the assumption that "in studying this reality it is possible to say: this is what's true."[16]

What is real cannot reveal what is true, in Ellul's terms. Therefore, in the light of the "permanent depth of the historical," it is impossible to state that his sociology can stand apart from his theology. Moreover, as his own statements in *A temps* clearly imply, his theology had one might say, an apocalyptic function when placed in dialogue with his sociology: to break the closed world open to the light of the End. His recovery of apocalyptic thus offers a polemical refusal of the social world as a "seamless web of relations . . . a sealed network of causally determined functions," without possibility of outside interruption.[17]

In what follows I will explore Ellul's account of these two decisive final sections within his "architecture": the Judgment of the Powers (Rev 15–19) and the New Creation (Rev 20–22). However, we cannot escape so easily

15. *Conférence*, 24. Ellul alludes here to the relationship of this book to the OT apocalyptic literature.

16. *Conférence*, 27.

17. Harink, *Paul among the Postliberals*, 74. Apocalyptic breaks open the closed relations perceived in social-scientific reason, projecting events onto a heavenly horizon "beyond," a horizon which cannot be directly described but which can be unveiled in symbolic form. What happens on earth is connected to the hidden horizon of heaven.

from the question of the future, but must pause at this point to ask, as the disciples asked Jesus, "When will these things take place?" (Luke 21:7).

Apocalypse When?

In *Sans feu*, Ellul envisages the end of time as the time of God's cosmic reconciliation of truth and reality, of heaven and earth. There are, so to speak, two eons: the present eon of Christ's "humble Incarnation": truth entering reality; and the future eon of the "new creation," when truth "rejoins" and "fills" reality.[18] This is again what we see in *Apocalypse*.

The language of *eons* is not Ellul's own but rather that employed by Marva Dawn in explicating Ellul's work. Dawn attempts to foreground Ellul's eschatology before exploring Ellul's contribution to a social theology of the powers, an exousiology, in my terms. This enables her to explicate the significance of Ellul's work against the background of earlier, more systematic studies of eschatology, leading her to claim that Ellul operates with the "objective dialectic" at the heart of biblical eschatology (a phrase coined by Théo Preyss and developed by Oscar Cullman). Christ's victory has not yet finally changed the being of the world, but it has changed its final destiny; therefore his victory is not a merely subjective victory for those who choose to see the world this way.[19] This is the basic shape of Ellul's theology, as developed most clearly in *Ethique*: the Incarnation has not effected what he calls a "magical" restitution of the world, as if it worked as an *opus operatum*. "There is no sort of reversal of the world's being, by virtue of the Incarnation, the Crucifixion, the Redemption . . . there is not a world that was once enslaved and now becomes free."[20]

For Ellul, these two moments of judgment and recapitulation are both a final work of God in the future eon and also an inaugurated process in the present eon of human history. That is to say, Ellul never looks to judgment and recapitulation as *merely future* events. Rather he clearly argues that they can be anticipated *now* in the present.[21]

The present judgment of powers funds Ellul's concept of "desacralization." Moreover, since in Jesus, the resurrection has already taken place and death has been overcome: the work of recapitulation can begin *now*. This work is a corollary of the work of desacralization, and the

18. As cited on 91 above, *Sans feu*, 308.
19. Dawn, "Principalities and Powers," 54; *Tabernacling of God*, 26.
20. *Ethique*, 13.
21. *Apocalypse*, 64.

characteristic expression Ellul uses for this dynamic in present human history is "reconciliation."

The outworking of these two eschatological moments in present history will be considered in detail in the next chapter on *Apocalypse Now*. However, it is important to stress now an essential point about this objective dialectic. That is to say that though the end is *more than* a future event, it is certainly *not less than* a future event. Indeed, it depends entirely the given future.

Therefore, we may ask, *Apocalypse When*? In other words, what does Ellul make of texts which speak of the *parousia* or physical presence of Jesus Christ, in recognizable person, in history?[22] A sympathetic critic of Ellul's apocalyptic eschatology contends that his argument comes close not only to "detemporizing" but even "platonizing" the biblical account:

> He sounds as though he believes in [a] temporal End. More than occasionally, however, Ellul's eschatology appears to be detemporalized. The End is not then a historical end but rather the Realm of the wholly other, the Beyond. The End doesn't intersect with history, except in the form of an individual "presence" and through a mysterious "hidden" adoption of our works.[23]

This is part of Gill's wider argument that Ellul has a weak understanding of God's presence in this space-time creation, the logical result of his strong emphasis on the alterity of God. Gill therefore questions whether Ellul's favorite description of God as "the Wholly Other" betrays an excessive divine transcendence, noting that the one chapter of Revelation Ellul does not deal with is chapter 4, which is all about creation![24]

What then is at stake for Ellul in emphasizing the presence of eternity in time? In earlier works like *Présence*, Ellul argues that the Parousia is not a "temporal and logical future," in order to mark that it is not a continuation of this present time.[25] By the time of *Sans feu*, he characteristically refers to the new creation in terms of the "myth of the heavenly Jerusalem," and he has in mind here its present meaning for us.[26] By the time of *Apocalypse*, he writes

22. The word occurs twenty-four times in the NT (Matt 24:3, 27, 37, 39; 1 Cor 15:23; 1 Thess 2:19; 3:13; 4:15; 5:23; 2 Thess 2:1, 8, 9; Jas 5:7, 8; 2 Pet 1:16; 3:4, 12; 1 John 2:28).

23. Gill, *Word of God*, 175. See also Fasching, who claims that Ellul's "merciless critique" of utopia is based on this framework (Fasching, *Thought of Jacques Ellul*).

24. Gill, *Word of God*, 177. We will explore the relationship between creation and apocalypse in Ellul's thinking in a later chapter.

25. See Dawn, *Tabernacling of God*, 147.

26. Goddard notes that Ellul says relatively little about the character of the future aeon (*Living the Word*, 88). In his contribution to the 2012 Bordeaux symposium, on the influence of *Sans feu* on Ivan Illich, the agnostic French urbanist Thierry Paquot clearly idealizes and Platonizes Ellul's hope, since he cannot share his faith. See in Chastenet, *Etre Ellulien Au XXIe Siècle*, 258.

of an "absolute end," implying that it is outside time. "The end helps us grasp what history has been and also, at the same time, what reality is now. But this is not a temporally successive end: it is an absolute end."[27]

However, in keeping with an objective dialectic, Ellul holds present and future in careful tension. Ellul clearly does not offer the accustomed modernist reconstruction of early Christian eschatology, turning away from time because of the infinite delay of the *parousia*, and gesturing instead towards an absolute Eternity which was realized in the universal church, for better or worse, depending on the perspective taken. Indeed, in discussing 1 and 2 Thessalonians, he clearly distinguishes his view from this modern "spiritualization," which rests upon the false move of "making the End of Time, the return of Jesus and the End of the World one and the same":

> However, these three elements are not necessarily linked and it is far from obvious that the first generation of Christians confused them. . . . What there is, is a warning against being convinced of a speedy return. . . . The fact that the end of the world and Jesus' return are not instantaneous does not preclude the actual and effective declaration of the End Times. On the one hand, "I'm coming soon." On the other hand, "The Time is near."[28]

Summarizing, Ellul notes that the *time is near* because it is inaugurated, even if the return of Christ has not yet happened. To say this return in glory will happen *soon* is not to speak of a small *quantity* of days but rather to mark the *quality* of the time we have now entered. We do not know the duration of time before the end of time but we know that these are the last days. Ellul argues explicitly here that this is not a "spiritualizing interpretation." and in concluding his commentary, he returns again to this *soon*, as it is repeated at the end of Revelation (22:20), and to which we respond, "Amen, Come, LORD Jesus," placing the emphasis on the gathering up of all things in the Eschaton. "*I'm coming soon.* This 'soon' includes all temporal dimensions, not only the future but also the present. Not just the spiritual but also the existential. Not only the individual but also the galactic. Not only truth but also reality."[29]

What is at stake for Ellul in this rather tortuous discussion? Once again, the influence of Karl Barth casts a long shadow. And indeed, perhaps in Ellul's concern to argue against history as progress, it is possible to argue, as Moltmann does of Barth's eschalotology, that in *Apocalypse* at

27. *Apocalypse*, 36.

28. *Apocalypse*, 135.

29. *Apocalypse*, 308, although in his final flourish, the emphasis is squarely on the objective achievement already established by grace.

least, Ellul does not offer enough hope for history *within* history. Moltmann claimed that in his polemical critique of liberal Protestantism's faith in the inexorable progress of history towards the kingdom, Barth severed the link between "the last things" of eschatology and history itself. Yet, as Moltmann noted of Barth, if "eschaton" means timeless eternity, then eschatology cannot easily provide concrete hope for this space-time world on this side of eternity. In practice, Barth's solution, Moltmann concluded, proposed too great a discontinuity from this world we know.[30]

Apocalyse Then: The Destruction of the Powers and Universal Salvation

We have set out briefly above Ellul's perspectives on history, time and eternity, and with these in mind we now turn to his treatment of the two great *future* moments of judgment and recapitulation. Indeed, perhaps the best-known feature of Ellul's eschatology is his advocacy of universal salvation, a doctrine which by its very nature is future.

It is perhaps intriguing, given the association between apocalypse and catastrophe, that Ellul contended that his universalism arose initially from his study of Revelation in the 1960s: "I believe, I do not seek to prove, but I believe in Universal Salvation. . . . I believe no one is damned and I find it in the Apocalypse."[31]

Although Ellul's advocacy of universal salvation is well known, what is rarely noted is its inextricable link to his view of the powers. We think again of the temporal relationship between the two moments of judgment and recapitulation: it is the prior judgment and condemnation of the powers which leads to the liberation and recapitulation of human works, and hence finally, to the end of death (this for Ellul is the meaning of "the second death" [Rev 20:14]) and from there, to universal salvation.[32] Ellul's movement towards universal salvation is therefore directly related to his reinterpretation of the

30. Volf in Bauckham, *God Will Be All in All*, 234. Jürgen Moltmann argues that the hope for history *within* history is signified in Revelation by the figure of the millennium. See Moltmann, *Coming of God*.

31. *Conférence*, 83. Quoting Barth, he then states more forcefully: "We do not believe at all in salvation if we believe that a person can be damned." See Goddard's chapter on Ellul in MacDonald, *Explorations in Universalism*. "Chastenet, presumably based again on personal correspondence, notes that it was when Ellul began a series of biblical studies on the book of Revelation in 1965 that he moved towards accepting universal salvation" (327). There is a hint to this time also in *A Temps* (70) where Ellul says he has "evolved" theologically.

32. As is noted in the preface by Rognon in *Apocalypse* (4), this interpretation of the "second death" is integral to Ellul's universalism.

judgment and condemnation of the powers in Revelation 15–19. Essentially, Ellul's argument for universal salvation boils down to this: he interprets passages about condemnation in Revelation in terms of the condemnation not of persons, but of powers. God's destructive wrath is directed against the powers, which are entirely destroyed, the very act by which he is able to reconcile himself both to humanity and its works.[33]

What *Are* the Powers?

We have already alluded to Marva Dawn's work on the powers as the vital connection between Ellul's theology and sociology, and *Apocalypse* provides much evidence that the structures Ellul studies sociologically are expressions of the *exousiai*.[34]

Dawn's 1992 thesis offers an extremely thorough survey of the topic, and two books popularizing Ellul's exousiology came out of it. Firstly, a collection and translation of a number of very early articles devoted to the powers which she had analyzed.[35] And secondly, a later reworking of the thesis itself published as *Powers, Weakness, and the Tabernacling of God* (2001). On Dawn's account, *Apocalypse* is perhaps the key work, although it is clearly related to more "typological"[36] accounts of the powers in his key books *Ethique* (1973) and *Subversion* (1984). Therefore, in what follows, I will begin with Ellul's writings on the powers in *Apocalypse* before comparing and contrasting them with his more systematic presentation of the powers in these two works.

However, as one begins such a task, evident problems present themselves. Firstly, because of his lack of explicit and rigorous exegetical work, it is far from easy to produce a coherent account of what Ellul argues about the powers. In the words of Gill, Ellul's definition of the powers in *Apocalypse* "leaves something to be desired in terms of rigor and clarity."[37] It is therefore almost impossible for any treatment of Ellul on the powers to escape

---

33. Ellul is clear that biblically, judgment and condemnation are not synonymous (*Apocalypse*, 204). This is outworked at length in chapter 6 of *Apocalypse*, "Le Jugement," later summarized in *Conférence* (77).

34. As she stated in her thesis, "though Ellul has never written an exegetical study of the traditional text associated with the concept of the principalities and powers [Eph 6], his commentary on Revelation includes large sections on the topic" (Dawn, "Principalities and Powers," 100).

35. Ellul in *Sources and Trajectories*, 24–25, referencing her thesis. Dawn especially draws attention to *Chronicles of the Problem of Civilization*.

36. Dawn, "Principalities and Powers," 91.

37. Gill, *Word of God*, 109.

being filtered through its reception and popularization by Dawn, Gill and other writers. It thus runs the risk I have already highlighted of preaching primarily to the Ellul guild.

Secondly, Ellul's exousiology is rather diffuse and complex, with a number of implicit assumptions, most obviously, as we shall see, a suspicion of the very exercise of power itself. It is, as Goddard notes, "one of the most difficult areas of his thought."[38] Unlike a number of systematic treatments of the powers, with which he shows himself familiar (see below), Ellul does not offer in *Apocalypse* a methodological preamble to explicate his understanding of the relationship between the spiritual and social dimensions of power.

Thirdly, and more significantly the task of interpreting Ellul's exousiology is fraught with difficulty against the wider backdrop of his entire oeuvre, quite simply because as one might expect over the course of over fifty years, Ellul significantly changes his position. In *Présence*, he posits two orders, the order of God's redemption, and the order of God's preservation of the world which, in Ellul's characteristic (and probably Calvinist) terms, is what makes life liveable in a fallen world.[39] Within "the order of preservation," Ellul includes not only institutions which support human life such as marriage and the family, but also at this stage what he will later consider as the unholy trinity of money, the state and technology, or "Argent. Etat. Technique."[40]

Ellul argues that all can share in this order of preservation, can make the world a better place, in the present time "as long as they are concerned for some kind of truth, an authentic justice."[41] Christians of course take an active part in preserving the world, although more is required of them. It is the particular role of Christians to work within God's order of redemption as well. It seems clear enough that by writing of preserving the world, Ellul has in mind a theology of creation, and indeed, in an earlier text, *The Theological Foundation of Law*, Ellul cites Colossians 1:16 to affirm that these social structures were created in Christ.[42] However, by the 1970s,

38. Goddard, *Living the Word*, 84.

39. *Présence* in *Défi*, 31.

40. Goddard, *Living the Word*, 113–14.

41. *Présence* in *Défi*, 31. See *Présence* in *Défi*, chapter 2.

42. Dawn, "Principalities and Powers," 93. Indeed, this is how Jacqui Stewart reads Ellul in an interesting article applying *Présence* to the ethics of Genetically Modified crops. From within the order of Christ's redemption of the world, Christians must ensure that questions of ultimate ends are not suppressed by the dominance of the means of preserving the world. However, Stewart rightly concludes from *Présence* that Ellul here holds to a view of orders of creation, arguing that, for Ellul, "God's creative activity is an ongoing gift in human affairs." See Jacqui Stewart's "Re-ordering Means and Ends," in Deane-Drummond, *Re-ordering Nature*, 257–74.

and especially Ellul's latest and most systematic treatment of the powers, in chapter 9 of *Subversion* (1984), we find an altogether different picture, as we shall explore.

Beyond these three particular difficulties, we note that explicating the powers is a spiritually demanding task. If the powers evade human understanding, it would be foolish and speculative to "explain" what is ultimately inexplicable to our (theological or socio-scientific) reasoning. This is something Ellul himself notes time and again, when he refuses to be drawn into speculation about the spiritual ontology of the powers. In this he claims to be following the NT which, in stark contrast to the complex angelology of contemporary Judaism and the fascination with magic of the surrounding Hellenistic world, offers only a stance of resistance based on the defeat of the powers.[43]

The Incarnations of the Powers

Despite these difficulties, Dawn gives a critical purchase upon Ellul's treatment of the powers by arguing that he "bridges the hermeneutical gap [between the ancient text and the modern world] by understanding the powers according to their functions and *by describing those functions of the powers as they are evident in social realities.*"[44] For Dawn, by this functional treatment, Ellul is able to hold the spiritual and human element in the powers in "*dialectical tension.*"[45]

In short, as Dawn states in a later summary of her work for a wider audience: "One of Ellul's most brilliant insights was that the biblical record never describes the essence or nature of the powers. We can know them only by their functions."[46] Following Ellul, she claims that we cannot give an account of the powers in isolation from these social functions; the starting point must be what is visible and to some degree explicable, that is, the social functions of the powers. Dawn thus sums up the most significant assumption underpinning Ellul's study of Revelation's exousiology: the fact that the powers *function* within society by *incarnating* themselves within *human works*, without being reducible to the people who do those works, or to those works themselves.[47]

43. Dawn, "Principalities and Powers," 62. See also 98, where she cites a letter from Ellul outlining his approach.

44. Dawn, "Principalities and Powers," 368.

45. Dawn, "Principalities and Powers," 106 (my italics).

46. Dawn et al., *Unnecessary Pastor*, 104.

47. Dawn, "Principalities and Powers," 103.

These distinctions between the powers, their works and people are what allow Ellul to argue for the salvation (through judgment) not only of human actors, but even of the salvation (through recapitulation) of the social works which they have done. And this provides a basic clarity. For if as Dawn states, "the basic disagreement in application of the biblical notion of the powers in the twentieth century derives from the debate about whether the powers will ultimately be reconciled or destroyed,"[48] it is quite clear where Ellul stands on this issue. Basing himself on Revelation 19 and 20, he is quite clear that the condemnation falls ultimately on the Dragon (Satan) and the Beasts, the great symbols within the book of opposition to God, Powers (capitalized by Ellul) which derive their power ultimately from the Power of Death. These, and only these, are ultimately destroyed, as they are thrown into the fiery lake of the second death (Rev 20:14–15). The people and their works will be judged, that is separated from these Powers, but not finally condemned and destroyed.

What then are these "incarnations," the social expressions of these Powers in Ellul's later work? It seems that they are the very institutions, such as the economy, the state and Technique which Ellul had treated within the providential order of preservation in his early writings. Let us consider now three key examples from *Apocalypse*.

Take, first of all, the two beasts (Rev 13). Rejecting a primarily historical-critical interpretation, Ellul argues that the first beast does not refer only to the historic Roman Empire, but to *the function of political power in all its forms.* This power masquerades in the clothes of divine power, but this is a parody. Moreover, he equates the second beast, disguised as a lamb, not simply to the imperial cult, but to the parody of the powerful divine Word which is intrinsic to all political power: that is, the *function of propaganda.*[49]

Secondly, take Ellul's interpretation of the four Horsemen of the Apocalypse (Rev 6). First and foremost, the white rider represents the Word of God, which alone rides freely within history.[50] The other three riders represent the powers, although they are not given free rein, but work within limits, a hint, Ellul contends, of the continuing sovereignty of God. For Ellul, the red rider represents the state, or "political power" permitted to carry the sword. The black rider with the weighing scales

48. Dawn et al., *Unnecessary Pastor*, 57. "Although there is much disagreement about the being of the powers, there is much greater agreement but different emphases on how to deal with the powers" (62).

49. See *Apocalypse*, chapter 6.

50. This is also, Ellul notes, a hint of the final victory of God's judgment. See for scholarly agreement, see the substantial discussion in Finamore, *God, Order, and Chaos*, 196–204.

represents money and "economic power," regulating purchasing power amid scarce resources. The pale rider represents Death itself. But here Ellul has in mind not so much death as a natural phenomenon, but Death as an annihilating force, unleashed against the earth and a quarter of its peoples. This is Ellul's apocalyptic account of history.

Moreover, this key passage provides a clear expression of his exousiology:

> I do not mean that the four horsemen exist in reality. But do they exist as concentrated power in a sort of being that acts with a will? Do we not enter here into demonology with angels, devils and concretized "powers"? . . . It all comes from humans; but finally we know well . . . that no person ever decides. . . . It all comes from humans, but in this domain all escapes us . . . Everything happens as if . . . there are all the human motivations and yet a strange kind of Transhuman which is disclosed. . . . People are the actors and the inventors. But there is more than people alone.[51]

Note how social reality and spiritual reality are held in tension—neither is denied. Yet Ellul refuses to proceed beyond observable social functions into speculation about "concretized powers." What apocalyptic reveals alongside the observable functions of the powers is an inexplicable "surplus" in any sociological accounting of the powers, that which remains beyond explanation, what Ellul terms interestingly a "transhuman" element.

Take thirdly the Great City of Babylon (Rev 17–18). As *Sans feu* suggests, Ellul takes Babylon as a figure not simply of Rome but of the City/Technique, urban-technological civilisation itself. It is the fall of the Great City in Revelation which precipitates the final destruction of the Powers of the Dragon and Death. The City of course contains people, who do its works, and yet Ellul notes a key distinction here between the Great City and its inhabitants, who, he argues, are liberated and saved amid and even by this very destruction. "It is Babylon the Great which is fallen; but we are not told that the people who inhabited Babylon the Great are condemned."[52]

For Ellul, Babylon can and must be distinguished from the people who worked within it and served it (in the fullest sense of the word). Moreover, not only the people, but *even their works*, can be separated from the Great City at the judgment. This final separating judgment implies for Ellul that there will be a universal judgment and subsequent salvation of all humanity and a universal judgment and subsequent recapitulation of

51. *Apocalypse*, 185. See also *Conférence*, 76–78.
52. *Conférence*, 85.

human works. The line of judgment does not fall between persons, the good and the evil, but within persons. And this is not a neat and painless separation of humanity from the powers but a deep cut which reaches to the very core of who we have become, and what we have done, as persons. It is worth citing him at length:

> We are faced here with the condemnation of the powers: the power of Death, the power of the State . . . the power of famine, the power of the great dragon, the adversary who wants to get rid of Creation, with all the powers of destruction. . . . And what about human beings? They are not condemned, but they are judged. . . . In other words [citing Heb 4:12–13], the Judgment will penetrate in order to separate what is to be preserved and what is to be destroyed. What will be destroyed is our sense of belonging, our affiliation to the powers, the fact that we have yielded to the love of money, the fact that we have yielded to the power of the state, and so on. This is condemned, but I am not, not in my being. . . . We are in our very beings saved. By grace we are forgiven.[53]

Ellul also cites here 1 Corinthians 3:10–15, another key text in his own understanding of the judgment of human works and lives. This separation of the people from the powers is why the people of Babylon at first mourn for its loss, because they are involved and invested in the city and in that sense are owned by it and belong to it. But just as they are ultimately saved by grace, so something can be saved even from the works of the fallen city. Basing his interpretation upon Revelation 22, Ellul argues that because the symbol of salvation is also a Great City, a New Jerusalem, wherein the wealth of the hostile nations are brought in tribute to God, whatever has been of value within the works of urban-technological civilization will be taken up and recapitulated, and brought into the immediate presence of God, a presence implicit in the promise that the LORD will be its Temple (Rev 22:21). The judgment of the nations does not therefore imply the condemnation of entire peoples or the wholesale destruction of their works. However, in keeping with his fundamental Personalism, this primarily corporate understanding has implications at the level of every single life. Even a person whose life disintegrates at the judgment of the powers may have made a contribution which lasts forever. "If in your life you have spoken a word, a single word worth keeping for eternity, it will be part of the heavenly Jerusalem, part of the work that God builds with our works."[54]

53. *Conférence*, 85–86.
54. *Conférence*, 92.

Ellul, Barth, and *Das Nichtige*

I have outlined above a fine-grained account of Ellul's development in *Apocalypse* of a dialectical treatment of the powers according to their functions, rather than their ontology.[55] This is to say, "the powers are important to Ellul not in themselves but only as they relate to the human world and human works."[56] Ellul's "functional" interpretation enables him to deploy the powers in his social theology and ethics without recourse to a speculative angelology and demonology. However, we must now pass to some more probing comments.

The *Chaoskampf* and the Meontic Tradition

I will argue below that although Ellul's emphasis in *Apocalypse* is on the functions of the powers, there is also an implicit denial of their being. It is this underlying train of thought which becomes more explicit in Ellul's later work. Indeed, Dawn expresses concern that Ellul's early emphasis on the functions of the powers is overtaken by his more "reductionist" explanation in *Subversion* (1984). Indeed, Dawn already notes of *Apocalypse*:

> Though his exposition is marred by his typical problem of overstatement, his greater problem is that his interpretation of Revelation stretches the text to fit with his preconceived notions about the powers. Though he did not formulate his specific listing of the powers according to their function until *Subversion*, we can see that Ellul's confidence in the adequacy of a functional definition for the biblical concept of the principalities and powers influenced his biblical interpretation from the beginning.[57]

We can find insight into what these notions are by attending not only to *Subversion* but to an even earlier, and more typological discussion of the powers in *Ethique*. As we noted above, in his earliest theological writings, Ellul quite simply spoke of powers within the providential order of preservation. Ellul then draws back from this claim towards a more functional approach, a trend already visible in *Sans feu*. In *Ethique*, relating at various points the theological horizon to the sociological horizon, Ellul credits the recovery of the powers language to Oscar Cullman and Karl Barth. In a

---

55. See Dawn's introduction to dialectic in her chapter on "The Call to Triumph over the Principalities and Powers," in Dawn et al., *Unnecessary Pastor*, 79–119.

56. Goddard, *Living the Word*, 85.

57. Dawn, "Principalities and Powers," 108.

section entitled *Liberté des Puissances*, he outlines four possible understandings of the powers:

> 1. Are we faced here with "demons" in the most elementary and traditional sense of the term? 2. Are we faced with "powers" (thrones and dominions) much more indeterminate but possessing an existence . . . an objectivity? 3. Or are we faced with a simple human disposition to "constitute" such a human fact as a power because we raises it up in this way? 4. Or, finally, are we simply in the presence of a "way of speaking," the use of imagery?[58]

Ruling out position 1, Ellul situates himself between positions 2 and 3, setting out his basic position in relation to money, to which he had devoted an entire book. Claiming to write out of the experience of actively confronting the powers, he contends: "I remain firmly convinced . . . that the 'exousiaï' referred to in the New Testament, or even the personalization of the power of money (as Mammon), correspond to actual realities, spiritual realities of course, realities independent of human decision."[59]

This is said to hold good not only for money but also for the state. And then, in a pregnant aside, implying an affirmative response, Ellul asks aloud: "I have wondered if Technique itself does not represent one of these powers. It's a straightforward enough question."[60] Two significant conclusions can be drawn from this key passage. Firstly, that position 4 has nothing to offer. Following Barth, and *contra* Bultmann, Ellul believed that the biblical language of the powers must not be "demythologized," but reinterpreted to denote modern forms of the powers implicated in the New Testament. Secondly, Ellul characteristically denotes by the powers the unholy trinity of money, the state and technology, or "Argent. Etat. Technique."[61] These three powers most concern Ellul in *Sans feu*; *Ethique*; *Parole*; and *Subversion*.

However, what is not so easy to clarify is the relationship between positions 2 and 3 in Ellul's thought. In *Ethique* (1977), Ellul seems not to exclude entirely position 2. However, by the time of a later treatment in *Subversion* (chapter 9), he basically asserts position 3, arguing that the powers do not have an objective existence. The genius of apocalyptic is to reveal the heavenly dimension of the powers—their false transcendence—while, in the very act of revealing them, casting them out of heaven, throwing them down to earth. It is worth citing Ellul at some length at this point:

58. *Ethique*, 174.

59. *Ethique*, 174. See also Dawn et al., *Unnecessary Pastor*, 106, citing *Ethique*, 174.

60. *Ethique*, 177.

61. Goddard, *Living the Word*, 113–14.

They are all characterized by their functions. . . . They do not exist as a person exists with their infinite complexity . . . their relationships and their inner mystery. What seems to me in this vision of anti-Creation is that there is no mystery. . . . There is nothing "behind" it. . . . They are certainly powers in the heavenly places but they have no existence apart from in relation to humanity. It is understandable that these powers attack what God has made, since they are expressions of the chaos, the nothingness that God put to work for his creation. . . . They are a disorganizing force. Not all chaos was absorbed in Creation, and Creation is always threatened. The relationship between the end of this Creation, humanity and its Creator is always disturbed, but not by an anti-god . . . or by an evil principle.[62]

In this rather cryptic passage, referring to a "vision of anti-creation," Ellul follows Barth in arguing that evil can only be understood as the absence and negation of the good. In other words, the presence of hostile powers in a good creation is understood by Ellul within what might be called the "meontic" tradition in Christian thought. Ellul here is clearly working with Barth's reworking of this tradition in terms of *Das Nichtige* or the Negative.[63] Ellul wishes to argue that there is an unwilled negative possibility implicit in the Creator God's decision for order over against chaos.

This tradition itself draws upon a scriptural motif often denoted by the German term *chaoskampf* in biblical scholarship. It is clear that the "expressions of chaos" Ellul has in mind is the *tohu wa bohu* (Gen 1:2), a theme present elsewhere in the canon in Job, as well as in Daniel and in later intertestamental literature.[64] In his late work *Genèse,* he repeats his argument that the primeval waters of Genesis 1:2 express the threat of dissolution, the possibility of the goodness of the earth melting away, like a sugar cube in water.[65] We will briefly revisit this theme in our account of Ellul's theology of creation, but most significantly for this discussion, this Barthian

62. *Subversion*, 206–7. Ellul claims that it is only in the "symbolic text" of Revelation that the powers are seen to exist in heavenly places—the emphasis of the gospels, as we shall see, is on their earthly activity.

63. Noble argues that Barth's Das Nichtige (*CD* 3, section 50) is best understood as a reworking of Augustine's concept of *privatio boni*, which is in turn derived from the Platonic idea of the *me-on*, the "not yet," the unfulfilled potential of something. Barth's concept is thus that evil is the negative potential, rather than sheer nothingness. See Noble in Lane, *Unseen World*, 218.

64. See Angel and Wright, *Playing with Dragons*, for an introduction to the *chaoskampf* in Hebrew literature, particularly in the books of Job, Daniel, and Enoch.

65. *Genèse*, 30.

framework seems to be in the background in Ellul's bold interpretation of the final chapters of Revelation in *Apocalypse*.[66]

Revelation 20

A most striking example of this approach is Ellul's interpretation of the fate of the *dragon*, or the *Diabolos* or the *Satan* in Revelation 20, bound at the beginning of the chapter (Rev 20:2), then released for a time before finally being destroyed (Rev 20:7–10). For Ellul, the spirits of power such as the state and money are merely the historic incarnations of this shadowy figure: they can rise and fall in the course of history without there being a fundamental change in the creation. However, the dragon itself represents a greater Power, a "replica" or double of God's power from the beginning of creation. "The spirits of power are but the emanations, as we have seen, of the Dragon . . . whereas the 'ancient serpent' the one who (without being the last) was there at the first . . . and the Satan who sits before God (Job) and the *Diabolos*, whose work is the exact replica of God's separating work in the creation—these powers are not of the same nature."[67]

As we have seen, Ellul argues that Genesis 1 presents creation emerging from a series of separations, elements from elements, creature from Creator and finally, and paradigmatically, humanity from God. The eventual wilful rupture of humanity from God appears for Ellul to be somehow a perpetuation of this "principle of division," as he calls it, not itself intended by God, but in some sense allowed, an inevitable process from separation to separation.

In other words, though separation brings order in creation, it also opens up the negative potential of rupture from God. In this light, we see the full significance of Ellul's theology of *rupture*. Our pursuit of power apart from God is a subversion of the original and good distinction between the Creator and the creature. As we saw with Ellul's interpretation of Cain, human actions affect not only the divine-human relationship but the very cosmos itself:

> Humanity is the climax of creation, and drags all creation down. The whole creation is separated from God and therefore what the Greeks will call the cosmos, the universe, is a universe that has broken from God and which, in Paul's texts for example, is necessarily the place where a whole set of elements of opposition

---

66. *Apocalypse*, 199.

67. *Apocalypse*, 247–48.

to God, of evil elements etc. gather together. . . . And as a result, this cosmos is called to make way for a new creation.[68]

Creation is thus destined to futility (Rom 8 is in the background here), and headed for a crisis of judgment.[69] In Ellul's formulation, it is because a right separation has now become a dangerous rupture, that all division must be overcome in a final act of reconciliation, a new creation. In other words, to remake the world, the dragon of division and rupture at the heart of creation must be destroyed. In characteristically bold language, Ellul claims this is nothing less than the reversal of the whole movement of creation.[70] To summarize Ellul's late account of evil powers, it is clear that he sees them as resulting from the negative potential of creation, not as created actualities.

Yet what are we to make of this approach in outlining a social theology of the powers, and in this case, above all, of Technique? Whilst he rejects a pre-mundane angelic fall, does Ellul, perhaps going beyond Barth, tilt at times towards a misleading metaphysical dualism? Anabaptist theologian Nigel Wright defends the value of Barth's concept of *Das Nichtige*, noting its explanatory power with reference to the problem of evil. In his book, *A Theology of the Dark Side*, Wright claims that Barth was right to argue against the traditional interpretation of an angelic fall, stripping the devil of his "personality," cautioning against the fascination that comes from considering him as a personal but fallen leader of the pack of rebellious angels.[71] Barth (and following him, Ellul), writing in the aftermath of the Second World War, grants an existence to "lordless powers," without giving them the validity of a created personhood.[72]

Wright does concede that Barth's reading of Genesis 1:2 is a classic case of creative eisegesis—of reading something into a text which is not present on the surface.[73] Yet he claims that *Das Nichtige* is not to be confused, but is to be held in tension, with Barth's concept of the Shadow.

---

68. *Genèse*, 62 (my italics).

69. Flying in the face of a good deal of scientific theology, Michael Lloyd bemoans the fact that in the light of evolutionary theory, the scope of the fall has been "reduced from the cosmic to the merely human" (Lloyd in Bimson, "Reconsidering a 'Cosmic Fall'"). Dave Bookless argues on the one hand that "the shattering effects of sin and fall include a breakdown . . . in the relationship between God and the created order" (*Planetwise*, 38). Yet on the other hand, he concedes that there are positive ecological consequences of natural death in the present age.

70. *Apocalypse*, 248.

71. Wright, *Theology of the Dark Side*, 41.

72. Wright, *Theology of the Dark Side*, 31.

73. Commentators as diverse as Henri Blocher and John Hick go further to suggest that Barth's exegesis of Genesis 1:2 imports a metaphysical dualism.

Barth's Shadow "signifies the positive and negative aspects of existence," which make it good in its totality (Gen 1:31), meaning "hours and days and years both bright and dark, success and failure, laughter and tears, growth and age, gain and loss, birth and . . . death."[74] However, although the clear distinction between these two concepts in Barth's thought is important, Barth wishes ultimately to say there is a sense in which Nothingness acts as parasitic upon the Shadow, using it as an "alibi."[75] It is the drama of human rebellion which gives it its opportunity.

Ellul's exousiology of "Money, State and Technology" is undoubtedly dependent upon Barth's use of the meontic tradition. As Scott Prather states of Ellul's exousiology: "it is hard not to hear Barth's claim that the wholly-oppositional, anti-creaturely power of Das Nichtige works in and through the powers in Ellul's claim."[76] Yet on the whole the significance of the Barthian and "meontic" element in Ellul's exousiology has been some-what neglected. Perhaps here again, Ellul's tendency to make unaccredited use of Barth, perhaps without fully articulating his conceptual framework, is a factor.

Ellul's ambivalent account of separation seems to be an echo of Barth's Shadow: necessary and good in creation, but open to deeper rupture. This underpins Ellul's interpretation of the new creation in *Apocalypse*. Distinguishing death as finitude, a "shadow" element of God's original good creation, and Death as the ultimate separating power of destruction, a corruption of death in its original purpose, Ellul is clear that new creation must now lead to the end of death in every sense.[77] Bodily death could have been received as creaturely finitude but once it becomes a lordless power, Death must be overcome within a new creation: "What is announced . . . is not the re-establishment of Eden: the original creation which death was part of, in order to eliminate what [death] had become, the last and abominable enemy, the ally . . . of chaos . . . of Nothingness—this original creation is now effaced by a radically new creation."[78]

As Ellul reads Revelation, this is why the transition from the judgment of the incarnations of the powers (Rev 15–19) to the new creation (Rev 20–22) is marked by a transition from the historical plane to the cosmic.

74. Wright, *Theology of the Dark Side*, 94.

75. Wright, *Theology of the Dark Side*, 95.

76. Prather, *Christ, Power, and Mammon*, 214. Goddard, Dawn, and Fasching have all to some degree explored the influence of Ellul's exousiology on his sociology.

77. Ellul's account of death is complex. See Goddard, *Living the Word*, 76–77, citing "De la Mort," a 1974 *Foi et Vie* article. We will consider it briefly in relation to Ellul's doctrine of creation.

78. *Apocalypse*, 253.

If the Incarnation is the reunion of God with creation, truth with reality, this creates a new order entirely without possibility of rupture. This must mean the destruction of all separation within creation, for God is now totally present. Destroying the Dragon in chapter 20, then, is another way of speaking of the destruction of Death itself, the second death (Rev 20:14) and the "remaking of creation."

But before this cosmic event, God's people on earth have work to do. This is, for Ellul, the meaning of the millennium, the thousand year reign of the saints on earth, during the time when Satan is bound (Rev 20:1–6).[79] The binding of Satan for Ellul signifies not a future time, a fulfillment of history at the end of history, but the present time of both delay and fulfillment: a delay which signifies that humanity now has the possibility of preparing lasting works of love and reconciliation. Indeed, only with Satan bound, are such works truly possible, though they are certainly not assured. Yet, Ellul credits the Incarnation alone with making possible what he calls "the great modern historical endeavor" to express fraternity, solidarity with the poor and the ideals of socialism and non-violence.[80]

As he puts it in a parallel treatment in the closing chapter of his testimonial book, *Ce que je crois*, his doctrine of reconciliation is a restatement of Pauline texts such as Colossians 1. While acknowledging too his debt to Irenaeus, Ellul notes that the patristic doctrine worked from an abstract, metaphysical idea of Humanity. For him it is *the works* human beings have undertaken which will be judged, some destroyed before others are preserved and taken up into the recapitulation of all things.

Moreover, this process, Ellul asserts, is paradoxically initiated in Revelation by the release of the Satan at the end of this time of the reign of God's people on earth (Rev 20:7). Satan must do his characteristic work of sifting, gathering all the evil works of history into a final assault against the Creator. In this text, for Ellul, the figure of Satan is a symbol, denoting not an individual supernatural power, but anticipating what the text then describes more realistically as the rebellious nations in battle ranks against God and his people (Rev 20:8–9).[81] "[The Satan] gathers together, in and among and through all the works of humanity, across our generations, our diversities, our cultures, what can be ranged against God, and therefore, what will be annihilated."[82]

79. *Apocalypse*, 250.

80. *Apocalypse*, 250. We have seen that Ellul deploys a similar argument about the impact of the incarnation in *Nouveaux Possédés*.

81. *Apocalypse*, 252.

82. *Apocalypse*, 252.

The Satan gathers these rebellious works together, but this merely leads to the very destruction of these works, along with the figure of the Satan whose work is now over. What is now left is God's new work of reconciliation: humans, having been separated from their evil works, are now saved, Ellul claims, and God will even gather up the good works they have done into the New Jerusalem. As he expresses it in *Ce que je crois*, a late summary of his view of recapitulation, this implies both absolute hope for humanity and radical uncertainty about our works.[83] "We may think we have clear data about our . . . works, those we deem good, which conform to God's will, but we cannot evaluate our political and technological works, and we will no doubt be surprised by what God keeps and what he destroys."[84]

The Unavoidable Questions of Being: A Dialogue with the Tradition

To sum up what we have learnt so far, we have seen that Ellul's complex eschatology in *Apocalypse* expresses his radical future hope, a hope which has clear implications for how we live out *Apocalypse Now*, the subject of my next chapter. However, while it is a major achievement, it still begs two unavoidable theological questions we must now briefly address in dialogue with the theological tradition.

Can People Be Separated from the Powers?

I have sought to show that Ellul's advocacy of universal salvation stems from his reading of Revelation. Although assessing his universalism is not my primary focus, it is inextricably bound to his exousiology. Whether we agree with Ellul or not about the impossibility of any person being finally destroyed depends in part on whether we find convincing his understanding of the powers which alone are condemned in order to liberate humanity.

We must then ask: is this a "cheap and cheerful" universalism, what Tom Wright refers to as "whistling *There's a Wideness in God's Mercy* in the darkness of Hiroshima, of Auschwitz, of the murder of children and the careless greed that enslaves millions with debts not their own"?[85] Writing after surviving the Second World War, having risked his life for the *Résistance*

---

83. *Ce que je crois*, 283.
84. *Ce que je crois*, 284.
85. Wright, *Surprised by Hope*, 193.

and moreover to save Jews fleeing Nazi terror,[86] Ellul would not recognize this characterization of his view: he would have us remember that salvation comes through a decisive judgment upon such acts as these, an escape through the flames (1 Cor 3:1–3). Moreover, he defends vigorously the continuing need to proclaim the gospel, for the Word of God alone brings this hope. Indeed, in Ellul's characteristic idiom, without it, we make this earth a living hell: "Is it still worthwhile proclaiming Jesus Christ and speaking about him? I answer yes without hesitation, for when I am in the presence of people who are utterly desperate, crushed by misfortune, by the lack of prospects, injustice and loneliness, I have to pass on to them the reason I personally have found for hope and for living."[87]

However, although Ellul's advocacy of universalism here and elsewhere attempts a biblical basis, ultimately, I am not convinced by his argument. He seems to exclude the possibility that the condemnation and annihilation of persons may in fact be necessary, for he refuses finally to countenance the radically indissolubility of evil acts from those who commit them, and the dehumanization they lead to. Is it really so easy to separate a person from their acts, and moreover, from the powers they worship?[88] Moreover, on exegetical grounds alone, I find it hard to reconcile with the many texts in Revelation which appear to speak plainly about the condemnation of persons.[89] Despite his avowed discovery of universalism in the text of Revelation, what is perhaps more significant for Ellul is the theological framework he adopts from Barth. Goddard's study effectively summarizes the influence of Barth, but notes that Ellul increasingly moved beyond Barth's hopeful universalism—to an atypically undialectical "absolute conviction" that all will be saved.[90]

86. "For his efforts, Ellul was awarded the designation 'Righteous Among the Nations' in 2001 by Yad Vashem, the Holocaust museum in Jerusalem" (Greenman et al., *Understanding Jacques Ellul*, 7).

87. *A temps*, 71.

88. See Wright, *Surprised by Hope*, 195, on the possibility of dehumanization. "Those who worship money increasingly define themselves by it and treat others as creditors, debtors, customers . . . rather than human beings . . . those who worship sex . . . increasingly treat other people . . . as sexual objects. Those who worship power . . . treat other people as collaborators, competitors, or pawns. These and many other forms of idolatry . . . damage the image-bearing quality of the people concerned and the lives they touch." Wright does not include those who worship technology as such but the same principle might apply.

89. Revelation itself contains a number of texts which suggest there will be an exclusion of persons (Rev 2:11; 12:14; 21:8; 21:27; 22:15). Gill notes the many other troubling biblical texts in the wider canon of scripture.

90. Goddard in MacDonald, *Explorations in Universalism*, 343–44.

Was Creation Good?

A second question presents itself, again concerning the status of the powers. If there is a relationship between God's original good "rupturing" or separating act, saying "No" to chaos, and humanity's rupture from God, we must ask: was the first creation then good or fallen, or at the least, destined to fall? Was it in that sense even *designed* to lead to further rupture, a *felix culpa*, before finally a new creation? Moreover, even more significantly, we can press further to the question: why will not the same process begin again with the new creation, if there is an unwilled negative potential implicit in God's first creative act? It is this kind of problem with the "meontic" interpretation of evil that has led some scholars to assert the value of the earlier patristic tradition, which speaks of a pre-mundane angelic fall, thereby safeguarding the goodness of created structures of society.

One such voice is conservative evangelical Pauline scholar Clinton Arnold in his book, *Powers of Darkness*. Offering a survey of Jewish cosmology and the wider Hellenistic fascination with cultic magic which is purported to inform the NT, Arnold argues that Paul can only be using the language of powers to denote real fallen angelic beings.[91] He therefore offers a critique of the entire tradition of applying the language of the powers to speak about the structures of society. Since, he contends, it is erroneous to equate the biblical *exousiai* with these structures, the powers should not be used for developing a theology of society for this would be to deny the creational goodness of given social structures.[92] However, he allows that there may be a relationship between personal evil powers and impersonal social structures, because the powers are able to exert an influence by corrupting the individual persons operating within basically good structures. Taking an illustrative example, he argues that the nation must never be denoted as evil in itself, although Satan can actively use people to corrupt a good creational structure. This is the case, he claims, with nationalism.[93]

However, the claim in Ellul's exousiology is precisely that this argument *for* creational orders and *against* individuals is at best naive. The challenge to Arnold, I contend, comes from attending to the socio-political implications of his theology, which are limited. Here is precisely a double-bind Ellul began to caution against in *Présence*: an inability to critique the structures, leading on the one hand to overspiritualized responses to structural problems[94] and

---

91. See Arnold, *Powers of Darkness*, chapter 13.

92. Arnold, *Powers of Darkness*, 195–96.

93. Arnold, *Powers of Darkness*, 209.

94. Dawn jokes that exorcizing the "spirit of poverty" will do little to deal with the problem of money, for the impact of Mammon upon us is not because "there are

on the other hand a reductive treatment of sin as an individual condition.[95] Dawn follows Ellul in arguing that it is "an exegetical mistake to equate principalities and powers with angels and demons," noting that Ephesians 6 suggests a correspondence between earthly authorities and spiritual powers, without suggesting that the authorities are themselves, quite simply, demons.[96] Over and against the witness of the deutero-canonical writings, shaped, she claims, by the fascination with magic within the then dominant Hellenistic culture, we must allow the "reserved attitude" of the NT towards the powers to shape our own.[97]

As we have noted, Ellul does not see personal, spiritual forces of darkness behind the trinity of "Money, State and Technology." His contribution is well summarized by Dawn:

> The connection he makes between the biblical category and contemporary realities is very profound, for by associating social, political, economic and technological mechanisms with the biblical concept of the principalities and powers he makes it possible to understand why these forces are able to exert such inordinate and inexplicable power over human lives.[98]

Although she does express a concern I share about Ellul's later "reductionist" approach to evil in *Subversion*, as outlined by Ellul in *Ethique* as position 3 above, still Dawn attempts to continue in Ellul's early functionalist vein in order to develop contemporary forms of "naming the powers," most notably technology criticism. Again she sticks with the earlier Ellul by considering the powers to be created good but now radically fallen from grace.[99]

A mediating voice in this debate is the Anabaptist scholar Greg Boyd. In his book, *God at War: The Bible and Spiritual Conflict*, Boyd argues explicitly against taking Augustine's "meontic" way in the area of theodicy and

---

demons flying around operating all by themselves" (Dawn et al., *Unnecessary Pastor*, 107).

95. This is what I suggested in my introduction about some theologies of the Cultural Mandate.

96. Justin Martyr articulated this view. This is position 1 above, which Ellul effectively rules out. John Stott, in his commentary on Ephesians, offers a similar argument for the viability of "biblical cosmology" today, noting that the *exousiai* of Ephesians must be understood as "personal cosmic intelligences." See Stott, *God's New Society*.

97. Dawn, "Principalities and Powers," 62, 83.

98. Dawn, "Principalities and Powers," 374.

99. See Dawn et al., *Unnecessary Pastor*, 83; Dawn, *Tabernacling of God*, chapter 1. For my assessment of Dawn's theological critique of technology, see chapter 6 below.

spiritual conflict,[100] but argues for a functional understanding of the workings of the powers. With Dawn he argues that the *exousiai* of Ephesians 6
are "qualitatively different to demons." What distinguishes the powers from
demons is precisely their scope of reference:

> These "powers" seem not to hassle individuals so much as foun-
> dational structures of society. There is something more general,
> more powerful and therefore more sinister (because less obvi-
> ous) about the working of the powers than there is about par-
> ticular demons. . . . Through prayer and social activism we are
> to labor towards exorcising the corrupted powers that structure
> fallen society.[101]

To refocus this discussion on the question of technology, I would add
that we can best retrieve Ellul's contribution by distinguishing between his
powers of "Money, State and Technoogy" at this point. If a particular power
has no basis in the goodness of creation, however we understand that, it
makes sense to argue for its ultimate destruction. Ellul argues this explicitly
of money and the state,[102] but as *Apocalypse* and indeed *Ethique* demonstrate,
he does not argue this for Technique.[103] As we will explore further in chapter
5 on creation, Technique is rather a distortion of a creational power for artifice, now diverted from its original purpose by our rupture from God. This
is why, I suggest, Ellul speaks of the recapitulation of human technological
works in a new creation, rather than their simple destruction.

Whilst it is of value to probe his exousiology, however, ultimately, the
question of the powers cannot be settled in ontological discussion, for it is
an existential element of Christian living. To this extent, Ellul's approach
coincides with Brian Brock's paradigmatic treatment of the Artemis cult
in Ephesus, which frames his Christian ethical account of technology.[104]
"It matters little in the end whether their god Artemis was a rebel spirit
possessing the community or the projection of the community's own

---

100. See also 175–77 below.

101. Boyd, *God at War*, 272. He writes of systematic "political corruption," "societal
racism," and "Western materialism" as powers. See also the chapters by Fernando and
Instone Brewer in McAlpine, *Facing the Powers*, for careful dialogues between biblical
exousioloy and contemporary society.

102. Ellul seems to say this of Mammon in *Money and Power* and we have noted
above his argument for the destruction of the Beast of all political power. On Ellul's
anarchism, see Goddard, *Living the Word*, chapter 7; Christoyannopoulos, *Christian
Anarchism*.

103. *Ethique*, 213–25.

104. Brock, *Technological Age*, 1, 374.

rebellion: this spirit is exorcised by Christ, and with it a whole way of life decisively upended."[105]

Conclusion

Building upon *Sans feu*, in his reading of Revelation, Ellul takes forward the technology criticism he had first voiced in *Présence*. However, the note of hope is the strongest, for he is concerned above all that reading Revelation as a series of historical catastrophes undercuts the true purpose of apocalyptic.

My concern in this thesis is with the power of Technique, and it is perhaps Ellul's concern that marks his prescient contribution. For Ellul, theologically speaking, the power of Technique rests in the sinful human desire for autonomy people invest in the technological enterprise. For El-lul, the freedom of Christ means freedom from Technique as a power over us—recovering the original freedom God intends, the freedom to have power over, that is, to use techniques. In *Ethique*, in keeping with the "ob-jective dialectic" between the present and future eons, Ellul argues that the powers exist still but they have been dethroned (Col 2:14), prior to their final destruction. They no longer have the power to create a shadow world, a parody of what God intended: "They remain powerful, but they lose this sort of demiurgical capacity, which enables them to create a world other than the divine and human world." This is the task of desacralization: "Let's say things are just things. And when we do that, we are called to live in a desacralized universe."[106]

Although Ellul has a universalistic future hope, Christians especially must undertake this work of desacralization, anticipating the final judgment and reconciliation. Those who conquer the powers in Revelation, he notes, are only those who witness to Christ.[107] What liberates us from the powers now, and what ensures that our works will have enduring value at the judgment is faith in Christ, the truly free person, as we shall see in the next chapter. As we shall explore there, Ellul's hopeful universalism never elides the significance of being in Christ now: "Here we find a decisive point, the distinction between

---

105. "So then, about eating food sacrificed to idols: We know that 'an idol is nothing at all in the world' and that 'there is no God but one.' For even if there are so-called gods, whether in heaven or on earth, as indeed there are many 'gods' and many 'lords.' Yet for us there is but one God, the Father, from whom all things came and for whom we live; and there is but one LORD, Jesus Christ, through whom all things came and through whom we live" (Brock, *Technological Age*, 375, referencing 1 Cor 8:4–8).

106. *Ethique*, 183.

107. See chapters 4 and 8 in *Apocalypse*.

the one who believes in Jesus and the one who does not believe. . . . The one who is outside the faith . . . remains vulnerable."[108]

Ellul affirms that the freedom of Jesus Christ is known only by those who believe in him and bear witness to him, and that is what it means to be church. Our rightful dominion can be anticipated even now, although the judgment of our works and victory over the powers belongs to God alone. The movement from this chapter to the next is well summarized by Markus Barth: "The power of filling, subjugating and dominating all things is reserved to God and Christ alone. But the function of demonstrating God's dominion and love is entrusted to the church. She is appointed and equipped to be a public exponent of grace and unity, the beginning of a new heaven and a new earth."[109]

108. *Ethique*, 184.

109. Barth in Stevens, *Abolition of the Laity*, 230.

4

Apocalypse Now

Desacralization and Reconciliation

Introduction

IN THE PREVIOUS CHAPTER, I have pursued my thesis by attending to Marva Dawn's groundbreaking theory that the powers are the uniting theme within Ellul's writings, sociological and theological. We noted that, in keeping with what he calls the "eschatological character of the Incarnation," Ellul clearly argues that the final judgment of the powers is anticipated in the present: as he states in *Apocalypse*, we live the last judgment in the course of history.[1] This is the process Ellul often describes as "desacralization." Moreover, he argues that the hope of recapitulation can also be anticipated in the Christian's present task of reconciliation. In the closing ethical coda of *Parole*, in a chapter entitled, precisely, *Reconciliation*, Ellul engages with the powers he has already outlined, outlining a model for reconciling word and image, language and Technique. "If the Apocalypse attests to the final reconciliation, the recapitulation, this reconciliation encompasses all reality."[2] For Ellul, in short, there is a double work of desacralization and reconciliation to be outworked *in present history*. In the previous chapter, we turned our attention to *Apocalypse Then*. In this chapter, we turn to *Apocalypse Now*.

As we have seen in chapters 2 and 3, Ellul believed that Jesus himself provided a definitive model for this twofold work. We have already briefly outlined in those chapters the significance of the Incarnation for Ellul in providing a model for the historic church (*Nouveaux possédés*) as well as for the church in the global city today (*Sans feu*). What can this chapter add to those discussions?

Indeed, using an image from the (post-)structuralism that Ellul flirted with, so central is the Incarnation to Ellul that working out what he means by it produces the effect of a *mise-en-abîme*, drawing the reader

1. *Apocalypse*, 206.

2. *Parole*, 267.

115

deeper and deeper into the corpus, but with the potential of getting rather confused, as in a hall of mirrors. Despite a keen awareness of his intellectual inheritance, Ellul was neither a patristic scholar nor a systematician. He does not treat the development of orthodox christological and trinitarian formulas at any length, but rather tends to mine the tradition here and there. Though gratefully indebted to Barth, Ellul's dialectical theology is not as sophisticated as Barth's, for his concern often lies in the social applications of Barth's theology.[3]

My central concern here is not to assess Ellul's relationship with orthodoxy, but to explore the the work of desacralization and reconciliation in the present time after the Incarnation but before the eschaton, *Apocalypse Now*, as I have termed it. In the previous chapter we began to explore Ellul's concept of divine non-power in Revelation, ranged over and against the powers of Argent, Etat and Technique. How does this concept relate to the theology of the Hebrew Bible? And what evidence for non-power does Ellul find in the life of Jesus as narrated in the Gospels?

To simplify, the chapter will be organized in two sections addressing those two questions. Firstly, I will assess the sources and trajectories of Ellul's Christology, considering especially his reading of the OT critique of idolatry, his understanding of the Logos in John's Gospel and the patristic influences upon him.[4] Secondly, I will consider Ellul's writings on the synoptic Gospels, most especially a particular narrative which stands out as paradigmatic: the account of the temptations of Jesus in the wilderness.

We turn first to Ellul's contrast of the Word and the idol.

The Word and the Idol

The second chapter of *Parole, L'idole et la parole*, opens with the assertion: "God speaks . . . from the beginning to the end of the Bible, it is all about a speaking God."[5] *Parole* deploys the dialectic of the word and the image to express a basic distinction between transcendent truth and created reality. However, with the Incarnation, we run up against an evident paradox, as truth becomes reality: the Word is made flesh (John 1:14).

Ellul approaches this fundamental mystery by following Kierkegaard and Barth's dialectical approach, arguing that the Word is at once transcendent

3. Gill, *Word of God*, 66, comments that Ellul is at odds with the tradition at points, offering occasional sketches of Trinitarian theology (e.g., chapter 13 in *Ce que je crois*, engaging with Moltmann), although skirting close to modalism in *Subversion* (e.g., 19).

4. In *Parole*, Ellul clearly demonstrates a grounded knowledge of patristic sources, especially Origen and Irenaeus.

5. *Parole*, 54.

and immanent, at once revealed and hidden in Jesus Christ. For Ellul, this paradox must be allowed to stand. The failure to grasp the dialectical nature of the Incarnation, to focus on one pole to the neglect of the other, is what leads, for Ellul, to theological error, an error which always has serious social consequences in the life of the church and the world.

Ellul is most often concerned with the loss of the transcendence of God. In *Subversion*, Ellul clearly associates this process above all with the Constantinian settlement of the church, since it constructed a visible religion in place of hidden revelation, leading to the "sacralization" of the Gospel. Ellul begins by affirming the importance of the immanence of God in Christ. "[God] is wholly and fully present in this Jesus Christ. God is nowhere else. All that we can know of God is here. . . . Everything given over to, devoted to humanity."[6]

However, he goes on to argue that the full and unique revelation of God in Christ does not elide the transcendence of God. God is hidden precisely in revealing Godself in Christ and he is revealed in Christ as the hidden God. "God Almighty is incarnate in a man. Yet he remains the Wholly Other. . . . If I say, God is transcendent, and I stop there, this is not the biblical God. If I say 'The God Jesus Christ,' that is not the Gospel."[7]

Indeed, the immanence of God in Christ has a paradoxical effect: it reveals the gulf between a transcendent God and humanity by localizing God's presence *in one particular, historical individual.* There is one sacrifice and one mediator, and all others are excluded. This transcendence is hence a power for what Ellul calls desacralization, as he explores in the *Coda for Christians* in *Les Nouveaux Possédés.* The Incarnation undercuts all other attempts at mediation with the divine.[8]

Idolatry: Desacralization and the Old Testament

Ellul sets this reading against the backdrop of the OT. There is for Ellul an essential continuity between the Testaments: he readily situates the Incarnation within the framework of Hebrew monotheism, over against the false gods of the nations. There is a clear continuity between the NT and the OT in the resistance to idolatry, expressed paradigmatically in the Decalogue. It is only against this background that we can rightly understand the claim that "the Word became flesh" in Jesus Christ.

6. *Subversion*, 56.

7. *Subversion*, 57.

8. *Subversion*, 70–71, in a chapter entitled, "Desacralization by Christianity and sacralization within Christianity."

In a pivotal passage in the theological second chapter of *Parole*, Ellul argues that God is never visble "image" because a representable god is by definition an idol: "God is no longer truly God when he is represented."[9] God is always "le Tout Autre," the Wholly Other, and his word has an immense power, but not a power which can be captured or compared to any other power than Word. Only the human being shares in that power by virtue of the Word. Indeed, Ellul argues that God's power as Word is a power held in and shared with his creatures. "He does not occupy all the space. The God who speaks also lets his creatures speak. God does not speak continually, drowning out all other sounds and expressions."[10]

Ellul can go as far to say that there are no genuine theophanies in the OT: in each case, Ellul claims the "vision" in fact is of an invisible God, perduring only for us in the word.[11] In a careful analysis of the programmatic narrative of idolatry, that of the Golden Calf, Ellul argues that Israel's idolatry did not consist in the desire to swap Yahweh for a foreign god, but rather to replace the spoken word of Yahweh with a permanent and powerful image of Yahweh.[12] The shining glory of God cannot be represented:

> This glory is invisible. It can only be grasped by an approximation in speech. It can never be reified. It is the manifestation of truth. It is the presence of a person. There is therefore an exchange of truth for reality, of the person for the object. . . . Now it is about vision, we have a change in the order of things, not a change of religion. We leave the order of truth and move into reality.[13]

Goddard's detailed commentary on this passage[14] suggests that it is important for understanding a central theme of the entire Ellul corpus. *Israel's history is, for Ellul, the very struggle to maintain faith in an invisible God, whose power is unconstrained by material representation.* "The condemnation of the Golden Calf . . . is not about the worship of foreign gods . . . idols . . . but rather it addresses the claim to represent in a visible way what has been revealed as invisible to Israel."[15]

Although the Golden Calf is a programmatic text, for Ellul, idolatry is a recurrent problem in the OT, which exhibits an internal struggle with idols, most especially at the site of the Temple; witness the people's

9. *Parole*, 101.

10. *Parole*, 75.

11. Exod 33:20 is cited as a paradigm text. *Parole*, 80, 104.

12. *Parole*, 96–107.

13. *Parole*, 101.

14. See chapter 14 in Barton, *Idolatry*.

15. *Parole*, 104.

idolatrous attachment to its sacred structure, critiqued by the Prophet Jeremiah, and Isaiah's critique of Temple sacrifice.[16] For Ellul, the meaning of the Temple is that it is an empty Temple, which bears witness to the "radical otherness" of God.[17]

Contrary to the common understanding that the NT overturns this transcendence, Ellul argues it both upholds and actually radicalizes it, arguing that it even desacralizes those elements within Jewish religion which had become sites of the "sacred." This is because, as we have seen in my account of *Sans feu*, Jesus desacralizes the Temple, since the Incarnation is now the unique tabernacling of God in creation. In an all too brief argument, typical of his polemical style, he suggests that the early church laid a greater emphasis on the creation texts of Genesis than was usually the case within Second-Temple Jewish thought, for he claims that these construe God's presence as Word in a way which fits with a Logos Christology. For Ellul, it is the book of Hebrews which definitively desacralizes all mediating elements within Second-Temple Judaism, interpreting Jesus' judgment on the Second Temple in the light of his once-for-all sacrifice and his supersession of the practice of ritual sacrifice and the cadre of sacrificing priests. Jesus' sacrifice is the only one needed, and all believers in him are incorporated into his priesthood.[18]

As a result, in keeping with what we have seen already, by virtue of the incarnation, Ellul asserts that "the world for Christians is entirely profane."[19] There is no longer a distinction between sacred and secular: everything has been desacralized, disenchanted but everything has become open to the wholly other Spirit of God.[20]

The point of this theological substructure in *Parole* is to move from the ancient text to the task of desacralization today. Ellul first takes aim at the idolatries he believes the historical church has succumbed and still succumbs to, namely bibliolatry and iconolatry.[21] Since any form of representation takes us away from the fleeting, living word to the fixed and powerful image, this implies for Ellul that the Bible cannot make the transcendent Word of God present: "The Bible is not a kind of visible

16. Jer 7:1–8. Ellul notes that a focus on sight fixes and limits the symbol's power (*Parole*, 99).

17. *Parole*, 105.

18. *Subversion*, 73.

19. *Subversion*, 74.

20. *Sans feu*, 251. Ellul's account of holiness was developed in the work of the theologian Sylvain Dujancourt, a former protégé of Ellul's, and editor of *Foi et Vie*, the Reformed Church journal, until 2004.

21. *Parole*, 106.

representation of God."[22] Even the written word is a "technique" of a kind, which inevitably conveys less than the spoken, embodied word. For Ellul, similarly the representation of the resurrected Christ in Eastern Orthodox icons ignores the fact that the tomb, like the Temple, was empty for a reason: "This God is truly the wholly other."[23]

Moving from judgment against the church and pursuing the essential polemic of Reformed thought against cultural idols, Ellul contends that far from being outmoded: "Iconoclasm is essential insofar as other gods and other representations are now visible."[24] And here, he turns to address "Money, State, and Technology," which he denotes as "invisible powers." Goddard argues that Ellul distinguishes between powers and idols in this way: whereas powers are immaterial but significant entities, idols are material yet insignificant entities. The example of this distinction Goddard draws from Ellul is that between the banknote, which is an idol, and money, which is a power.[25]

Although we find here some provocative insights we shall explore in chapter 6, there are however significant problems with Ellul's exegesis, problems which will come back to dog many of his ethical conclusions. In the same volume as Goddard's article on Ellul, in an article outlining a view which has become widespread in biblical scholarship, Nathan McDonald suggests that Exodus "splices together" the narratives of the Golden Calf and the Tabernacle in order to make a contrast between the "illegitimate representation" of the Calf and the right worship involved in the making of the Tabernacle, the place where the presence of God can truly dwell.[26]

The Tabernacle and the Temple have indeed become significant themes in recent theologies of work, production and technology. "Nearly every book in the past decade on work by a theologian or Christian ethicist has included some brief reference to the Tabernacle account."[27] Ellul does not read Tabernacle and Temple texts in terms of the gracing

22. *Parole*, 70, for his discussion of the stone tablets. This connects to my consideration in chapter 3 of Ellul's doctrine of scripture. It also points toward 238–42.

23. *Parole*, 106.

24. *Parole*, 106.

25. In Barton, *Idolatry*, 230–45, drawing upon *Parole*, 97–99. We might extrapolate from this to consider the relationship between a technological device and the spiritual power it exerts.

26. In Barton, *Idolatry*, chapter 2. Recent scholarship on Israelite monotheism has called into question many of Ellul's interpretations here. Theophany seems a well-established notion, and it has even been suggested that the OT is open to the idea of "bodies of God." See Sommer, *Bodies of God*.

27. This is the opening statement of Jeremy Kidwell's thesis, "Drawn into Worship," 25. We will return to this argument in chapter 6 below.

of human manufacture. However, for Ellul the "Empty Temple" within Israelite monotheism posed an ethical challenge. The wholly other God was not to be visible in one place, because the glory of the incomparable LORD was present in every place throughout creation, concealed and revealed at the same time. God's people are directed away from religion and outwards into right action in the world.

Particularity: Desacralization and the New Testament

It is this same dialectical pattern of interpretation that Ellul brings to the NT. He strongly upholds the particularity of God's presence and "tabernacling" on earth in Jesus. In alluding to the word used to translate John 1 in French, "le Verbe," Ellul is clear that Jesus is the only means of God's revelation. "The Word of God is the very person of God incarnate. There is no contradiction in the fact that the word is spoken by God and also incarnate in Jesus, since this word is that which reveals God, and *God has effectively revealed himself only in the Incarnation of his Son.*"[28]

Again, Ellul sets this within the framework of God's words to Israel, for he does not wish to let the Word of Christ reduce the significance of that history. In writing thousands of pages about the OT, Ellul demonstrates an understanding of the corporeal election of Israel to bear the word of God, a calling, moreover, he did not believe has been revoked. Word need not be opposed to flesh.

Ellul is therefore not "Christomonistic," for he is clear that "the personalizing of the Word does not lead to its deverbalizing."[29] Although he points at times to the Jerusalem Temple as an image of the Incarnation, the model he privileges is Israel's prophetic calling. The written words of the prophets can truly be the word of God in relation to this incarnate Word, insofar as they send us to Jesus Christ: "The personality of the Word of God cannot contradict its literalness and intellectuality. The word spoken in ancient times by the prophets becomes fully the Word of God because it refers to the incarnate Word."[30]

He hence reads the Old Testament christologically. In his account of creation and in his account of the covenant with Israel, Ellul argues that the word implies immanence, Emmanuel, God with us: "God creating through the Word means: God inaugurates history with humanity. Humanity will

---

28. *Parole*, 58 (my italics).

29. This is Kevin Vanhoozer's way of defending Karl Barth against this charge. See Vanhoozer, *Remythologizing Theology*, 202.

30. *Parole*, 58.

not be without God. . . . The God who speaks is 'God with humanity,' Emmanuel, and then God in a human being."[31]

However, the use of the singular is significant here, for the Incarnation does not reveal the divinization of humanity *in toto*. Ellul's universalism is cautiously hedged around with the caveat of the objective dialectic we considered in the last chapter:

> We must not stretch this too far, and say in a metaphysical leap that God in a human being means "in every human being," implying that human beings are divine, and all that follows from that premise. . . . Only one person is called Emmanuel; God became incarnate in just one man. We must not leap to the generalization, even if every person is saved by this Incarnation and even if this Incarnation is in a sense a model.[32]

Following Barth again, Ellul offers a universal hope, while resisting what he sees as a "metaphysical universalism." He sees this as a disastrous trend within the contemporary church, offering "a sophisticated effort to justify and legitimize our modern ventures through Christianity."[33] Ellul's implied interlocutors are mostly silent in *Parole* but elsewhere, he is bitterly polemical about his near-contemporary, the French Jesuit scientist and theologian, Teilhard de Chardin:

> And that's the scandal of the terrible heresy of Teilhard de Chardin: the attempt to sanction the world and all that it represents in the name of Christianity. But it can only be made possible, as becomes clear in his writings, by pushing aside the Incarnation of Christ in the person of Jesus. This is what leads to the denial of God's personhood, making Christ a point, the most perfect geometric abstraction.[34]

Over against the tendency he perceives to create around the concept of incarnation a perfect system, Ellul argues for the punctiliar moment of Incarnation in the person of Jesus, with its earthly duration ended by his Ascension to the Father. That is why, he claims, Jesus was not recognized as God in his earthly life, and his ministry constantly points to the word, not the image. Ellul lays emphasis on the hiddenness of God in Christ, veiled in flesh. "What is incarnated is still a word. It is the Word that is made flesh.

---

31. *Parole*, 63.
32. *Parole*, 63 (my italics).
33. *Parole*, 91.
34. *Fausse*, 182.

Nothing else. . . . It is the *invisible* God who came *as the word.*"[35] Granted, the Word of God was seen and apprehended by the senses, but this state of affairs was only temporary:[36]

> The Word entered into the world of the senses. . . . The Incarnation is the only moment in world history when truth joins reality, when it completely penetrates reality and therefore changes it at its root. . . . But this is temporary; it is limited to the period of the Incarnation. Once the incarnate life of Jesus is over, the two orders become separate again.[37]

The language of separated orders and a temporary vision of the Word seem reminiscent of the Christology associated with Antioch, which emphasized that the Logos assumed a specific human being for a time, rather than human nature for all time. There is perhaps a legitimate question here about whether Ellul claims less than Nicene orthodoxy by making such a sharp distinction between the two natures in Christ. As McGrath notes of writers such as Theodore of Mopsuestia, this understanding "leads to the suspicion that the Logos merely puts on human nature, as one would put on a coat: the action involved is temporary and reversible, and involves no fundamental change to anyone involved."[38]

However, Ellul's view of assumption is decidedly stronger than this, as we shall see. But what Ellul seeks to safeguard in this emphasis on the particularity and the temporal moment of the Incarnation is the eschatological framework we have already considered. Citing popular formulations of his day to speak of an already "sanctified matter," "transfigured flesh," and "christified nature"—an effected metaphysical restitution of humanity and creation—he argues that this loses sight of the dialectic between the promise and its fulfillment, as if the Incarnation enables us to see all things already transformed in Christ.[39] This is to assume that the Incarnation has an automatic effect. Ellul refutes the *opus operatum*, we recall, and we cannot capture the Incarnation any more than the disciples could capture the moment of Transfiguration. "Of course the Incarnation is the coming in human flesh of the absolute God and

---

35. *Parole*, 63. Jolyon Mitchell in *Visually Speaking* has disputed this account and its implications for communication ethics, as we will explore in chapter 6. Ellul clearly downplays the significance of Jesus' visible "works of power," which is part of his general ambivalence about the language of power.

36. *Parole*, 63.

37. *Parole*, 89 (my italics).

38. McGrath, *Christian Theology*, 339. McGrath notes the Antiochene writers did not intend this conclusion to be drawn.

39. *Parole*, 115.

the truth of his love. But that happened once, in a given time and place. It is as fleeting an event as the Transfiguration."[40]

As with the Transfiguration, Ellul marks that the resurrection appearances at Emmaus and Lake Galilee were particular moments, and particularity is the watchword of his account. In concluding his anthropology, Ellul argues in brief that we have not been divinized simply by virtue of the Incarnation. The image of Christ is inscribed only on the human Jesus. It is in the particular, singular, exemplary life of Jesus of Nazareth that God is incarnate:

> We must not try to find humanity's deification in God's humanization, as if God became human so that humanity might become God. . . . This is applied very concretely: to material, corporeal, visual humanity. The human being in themselves, as we see them, is said to be the face of God. One wonders then why the Gospels find it necessary to say of Jesus: "Behold the man." He is the *only*, the *unique* case of a human being as the image of God. But he is God's image precisely in the visible image of the condemned, scourged individual.[41]

Ecce Homo—this is the exemplar Jesus leaves for his followers, a suffering, challenging presence rather than a general, affirming presence. What Ellul wishes to show is that the image of Christ is only taken on by those who believe in him: being made *in imago Dei* does not mean that the human being is automatically *in imago Christi*, and Ellul rejects the notion of salvation as deification.[42] If there is a continuing Incarnation after the Ascension, it is not in every human being, but the vocation of those who believe, who hold out this particular vocation for all. In other words, it is the church which is to embody Christ, and here ecclesiology comes to the fore. And yet once again, we will find here at the very least an incomplete agenda in Ellul's oeuvre.

40. *Parole*, 91.

41. *Parole*, 117. The later Barth went as far as to speak of "the humanity of God," arguing from Romans 5 that man is in Christ before he is in Adam (see Barth, *Humanity of God*). James Dunn strikes down Barth's exegesis, following Bultmann in claiming it results in a Gnostic Christology (*Romans 1–8*, 277). According to Rognon, Ellul wished to recall the later, more optimistic Barth to his earlier "No" (Rognon, *Pensée*, 241).

42. *Parole*, 63.

Incarnation, Church, Spirit

The majority of Ellul's references to the church in *Parole* and *Subversion*, and elsewhere in his writings, are at best ambivalent. For Ellul, Christian presence in the modern world did not simply mean the historic church. Marva Dawn notes this tendency and seeks to mine valuable gems from Ellul while not quite confronting an important problem we will return to below, his emphasis on the individual Christian over against the corporate church.[43] *Parole* is typical in this regard. Ellul devotes an entire section of a chapter on iconoclasm to the "invasion of the church by images," suggesting that the contemporary obsession with images is analogous to the medieval church's obsession for visible power and success. Indeed, he makes a bold historical claim that the institutional church bequeathed this concern with the power of the image to modernity.[44]

Ellul's critique of the "audio-visual church" is essentially rooted in his reading of John's eschatology. At one level, John, known as the Book of Signs and Book of Glory, does not seem to be very fertile ground for this case and yet Ellul tackles head-on the notion that John leans towards a more realized, almost Gnostic eschatology.[45] Indeed, for him, two significant affirmations frame the Gospel, pointing to what is yet to be realized: "The first is: 'No one has ever seen God' (John 1:18). The last is: 'Blessed are those who have not seen and yet believe' (John 20:29)."[46]

Ellul wants to stress that the language of sight in John's Gospel points to the vision of the future, what he calls "the presence of the end."[47] Only the Holy Spirit enabled the first disciples to see the LORD by faith; others saw him and did not believe. Although that moment has passed, John's Gospel stresses that sight is still possible, by faith, most evidently in the apprehension of Jesus now ascended and glorified, but also visible in the body of Christ, the body of believers, and in the Eucharist, as well as in the poor and the suffering, all through the work of the Spirit promised by Jesus (John 14–16). The disciples are told they will receive the Holy Spirit, to transform sight, making them capable of seeing the invisible. "Thus they would see him again, but in a different way, with a plural dimension: they would see

---

43. See Dawn et al., *Unnecessary Pastor*, 137–39.

44. *Parole*, 211. A recent work of missiology (Frost, *ReJesus*) takes hold of Ellul's critique of false images and religion. Citing Ellul, Frost argues for "orthopraxy" over against a philosophical "orthodoxy" (53, 142–44).

45. Ellul claims this is a misconception, for it is in fact concertedly "anti-Gnostic." Richard Burridge concurs (*John*, 22).

46. *Parole*, 269.

47. *Parole*, 278.

Jesus himself glorified, but they would also see him in the body of Christ which is the church, and in the Eucharist. They would also see him present in the poor and the suffering. We see because we believe."[48]

We see here that Ellul's understands the work of the Holy Spirit to be a desacralizing and reconciling work, anticipating the final judgment and recapitulation. Key here is Ellul's understanding of Jesus' resurrection as a prolepsis, an inauguration of the final resurrection. As the deposit of the Spirit, the resurrection of Christ is the promise in time of the resurrection of the dead at the end of time. There is an *already*—death and evil have been defeated once for all—and there is a *not-yet*, and we live by the promise.[49]

This does not mean that the church is simply a passive recipient of moments of revelation from the Spirit. For Ellul, the church incarnates the body of Christ primarily through its Spirit-breathed words of witness. As Ellul puts it in a subtle closing section entitled *The Word of the Witness*, just as human flesh was necessary for the Incarnation, so the Word of God still today needs the embodied human word.[50] This embodied word is never coercive, never power over, but invitation and summons. If Jesus incarnates the Word of God, we for our part are called to bear witness to that Word by our words. Indeed, though a fierce opponent of idealism about the church, Ellul himself was by no means an armchair critic: he preached in and led forms of church for almost his entire Christian life. Despite attempts to downplay this in some circles, perhaps due to ingrained French anticlericalism, his close friend Patrick Chastenet highlights Ellul's commitment to the gathered church: "He returned in 1953 to the local church activities he had already tried out during the Occupation. He began by organizing monthly worship in the large dining room of his house in Pessac, and then increased its frequency. He eventually ran out of space to

---

48. *Parole*, 277. This is the third of a crescendo of four points about sight and the Incarnation Ellul perceives in John's apocalyptic passages. Firstly, that there is a discrepancy between what is seen and what is said about what is seen. This Ellul refers to as "seeing as," in the sense that Jesus constantly speaks of one thing through another thing. Secondly, the witness claims to see something physically, when in fact it is a spiritual insight, a certainty witnessed to. Thus, in this Gospel, John the Baptist sees Jesus as the "Lamb of God." Thirdly, other passages say that seeing does not mean believing, for we need not evidence but faith. John's Gospel is constantly showing that Jesus was seen but not believed. Finally, in John's Gospel Jesus' presence relates to the end of time, a theme taken up within apocalyptic literature. His presence anticipates the end of time within time.

49. *Parole*, 91–92. In this respect, Ellul's argument seems to parallel the idea of prolepsis developed by Pannenberg. Ellul accepts as foundational the truth of Jesus' resurrection—and any questioning on the basis of historical criticism he dismisses as reducing truth to reality.

50. *Parole*, 119.

accommodate all the Protestant families, and so in 1959, the Presbyteral Council of Bordeaux agreed to put at their disposal a small building adjoining the property. Although not registered as a pastor, Jacques Ellul was accorded a permanent pastoral license."[51]

Summary: Discipleship before Imitation

Parole is perhaps Ellul's most complex work and an enduring contribution and achievement, arguing, in short that whereas God has become human, humanity has not and will not become God. We cannot and must not dissolve the distinction between humanity and God in this way. God's being is "neither universalised nor universalisable," but universal salvation does not depend upon our divinisation or deification.[52] For Ellul, the distinction between God and humanity must remain, even in eschatological perspective. This is symbolized in Revelation by the fact that there is no Temple in the New Jerusalem. God is immediate to humanity and yet not contained: "God is everywhere in the city. Yet he is infinitely beyond it."[53]

The divine Son enters the world not merely to reveal who we really are, but to do for us something that we cannot do for ourselves, to deal with our rupture from God and restore our relationship of free and loving obedience to God. He comes to resist and break the powers which enslave humanity. This is what we will explore in section two.

However, it is important briefly first to acknowledge the weaknesses in *Parole*. It is easy to get somewhat lost in this interweaving of so many different strands; one wonders if Ellul could have argued his case more simply. In seeking to simplify Karl Barth's complex christological anthropology, Brian Brock provides an apt summary of what I believe Ellul, following Barth, wishes to argue. Brock argues that Barth's account can obscure the essentially simple point he wishes to make: that human beings do not overcome the Fall by our own work. Drawing on the language of Ephesians, Brock writes: "The Christology this suggests is one in which the head is not identical to the body, and in which Christ is the worship leader opening up a proper enjoyment of creation, the Trinity and one another.

---

51. See Ellul and Chastenet, *A contre-courant*. There has been some speculation, too, that in the 1930s, Ellul almost joined the French Assemblies of God, a Pentecostal denomination often considered a "sect" in French society. Ellul's faith was birthed in a profound spiritual experience or baptism in the Spirit, and he never lost his thirst for experience of God.

52. *Parole*, 91.

53. *Sans feu*, 336. See also chapter 7 in *Apocalypse*, on the new creation.

This is to emphasize that Christians are first disciples rather than imitators of or analogues to Christ."[54]

With this in mind we turn to engage with Ellul's account of the unique work of the Son of God over and against the powers.

"If You Are the Son of God . . . ?" (Luke 4:3)

Any engagement with Ellul's writing on the Gospels must begin by noting his general suspicion of the historical-critical method. He was unconvinced of the value of the burgeoning "Quest for the Historical Jesus," considering that it tended to reduce truth to reality.[55] He essentially operates with a canonical reading, considering himself an "amateur" biblical scholar—a lover of the Gospels who pored over them in fine detail. And for that reason his unconventional approach often throws up acute, interesting although often idiosyncratic insights. We have already glimpsed this style of engagement with the Gospels in Ellul's account of Jesus in *Sans feu*. Here we will see that Ellul offers a suggestive exousiology in his reading of the Gospels.

The narrative of the temptations in the synoptic Gospels (Matt 4; Luke 4; Mark 1) is clearly paradigmatic for Ellul. The desert is the place where Jesus resists evil powers and so lives truly with the freedom of the Son of God. It is a motif in the central chapter of Ellul's first significant work of theology, *Sans feu*, and is a refrain within *Ethique*. In *Si tu es le Fils de Dieu: Souffrances et tentations de Jésus* (hereafter *Si*), a short, eighty-page text and one of Ellul's last theological works, Ellul revisits and expands upon his previous writings on the temptations, offering a Christology from below.[56] Ellul believes that in studying these tests, we learn the truth about God, but also, moreover, a truth which impacts every person, in every society, even if the human condition varies over time and space, for "What is not assumed is not healed."[57] Goddard notes especially its significance as a statement of Ellul's mature theology of atonement: "How Christ fully assumes, suffers and overcomes the death, closure, Eros and necessity of the fallen world is most fully described by Ellul in . . . *Si*."[58]

---

54. Brock, *Technological Age*, 295. See also Williams, *Being Disciples*, 12–14.

55. For an example of Ellul's critique of the Quest, see *Si* in *Défi*, 938–39.

56. The original was published in 1991, but in 2014 Wipf and Stock published an English translation by Andreasson-Hogg, *If You Are the Son of God*. My engagement with the original French version in this text predates this work.

57. This expression belongs to Gregory of Nazianzus.

58. Goddard, *Living the Word*, 96. As the language of assumption hints, in *Si*, we find a lively engagement with classical, patristic theology.

Ellul's starting point in *Si* is reminiscent of *Parole*: God is fully incarnate in just one singular historical person, Jesus of Nazareth, not the ideal human superhuman, but an ordinary person, entirely human:

> Such is the humanity of Jesus: a man, not the superman, the total man or the perfect man, above the human condition, no, a little Jewish man with his joys and sorrows. This is precisely the terrible scandal of the Incarnation: God, all of God, has come into this *uomo qualunque*, this "ordinary person," who, though God-bearing, remained entirely subject to the human condition. I have no other claim than to show this.[59]

Indeed, it is perhaps because testing is both a particular but also a universal human experience in a fallen world that Ellul looks to this moment of Jesus' earthly life. In overcoming temptation, Jesus demonstrates his freedom from the powers and thereby frees us from them. This is what we will explore in a cascading argument below, following the movement of Ellul's thought.

Limits Bring Temptation

This first conviction is a presupposition for all that follows. *Si* is essentially a survey of texts linking suffering and temptation in Luke's Gospel, but at significant moments Ellul draws upon material from elsewhere in the scriptures. Indeed, he frames the entire discussion with a reference to Heb 2.18, arguing temptation arises from our experience of suffering, finitude and limitation. Ellul argues that we see this typified in Jesus, for whom every moment of suffering—whether the physical suffering of hunger or tiredness, or the psychological suffering of misunderstanding and rejection—is a moment of temptation. The temptation Jesus constantly faced, Ellul claims, was to renounce the limits of the human condition, *and to assert his status as divine Son*: "All temptation was suffering for him, and all suffering involved a temptation. . . . He could have escaped it, but to remain on the human level, he refused to. . . . We will therefore try to follow the Gospels, which show us perfectly Jesus' human, fully human, condition."[60]

The entire rationale behind *Si* is this: to show that as divine-human Son, Jesus has identified with us in all things, assuming all human experience rather than assuming an abstract and essential human nature.

59. *Si* in *Défi*, 943. "Uomo qualunque" is the name Ellul gives elsewhere to the "ordinary person" who is the explicit subject of his sociology (*Parole*, 227n1). It had political overtones in communist and anti-communist parties of the 1940s and 1950s.

60. *Si* in *Défi*, 938.

Granted suffering and finitude provides a route for temptation, but what exactly is temptation? In order to define it, Ellul reaches for James 1:13–15, arguing that it is a typically human experience; God does not tempt us. In fact, it is *the* archetypically human experience because, as James suggests, temptation results from the human desire to escape our limitedness, to become like God.

Genesis 3 is clearly a fundamental text here, and Ellul defines what he means by "the spirit of power" in terms of "absolute covetousness," the desire to be like God.[61] This is why, Ellul notes, the prohibition of covetousness provides the summary to the Ten Words given to Moses: "First, in the Decalogue, the last commandment is 'you shall not covet.' And I say that if it is the last, it is that it is at the same time the conclusion, but also the summary."[62] In short, "spirit of power" and "covetousness" together denote the root of temptation.[63]

Jesus Overcomes the Spirit of Power by Submission to the Father

This identification of covetousness and power becomes clearer as Ellul considers what it means for Jesus to be fully human. If he was a finite human being, he was not immune from temptation, and therefore not immune from the spirit of power. Following Hebrews 4:15, Ellul is concerned to stress that Jesus really embraces our humanity, to the point of embracing the rupture, and our alienation from God. The burden of Ellul's account is to show that the humanity of Jesus is humanity just as we experience it. "Jesus was made like us in all things—that is to say, he is constantly faced with choices to make. . . . Jesus does not have the sovereign freedom of God. It is precisely because he is found not only in a situation of finitude but also in the alienated condition that its freedom is radically meaningful."[64]

Being alienated means being tested. Being declared as the Son of God at his baptism is not for Ellul a declaration of divinity, but rather an affirmation of his perfect humanity, for he is loved as humanity was loved "in Adam." However, coming after the rupture, Jesus recapitulates Adam's role in a world of powerful temptations. In this world, it is the refusal to grasp at power, the willing obedience that Jesus offers to God, as the true

61. *Si* in *Défi*, 946.

62. *Si* in *Défi*, 945.

63. Girard sees the tenth commandment as the summary commandment and a paradigmatic prohibition of mimetic desire. See Girard, *I See Satan Fall,* chapter 1.

64. *Ethique,* 61.

Human, that opens up a new way of being human. "The new Adam overcame the trap and did not usurp the glory of God. The temptation was to come from all sides, in multiple circumstances, corresponding to the roots of covetousness-power, which, since Jesus was human, must have existed in him too but which he knew how to uproot."[65]

Jesus refuses to give in to this desire to be Godlike, even though he has a unique divine-human vocation. Three times Ellul cites Philippians 2.6 to show that Jesus refuses to claim equality with God and thereby to follow the way of the first Son of God.[66] Instead of doing so, Jesus models a relationship of perfect freedom and obedience towards God the Father, overcoming sin by living a sinless, yet tested, life. Because he succeeds where we fail, we can be free as he is free, for perfect freedom is grounded only in the non-competitive, free relation between the Father and the Son: "The will of God in Jesus Christ for us is freedom (Jesus being perfectly obedient and perfectly free). The Father gives complete freedom to the Son."[67]

Jesus Desacralizes the Powers by Divine Non-power

The narrative function of the three paradigmatic tests that Jesus overcomes in the wilderness before he begins his public ministry is thus to reveal Jesus' sinlessness as the Son of God, the true Human.[68] However, in keeping with his exousiology as outlined in the previous chapter, Ellul interprets this narrative not first and foremost as historical but rather as a kind of "overture" to the synoptic Gospel accounts. The historical sufferings and testings of Jesus at the hands of human agents, which are the subject matter of the synoptics, are here given their full theological meaning at the outset. Ellul takes this to an extreme conclusion: if it is humans who test Jesus in concrete history, then it is legitimate to read the figure of the devil in this narrative as a symbol of the way human powers put God to the test:

> I am going to shock people now: it was human beings who put
> the Son of God and God to the test, and who do this indeed
> precisely because he is the Son of God and God himself! And
> I venture to say that these three temptations at the beginning
> have been included or written by the evangelists retrospectively,

65. Si in Défi, 1001.

66. "Jesus does not claim at this time to be more Son of God than all those to whom the word of God has been announced! . . . He is the bearer of the word of God, but at a point so extreme and complete that this word is incarnated in him" (Si in Défi, 1000).

67. Ethique, 13.

68. Si in Défi, 1012.

that is to say that in understanding the temptations that Christ underwent throughout his ministry, they summarised it all in these three preliminary temptations. The devil is then only the representative of all humankind, speaking in our name. He is only a symbolic and artificial figure, the true tempter being human persons and society.[69]

Following this familiar reductive logic, Ellul claims that the sum of personal and social human desires, the collective spirit of power, is an adequate explanation for the phenomena of the powers and principalities. "Covetousness and the spirit of power have an individual character, living in every human heart, and since we are all inhabited by this covetousness, as a result the entire social body exalts it, leading to the phenomenon of the 'exousiai.'"[70]

In keeping with the hermeneutic we noted in chapter 2, Ellul claims that this analysis holds good for humanity in this and every age, and so he reads the wilderness temptations within the framework of powers we find in his sociological critique of modernity. In the desert, Jesus refuses the "economic temptation" of fulfilling every need, the "political" temptation of establishing a forceful theocracy and the "religious-ideological" temptation of "using" the spectacle to prove his status.[71] Ellul's account of the first temptation is most suggestive for his theology of Technique, for here in a very compressed form Ellul summarizes the analysis he develops elsewhere: the "artificial creation of needs" through technology is the driver of modern economic life. In turning away from the (legitimate) need for bread, Jesus finds his being in desiring the word of God and not in the fact of desire itself. "How can we not think of our present society, where, thanks to technique, we have indeed gained the world, but where humanity today has manifestly lost a sense of who we are. We have become empty of all being. An emptiness filled by desire and distraction."[72]

But Jesus is not only truly human, he is also truly God. And this begs the question: if we take seriously Jesus' own experience of suffering and finitude at the hands of humanity, and *if Jesus is truly the Son of God*, what does this imply about the character of God? Ellul argues that it is ultimately God in Christ being tested, *a test endured within the relationship between the Father and the Son*. "Moreover, one must realize that if Jesus is truly the Son of God,

69. *Si* in *Défi*, 947–48.

70. *Si* in *Défi*, 946.

71. See Yoder, *Politics*, chapter 2, for a similar treatment.

72. *Si* in *Défi*, 988. In *Bluff*, he develops this argument in a sociological vein, but underpinned by this theological framework.

this suffering, entirely human, is a temptation that is thrown at God Himself So it was not simply curiosity that made me re-read the Gospels in this light, but rather the desire to plumb the relationship between the Son and the Father, and in so doing to learn to know the Father better."[73]

We recall with James that temptation does not come from God; it comes from us. Therefore Ellul argues that we tempt God to "anger, vengeance, extreme domination, which are possible for God." In short, we tempt the Father to cease being the Father of love, which is his true mode of power.[74] This interpretation of God's inner life is implicit for Ellul in John 1:5: The light enters the darkness, and refuses to overwhelm. Rather, it allows itself to be suppressed but not overcome:

> To be a true light, he could not impose himself, conquering by force. He would have ceased to be a light if he started to play darkness' game, thereby becoming darkness. Just as the light which has come to enlighten the world suffers rejection, so the risen, glorified Christ does not enter by force. . . . The "light from light" was tempted to get rid of the darkness once and for all. This light suffered from his refusal to do so, in order to overcome by love, and without coercion. That sums up Jesus' life. There we come face to face with the deepest love. "Come, but I will not coerce you. I'll set you free. And now, come."[75]

The Power of New Creation Is Unleashed by the Cross and Resurrection

This interpretation is carried through in his reading of the final test within the relationship of the Father and the Son, anticipated in the Garden of Gethsemane, and enacted on the cross. Ellul cites a number of times Jesus' decision not to call on the Father for angelic deliverance at the time of his arrest, as recorded in Matthew 26:52–54. Attaching momentous significance to this refusal of self-defense, it signifies for Ellul not only a choice for *non-violence* but also for *non-power*. This is the moment when Jesus refuses to call on the Father, but trusts the Father enough to remain undefended. "These words, whose meaning corresponds exactly to how Jesus chooses to live, are extremely rich: they denote first of all the fundamental choice for 'non-power.' This goes far beyond non-violence. Non-power is not powerlessness, but the

73. *Si* in *Défi*, 940–41.
74. *Si* in *Défi*, 948.
75. *Si* in *Défi*, 949.

decision on the part of the one who has power not to use it, not to use the power he could unleash, not even to defend his life."[76]

Moreover, in this decision, a new kind of power, fully divine, is revealed—fulfilled in the decisive vindication of the Son's obedience three days later. Drawing on 1 Corinthians, Ellul sees the cross and resurrection together as an act of destroying the powers. "God made a choice: it was necessary for God's Chosen One, his Messiah, to be weak and foolish in the eyes of the world. . . . But 'the things that are not'? Exactly so, for Jesus plunges into death: he is no longer. However, when this 'thing which is no longer' rises again, he nullifies death, and with it all the powers that claimed to govern the world."[77]

The cross and resurrection together are the decisive liberation from the powers, exposing them for what they are, parasites upon God's good creation. Ellul expands on this victory in an important passage in *The Ethics of Freedom* where he outlines the "objective work" of Christ:

> The objective intervention of Christ against the powers can defeat them. Man alone cannot escape. What overcame them is the fact that on the Cross, as in the Temptations, and throughout the Temptations, and in Christ's stripping away of divinity (Kenosis), Christ did not fight power with power. . . . So these powers were deprived of the only thing they had, their very power to conquer, because they had nothing precisely to conquer. . . . The Powers are defeated because Jesus can say: "Nobody takes my life, but I lay it down."[78]

Jesus disarms the powers by denying them any victory, by absorbing their impact in his person. He freely refuses to fight on their terms, giving no doctrine of power but pointing only to his Father. "Jesus' entire life and work is a finger outstretched to point only to the Father. As regards power, we revisit what we have said about goodness: 'Do not look at me, look only to the Father.' And his entire life of prayer always comes back to: 'I praise you, Father' . . . and 'Not my will, but yours.'"[79]

This non-competitive imitation of the Father by the divine-human Son, the pointing away from self to God, is the basis for Ellul's ethics of non-power, which we shall explore in chapter 6.[80] Thus, to conclude, Ellul's

76. *Si* in *Défi*, 1007.

77. *Si* in *Défi*, 1005.

78. *Si* in *Défi*, 1182–183. This is for Ellul the meaning of Jesus' self-emptying or kenosis.

79. *Si* in *Défi*, 1005.

80. *Ethique*, part 2. For Ellul, freedom is the key motif of St. Paul's theology of the

account clearly echoes the ancient understanding of *Christus Victor,* an objective and decisive victory over all usurping powers, with the promise that God will one day be all in all.[81] Though an objective work, as "sons and daughters of God" we can subjectively respond by living freely, as the Son did towards the Father.

Yet, throughout his account of Jesus the unique Son of God, the dominant patristic motif Ellul employs is assumption: what happens from God's side.[82] In closing, Ellul returns to the "Last Temptation of Christ"[83] implied in the cry of dereliction on the cross: "My God, my God, why have you abandoned me?" (Mark 15:34). For Ellul, this is quite simply the temptation to utter despair, and at this moment, we see that the Son enters into what Ellul sees as the lowest human experience, the temptation to lose hope in God. And yet at that moment, he declares "It is finished," for he takes all suffering and testing away from humanity and takes it into God.

Moreover, Ellul here reaches for the language of substitution. "As for the condemnation of suffering, yes, he substituted himself for us. . . . God himself has assumed this evil in himself."[84] Jesus takes on the rupture from God we know only too well. However, pointing away from Anselm's concept of satisfaction for sin, Ellul celebrates the assumption into God of both all evil and all suffering: "'Why have you forsaken me?' 'It had to be this way.' It had to be, not to satisfy God, but to bring the totality of human misery into the heart of God."[85]

---

cross. Freedom in Christ is, for Ellul, the center of Pauline theology; his paradigm texts here are Galatians 5:1–13; Colossians 2:15–23; and 1 Corinthians 8; 9:19–23, because at issue in each, and most obviously in Colossians, is the freedom Christ has won in relation not only to sin but also in relation to the powers. Ellul's concept of freedom is close to what Girard calls "positive mimesis," based on a strikingly similar model of atonement.

81. Gustav Aulen's statement of his understanding of the "classic" theory of atonement shows some affinity with Ellul: "*Christus Victor* . . . fights against and triumphs over the evil powers of the world . . . and in Him God reconciles the world to Himself" (Aulen in McGrath, *Christian Theology*, 398). See also Boyd, *God at War*, chapter 9.

82. *Si* in *Défi*, 1016. See also 938, 951, 957.

83. Ellul hints that one influence on the writing of the book was the release of Martin Scorcese's film, *The Last Temptation of Christ.* He also suggests that the novelistic account of the Jesus Quest, *The Shadow of the Galilean* by Gerd Theissen, provoked him to write.

84. *Si* in *Défi*, 951. See also *What I Believe*, 191.

85. *Si* in *Défi*, 1016.

The Historical Responsibility of Christians: A Dialogue between Ellul and Yoder

In considering his work on the incarnation, we have begun to sketch Ellul's ethics of non-power. His ethics are a challenge to all ethics which displace the biblical Jesus, offering a less particular, more universal framework. Especially Ellul sees in theologies of *homo deus*, past and present, such an ethical framework, a temptation he intuits as frighteningly close at hand in our technological hubris. Here the tempter shouts, urging us to trust in who we can be. "No faith in humanity is possible, nor is the theological formulation: 'God became man so that man could become God,' which is the ultimate demonic temptation offered to us. No, Jesus became man so that we can be truly human, truly creaturely, free, loving freely our God, Creator and Saviour, in obedient faith."[86]

Jesus became human *so that we can be human, creaturely*. Granted, freedom in Christ is not automatically conferred on all yet it is, as he argues in part 3, chapter 3 of *Ethique, The Historical Responsibility of Christians*, Christ's work is an objective work: "The Incarnation of Christ has effectively changed history," implying new relationships between humanity and God, humanity and society and humanity and nature.[87] Christians must live *as if* they believe that human suffering, misery and death *are* assumed into God, and *have been* overcome.

But they must also live realistically between the times, and hence this responsibility is primarily a "negative responsibility."[88] The Incarnation has threatened the powers of the world, which provided some stability and made life livable in a fallen world. In *Ethique*, Ellul concedes that these powers have validity as necessary human responses—coping mechanisms, we might say—within the world we live in. This is what Ellul characteristically refers to as "necessity."[89] They are part woven into the fabric of a world ruptured from God. The problem arises when they are erected into "a total system," given a false transcendence, thereby oppressing humanity and working actively against God's good creation.[90]

---

86. *Si* in *Défi*, 1012.

87. *Ethique*, 311.

88. *Ethique*, 311.

89. *Ethique*, 311.

90. In *Ethique*, it is clear that "total system" is what Ellul understands by the Pauline *stoicheia*. Ellul's book *The Technological System* on this account is hence an exploration of the "elements" of the technological society.

However, in the movement of the Gospels, we see Jesus challenging these powers, throwing Satan down from heaven.[91] Shattering the peace of the world in the name of a greater peace, he calls people to break existing ranks, and his parables witness to a new order hidden within the old. This is why, paradoxically, therefore, the Incarnation first brings judgment, plunging that world into crisis, disturbing its order.[92] Yet, Christ also brings a new order, the order of love: "Hence, through the Incarnation, society, the human world, becomes chaotic, truly plunged into chaos. But Christ replaces these old forms of relationship with new relationships of love and freedom."[93] Ellul insists that this true order is livable in this world, as long as it is incarnated in actual realities by those who are in Christ. It is not even premised on the total conversion of the world: "The new order, the order of the Beatitudes, is perfectly liveable and possible. It is not even necessary that all people without exception live in love and freedom, but this freedom must be present and incarnate."[94]

In a motif of significance for Ellul's approach to technology, he states that our present task is to live "in a world where there is no longer any distinction between the sacred and the secular," that is to desacralize the powers, in anticipation of the final reconciliation of all things. This is then an individual but not a private morality; it is a task which Christians undertake for the world.

However, despite this emphasis on our responsibility, we touch here upon features of Ellul's ethics which many find frustrating: his tendency to criticize the historical church and propose, as some see it, the need for a Christian contrast society while refusing to give detailed examples or generating concrete practices readily applicable today.[95] On the one hand, Oliver O'Donovan speaks for many when he expresses sharp disagreement with Ellul's anti-Constantinian stance, claiming that Ellul regards Christendom with unjust suspicion as a mistaken power-grab and "social-engineering" project, rather than viewing it more soberly as a process fuelled by the conversions of people with social standing.[96] And on the other, Ellul is far from the confidence

---

91. In Ellul's brief account in *Subversion* (213–14) there are clear echoes of Girard in *I See Satan Fall*.

92. *Ethique*, 314. In *Apocalyse*, this is how Ellul interprets the meaning of Satan's expulsion from heaven in Revelation 13.

93. *Ethique*, 315.

94. *Ethique*, 315.

95. See, for example, *Subversion*, 221.

96. O'Donovan, *Desire of the Nations*, 196. Brian Brock argues similarly, following Wannenwetsch: "Wannenwetsch's suggestion is that the anti-Constantinian stance of political theology breeds political pessimism by assuming that the only way Christians

that the corporate church can serve as "the Basis for Social Ethics,"[97] since he characteristically speaks of the choices facing individual Christians immersed in the world, rather than of the body of Christ.

Indeed, noting the popularity of Ellul's accounts of the laity scattered in the world, a recent book popularizing Ellul for seminarians argues that he missed a valuable opportunity to contribute to the life of the gathered church:

> Ellul emphasizes the church's scattered life, as the people of God are dispersed across society throughout the week, to provide a Christian presence in various arenas, making life livable in the "penultimate" realms of life while pointing people to "ultimate" ends of life found in Jesus Christ. His emphasis upon the laity's critical role in the world is commendable. Yet, he mentions only in passing that such laypeople are dependent upon the gathered Christian community for their development. A vibrant gathered church is logically necessary to accomplish his vision, yet where is an account of the church's corporate life? The overall picture so stresses the Christian in the world that Ellul has neglected the formative context of the Christian in the church, the fellowship of shared faith. *Ellul's theology never develops a positive role of the corporate body of Christ.*[98]

It is perhaps true to state therefore that critiquing Ellul's ecclesiology involves too much inference and too many arguments from silence.[99] It is perhaps then more fruitful briefly to compare and contrast Ellul's negative emphasis with the work of a similarly radical Anabaptist thinker, John Howard Yoder. Yoder's seminal book, *The Politics of Jesus* shares many of Ellul's critiques, and yet it outlines more clearly than Ellul a positive account of the church's present role in desacralization and reconciliation. In other words, Ellul's reading of the temptations, while suggestive, is somewhat restricted by his attention to the question: "freedom from what?"

---

can influence secular society is by protesting against it. The church ought to stand amidst the world . . . made up of people very much within it" (Brock, *Technological Age*, 241).

97. Hauerwas and Willimon, *Resident Aliens*, 69.

98. Greenman et al., *Understanding Jacques Ellul*, 124 (my italics). Ellul seems most of all to have the heroic Christian individual in mind as he writes. Charles Ringma has produced a year of devotional readings mining Ellul's reflections upon connecting "personal faith and social responsibility." See Ringma, *Resist the Powers*.

99. The Lutheran theologian Paul Zahl provides a pithy description of his approach, which could equally apply to Ellul: "A theologian of grace has no ecclesiology" (Zahl, *Grace in Practice*, 252).

to the detriment of the question: "freedom for what?" And whereas Ellul finds little material in the Gospels for concrete social ethics, Yoder finds much in Jesus' teaching to commend a form of social and political life, alternative yet embedded in the world.

Granted, Yoder's approach shares common ground with Ellul in at least four important respects. Firstly, Yoder basically agrees with Ellul about the need to articulate an "exousiology" which is not confined to discussion of "the orders of creation."[100] For him, such an approach elides the fall, and most of all, does not affirm that "it is in Christ that these values find their meaning and coherence. As a matter of fact the theology of the orders of creation has generally affirmed that Jesus Christ has little directly to do with them."[101] Secondly, therefore, he argues that we must start with the Jesus of the Gospels, Christology from below, if we want to explore the themes traditionally dealt with in "systematic" theology, such as Incarnation and Trinity.[102] Thirdly, moreover, he argues that Jesus *is* a model for Christian ethics, a case he constructs around a rather Ellulian interpretation of the temptations narrative, arguing that the three powers in question here are economics, politics and religion. Noting that these modern concepts are "structurally anomalous" to the biblical powers,[103] he outlines a vision of what he calls "revolutionary subordination," an approach broadly similar to Ellul's non-power.[104] Fourthly, Yoder's approach to these powers shares with the early Ellul a reluctance to move beyond a functional interpretation. Noting Ellul's later shift from a "realistic" to a "metaphorical" approach, Yoder concludes that asking "What are the powers?" is itself a very modern question: "I doubt that our concern to interpret the witness of the scriptures in their setting is much served by our importing this kind of modern question into . . . first-century literature."[105]

And yet, there are a number of significant differences too. First and most significant of all, Yoder does wish to affirm loud and clear the goodness

---

100. The Pauline vision is "a very refined analysis of the problems of society and history, far more refined than the other ways theologians have sought to describe the same realities only in terms of 'creation' or 'personality'" (Yoder, *Politics*, 144).

101. Yoder, *Politics*, 144. He has in mind here the "sphere sovereignty" of Dutch Calvinism, although this assessment holds too for the "natural law" theology of Roman Catholicism. "It would not be too much to say that the Pauline cosmology of the powers represents an alternative to the dominant ('Thomist') vision of natural law as a more biblical way systematically to relate Christ and creation" (Yoder, *Politics*, 159).

102. Yoder, *Politics*, 56.

103. Yoder, *Politics*, 142.

104. Yoder, *Politics*, 24.

105. Yoder, *Politics*, 161, thereby turning away from the work of Walter Wink.

of the powers in God's creation, rejecting what he refers to as Cullman's view (which is also Ellul's) that the powers will ultimately be destroyed. He argues that we cannot live with or without the powers, for "our lostness and our survival are both totally dependent on [them]."[106] Rather, he holds to an understanding of the powers as part of God's preservation of the world, a view held by Berkhof, who described the powers as the invisible background of creation, "the dikes with which God encircles his good creation, to keep it in his fellowship and to protect it from chaos."[107]

Secondly, therefore, to save creatures in their humanity, these powers cannot simply be destroyed. "Their sovereignty must be broken," and this is the freedom won by Christ's victory.[108] In this emphasis on the liberation motif (drawing on Col 2:13–15), Yoder agrees with Ellul about this freedom *from* the powers, and the need for resistance. However, whereas Ellul has little to say about what this freedom is *for*, Yoder finds a positive, reconciling content for a Christian social and political life by turning to Jesus' clearly programmatic sermon at Nazareth. Its setting is, precisely, as Luke's Gospel relates, after Jesus' time in the wilderness. Drawing upon the riches of historical scholarship (a resource to which Ellul sadly grants too little value), Yoder builds his ethics around the Nazareth sermon (Luke 4:14–21), and its background in the Old Testament hope of the Jubilee as it is expressed in Isaiah 61. By emphasizing the significance of Jesus' proclamation, Yoder makes sense of "the implications of the Jubilee" by showing how each of its four prescriptions are interwoven into Jesus' teaching in the Gospels.[109]

Conclusion

Although Ellul's use of the temptation narrative offers a powerful meditation on the significance of Jesus' sinless assumption of our alienation, as Gill notes, "his approach fails to develop Jesus' teaching and example as fully as it might have been developed."[110] Moreover, we have seen with Yoder that Ellul's account of creation is open to question. It is to this task we now turn.

---

106. Yoder, *Politics*, 143.

107. This is how Paul Stevens characterizes this view, aligning Yoder with Berkhof (Stevens, *Abolition of the Laity*, 226).

108. Yoder, *Politics*, 144.

109. Yoder, *Politics*, 28. See also Yoder, *Politics*, chapter 3. An example of this more positive approach can be found in the recent Church of England Pastoral Letter, *Who Is My Neighbour?* The Bishops speak of almost Ellulian "concentrations of power," but offer a platform for liberation based on the idea of redeeming intermediate institutions.

110. Gill, *Word of God*, 173.

5

The Apocalypse of Creation

Is There a Doctrine of Creation in Ellul?

WE HAVE APPROACHED ELLUL's theology back to front, as a function of his own apocalyptic framework. As I have argued over the course of the previous chapters, for Ellul, grace breaks in from the end into the present, and Christian theology and life for Ellul is a task of "actualizing the eschaton."[1] We now come at last to the question of *beginnings,* what we might call Ellul's doctrine of creation, if indeed he has one at all.

We have already noted that critics have assumed creation to be a basic lacuna in Ellul's thought, which is justly seen as concerned with a post-lapsarian world: "yet we must keep returning to the rupture."[2] In the popular theological imagination, Ellul has long been caricatured as a strange Marxist-Calvinist crossbreed, calling for revolution but not expecting much to happen before the eschaton. For example, in the 1989 Gifford lectures, later published as *Ethics in an Age of Technology,* the influential American theologian and historian of science Ian Barbour dismisses Ellul's technology criticism as an outworking of an excessive view of divine transcendence and human sin, and a correspondingly false anthropology:

> Ellul holds that biblical ethics can provide a viewpoint transcending society from which to judge the sinfulness of the technological order and can give us the motivation to revolt against it, but he holds out little hope of controlling it. Some interpreters see in Ellul's recent writings a very guarded hope that a radical Christian freedom that rejects cultural illusions of technological progress might in the long run lead to the transformation rather than the rejection of technology. But Ellul does not spell out such a transformation because he holds that the outcome is

---

1. *Présence*, chapter 3, in *Défi.*
2. *Parole*, 107.

in God's hands, not ours, and most of his writings are extremely pessimistic about social change.[3]

In their very conception Ellul's sociological writings often support this hopeless conclusion, yet Barbour clearly glimpses something of Ellul's emphasis on God's apocalyptic action breaking into the present. However, in commenting that Ellul starts with sin and "holds that the outcome is in God's hands, not ours," Barbour effectively accuses Ellul of promoting quietist ethics. In making his counterclaims, Barbour offers a theology and ethics of creation almost directly contrary to Ellul's. He sees humanity as essentially co-creators with God, and offers process theology as a model to "overcome this sharp separation of humanity from nature and God from the world. It affirms divine immanence as well as transcendence, and it understands God's power as empowerment."[4]

In this chapter, I will argue that this dismissal of Ellul is a function of a general ignorance about the full trajectory of his career and the neglect of his writings on creation. Indeed, it is, I will contend, grossly inaccurate to suggest that Ellul did not offer over his theological career plenty of resources in this area. This is in fact one of Ellul's dominant concerns. In what follows, I will seek to outline what I call the Apocalypse or revelation of creation, drawing upon Ellul. Yet this is not a perspective unique to Ellul but one which sits within the Protestant tradition which nurtured him, which presents creation as a truth that we can affirm only in Christ. As Stanley Hauerwas states: "We do not believe that 'creation' is something all people can affirm. Rather the confession of creation is something made by a group of people called to be a 'church' in a world of people who do not in fact know that they are creatures."[5]

What Ellul wishes to say, quite simply, is that we cannot construct a theology as if what we see around us represents God's good created order. And yet Christians can and should expect to find much to say about creation, for as Ellul puts it, "In Jesus Christ, we find again a meaning that connects us to this creation."[6]

This way of putting it suggests at first sight an adherence to a temporal framework of Creation—Fall—Redemption, along the lines of "Creation Regained."[7] And yet as we have begun to glimpse, Ellul develops Irenaeus's doctrine of *anakephalaiosis,* or recapitulation, and points instead towards

---

3. Barbour, *Ethics in an Age of Technology*, 12.

4. Barbour, *Ethics*, 263.

5. Brock, *Technological Age*, 324, citing Hauerwas, *In Good Company*, 195.

6. *Genèse*, 77.

7. See, e.g., Wolters, *Creation Regained.*

what we might call "Creation Fulfilled." The Apocalypse of creation, as I shall expound it, therefore connotes both creation's revelation through faith and its final completion in Christ.

Almost all of Ellul's major theological texts, beginning with *Présence*, have much to say about creation, although perhaps *Parole* is of particular note. *Parole* especially is Ellul's first sustained attempt to articulate what Christians can say about creation, and precisely within a major work which seeks to bring theology into dialogue with his sociology, operating the "internal dialectic" between the two that Rognon refers to as characteristic of all those texts within the Ellul corpus categorized as "theological."[8]

However, Ellul's most sustained writing on texts which are traditionally at the heart of a theology of creation is found in lesser known articles and in later, untranslated French writings. To that extent, the neglect of Ellul's doctrine of creation in non-specialist and English-speaking scholarship is perhaps a function of the neglect of these writings.[9] Two such texts will be particularly significant in this chapter, namely a late study of the early chapters of Genesis, *La Genèse Aujourd'hui* (1987, hereafter *Genèse*) and *Théologie et technique: pour une* éthique *de la non-puissance*, which exemplifies my thesis. Rognon's preface to this recently published text argues that it uncovers for today Ellul's theology of creation, with many of his earlier articles on creation, Technique and nature incorporated within the text. I propose in this chapter to make original use of these two lesser known texts, as well as tapping into some of the neglected riches of the better-known works.

In short, then, Ellul does have a theology of creation, and one not without ethical implications, especially in relation to work and technology. I will tackle below in two sections the two most significant questions in a theology of creation. Firstly, who is God the Creator for Ellul? And secondly, who is humanity the creature for Ellul?

God the Creator

Genèse is a collection of biblical expositions of the first two chapters of Genesis given at a national conference of psychoanalysts in 1985. This makes them especially interesting in that Ellul operates an "internal

8. See chapter 2, "A Faithful Betrayal."

9. In France, indeed, Ellul has latterly become known for his theology of creation, typified by leading French Protestant Theologian Antoine Nouis's book, *L'aujourd'hui de la Création*, based in part on what he sees as Ellul's concern with rabbinic interpretation in *Genèse*. The French United Protestant Church weblog, *Bible et Création*, has a section devoted to Ellul.

dialectic" between the ancient theological symbolism of Genesis and contemporary understandings drawn from scientific and sociological sources. Ellul's conclusion, *Actualité de la Genèse,* added for publication and dated November 1987, confirms that this dialogue was his intention.[10] We will touch below at points upon the connections between Ellul's theology and sociology in his writings on creation.

Genèse well demonstrates the hermeneutical approach we explored in chapter 2. In his use of the truth-reality dialectic, he is concerned to show that Genesis, though a product of a particular moment in Israel's history, the context of the Babylonian exile, can become the true and living word of God to the attentive contemporary reader—although how this plays out is certainly open to criticism.[11] Above all, Ellul attempts a close and faithful attentiveness to the original Hebrew text, offering some interesting and often surprising interpretations. However, he does also reveal the sources he is drawing upon. He engages particularly with Talmudic interpretations of Genesis, accessed through his friendship with the French Rabbi and Bible translator, André Chouraqui, whose translation of Genesis 1–3 is included as an appendix. Ellul also demonstrates a familiarity with patristic interpretations, although he sharply critiques these at points. In contrast, he refers appreciatively to then contemporary biblical scholarship, in particular the work of Gerhardt Von Rad and Paul Beauchamp. It will come as no surprise to note that another considerable influence upon Ellul's theology of creation is Karl Barth.[12]

Following Barth, Ellul dissents from the *analogia entis.* However, there is not an entire rejection of natural theology, but rather a redefinition in terms of what Barth himself called the *analogia relationis,* the analogy of

10. It is not clear to what degree this represents a move away from earlier perhaps more contrarian stances. Each exposition is followed by dialogues between Ellul and questioners exploring the implications of what he has said. Following Ellul's contribution is a set of dialogues with Francois Tosquelles, a psychoanalyst who addresses the biblical text from his anthropological perspective. However, Ellul admits his basic ignorance here (*Genèse,* 55), and for Rognon, there is scant evidence that Ellul is particularly interested in psychoanalytic theory (Rognon, *Pensée,* 302). Elsewhere, indeed, Ellul calls Freud a "criminal against humanity"! See Rognon, *Pensée,* 275.

11. *Genèse,* 213. I will not spare from criticizing possible deficits and blind spots, as in this chapter and the next we bring Ellul into dialogue with other recent writings on the theology of creation, e.g., Blocher, *In the Beginning*; Moltmann, *God in Creation*; Boff, *Cry of the Earth*; Bookless, *Planetwise*; Brock and Parker, *Saving Paradise*; Brock, *Technological Age*; Northcott, *Moral Climate*; Scott, *Political Theology of Nature*; Ward, *What the Bible Really Teaches.*

12. This influence is largely implicit in various similarities, although Ellul explicitly founds his understanding of the revelation of the name YHWH on Barth.

relation. What Ellul offers is essentially a relational account of God the Creator, with three key elements which I will explicate below.

First, both transcendent but also revealed as "the wholly other" ("Le Tout-Autre"), the Creator is shown to be beyond creation and only thereby entirely free for relationship with it, and paradigmatically with humanity.[13] However, by blessing creation (Gen 1:4), God is not absent from what he has made. Indeed, he sustains created space by his blessing, while being in no way immanent within it.

Secondly, God is sovereign LORD over time and history. Ellul argues that the Sovereign Creator does not create from nothing, but creates over and against nothingness. In this respect, Ellul offers an interesting re-interpretation of the doctrine of *creatio ex nihilo* (Gen 1:2) in terms of the powers of chaos, and without which it is impossible to understand Ellul.[14] Indeed, Ellul's account of human dominion (Gen 1:28) flows directly from this notion of divine dominion over chaos upon which it is predicated.

Thirdly, for Ellul the Sabbath rest at the conclusion of the first creation account (Gen 2:1–3) reveals something fundamental about God and about the purpose of the entire creation, of which the Sabbath observance is but the rich symbol.[15] Sabbath is a key theme developed in later writings, and serves perhaps as the summary of Ellul's mature doctrine of creation. In short, Ellul wants to argue that God's rest reveals a vision of both time and eternity, of our historical freedom in the present time and our ultimate eschatological freedom.[16]

A Relational Creator

In the first and second expositions in *Genèse*, Ellul engages with Genesis 1:1–2:3, which he takes to have universal scope. The first thing Ellul wishes to establish is that God speaks creation into being. Indeed, elsewhere, Ellul speaks of a "connaturality," or commonality between creation and the Word.[17] Therefore, creation by the Word of God in Genesis implies that the very existence of creation itself is a revelation of God's love. For Ellul, God's free decision to create flows from God's love.[18]

13. "The hidden God who reveals Godself" (*Genèse*, 109).

14. See my earlier discussion of the *chaoskampf* in chapter 3.

15. See *Ce que je crois*, chapter 12.

16. Ellul states he intends to redefine both the doctrines of providence and *creatio continua*.

17. *Parole*, 72.

18. Ellul often refers to the relationship between freedom and love. See Goddard, *Living the Word*, 67–70.

However, *the Word alone* also implies a fundamental distance between creation and the Creator: "creation by the word means what is created is truly different from God."[19] Moreover, this separation Ellul understands in terms God's *transcendence over* creation. "Biblical creation is totally desacralizing because it is in no way a theodicy . . . on the contrary, the biblical account of creation is stripped bare: God speaks and things are. That's all. This means that God is really outside the world, totally transcendent."[20]

For Ellul, if God creates by his Word, created things are just that, *things.* "Desacralization" for Ellul is a function of God's otherness from the material world he has created. However, Ellul states too that although the Word is distinct from God, the Word is God himself at the same time, and where the Word is present, God is present.[21] For Ellul, indeed, God's very power and presence within creation is expressed, mediated through the one who receives God's word, the human being:

> Speech carries at the same time meaning as well as power. This word which created the elements and the world is the same word which when addressed to humanity says something about God. . . . God creating by his word is God not outside creation but God with it, and first of all, with the man who is made precisely in order to listen to this very word, to create this relationship with God, and who having received the Word himself, can respond to God in a dialogue.[22]

Therefore the creature made in God's image is no mere "created thing."[23] Rather, as Genesis 1:28 makes clear, humanity bears something of God's transcendence over creation. The image is not merely relational but also "functional" for in receiving the command to fill the earth and be fruitful, humanity is placed "at the summit and the center of creation." In a surrounding world that "sacralized" the forces of nature, Genesis affirms that: "Human beings are not subjected to a play of superior forces."[24] For Ellul, the Bible tells us that creation is not sacred, since it gives, moreover, humanity a mandate to desacralize.

Here we see the stark difference between Ellul's account and ecological theologies of creation influenced by the natural sciences and process theology, which have tended to look back to Gen 1.2 and the Spirit brooding

19. *Genèse*, 35.
20. *Subversion*, 70.
21. *Genèse*, 30.
22. *Parole*, 56–57.
23. *Subversion*, 70.
24. *Subversion*, 70.

over the waters, to construe an incarnational presence of God within all creation. Numerous recent interpreters have decried the purported "disenchantment" and "androcentrism" justified by Genesis 1:28 along these lines.[25] For Ellul, as he outlines in *Subversion*, to identify creation with the body of God, far from being novel, is but a new moment of "resacralization." As we have already seen, the chief modern culprit here is Teilhard de Chardin, who for Ellul merely employed Christ within a "metaphysical system" determined first of all by his scientific worldview. In contrast, the only place Ellul finds Christ in Genesis 1 is in the world-creating Word (Gen 1:1) and the divine image (Gen 1:28).[26] Indeed, drawing on rabbinic sources, Ellul concludes that the Genesis account of God speaking leads, inevitably for Christians, to Incarnation.[27]

Therefore, on the whole, as Goddard notes, it is the case that "within Ellul's doctrine of creation, his primary concern is with humanity."[28] However, Ellul is concerned to move away from a crude anthropocentrism. For example, he states that the divine spirit is not only given to humanity, but also to animal life in Genesis. The Spirit is a gift, not an inner possession. The Creator breathes in his breath (*ruach*) in creating a living-being (*nephesh*): "The spirit of God comes, it breathes in you, but you cannot keep it."[29]

Moreover, the biblical text makes it abundantly clear by repetition that God's relationship with all he has made is a relationship of blessing. This blessing is interpreted by Ellul in terms of the concepts of holiness and separation. The cosmos is created through separation, and this is how his Spirit *sanctifies* the non-human creation: "This work of separation that God performs is at the same time a work of sanctification."[30] For Ellul, the repeated blessing pronounced on the created forms is given only as God sees them in relation to him. Created things have no intrinsic goodness,

25. For example, Leonardo Boff reproaches Genesis 1:28 for mandating technology and the will to power (*Cry of the Earth*, 75–81) and follows Teilhard in arguing for a Trinitarian immanence in creation (chapters 7–9). See also Parker and Brock: "Like the breathing of a human body, the images said that God blessed the earth with the breath of Spirit. It permeated the entire cosmos and made paradise the salvation that baptism in the Spirit offered" (*Saving Paradise*, xv). In contrast, Peter Scott critiques the tendency to construe the divine Spirit as an immanent force or energy within creation and to deny a "determining place" to Jesus Christ as God's particular presence (*Political Theology of Nature*, 20).

26. *Genèse*, 71.

27. *Genèse*, 30. There is no developed Trinitarian reading of these texts, although Ellul does note in passing that it is not unjustified to find hints of the Trinity in Genesis.

28. Goddard, *Living the Word*, 68.

29. *Genèse*, 116.

30. *Genèse*, 34.

rendering them sacred; they have goodness in relation to God, who alone declares what is good: "They are good insofar as there is the word, there is [God's] looking, there is relationship."[31]

In conceiving of the cosmos in terms of relationships and not in terms of orders, Ellul offers a direct challenge to the Greek theory of an ordered and self-existent nature assumed in the theologies of creation produced by the Greek and Latin Fathers, and taken forward in the work of Thomas Aquinas.[32] This too is to deny biblical desacralization. For Ellul, there is no essential nature, but a creation entirely dependent on its relationship with God for its continued emergence, "It is something that always has a new aspect."[33] Moreover, although creation is primarily for God, something which overwhelms humanity, in our daily experience, creation is not a static megalith but an event becoming, arising, emerging before us.[34] "In other words, there is no existing nature in which the human being finds himself, where we have a certain place. There is a world in relationship to the human being which can only be understood within this relationship, and a world in relationship to God, which can only be understood within this relationship."[35]

What Ellul therefore proposes is a relational account of creation rooted in the Bible's account, with an emphasis on the vocation of humanity within this nexus. On this account, the Creator God is "a passionately involved personal being [who] upholds each thing in its distinctness—but things have their distinctness only through their relationships."[36]

31. *Genèse*, 41.

32. A recurring theme in Ellul is his faithfulness to a Hebraic way of reading. Indeed, he echoes here his consistent rejection of traditional Greek metaphysical modes of thinking, a rejection which is also significant for his treatment of the incarnation (see also *Subversion*, chapter 2). Ellul however considers that of the Greek and Latin Fathers, only Saint Jerome knew Hebrew sufficiently to understand the creation accounts (*Genèse*, 33).

33. *Genèse*, 33.

34. *Genèse*, 33. There are perhaps echoes of Martin Heidegger's concept of the unveiling of being here (Brock, *Technological Age*, 58).

35. *Genèse*, 34.

36. Thus, Loren Wilkinson contrasts the "New Story of Creation" with the "Old Story of Orthodoxy," cited in Stevens, *Abolition of the Laity*, 99. In more recent ecological theology, there has been a tendency to see this relationality in terms of James Lovelock's Gaia hypothesis (see, e.g., Northcott, *Moral Climate*, 69–71, for a discussion of relationality).

The Creator's Power

The second implication of Ellul's understanding of God as Word is that the Creator is sovereign over time, and therefore history. The first creation account presents the Creator as *speaking* light into being to signify that light, and therefore time, are his primary creations. This, Ellul claims, shows that "biblically, space is neither primary, nor essential": God is not located in space, as we are, and this is a mark of God's alterity.[37] But as a speaking Creator, he is not timeless in the sense of beyond time, and yet neither is he subject to time, as if a Greek god or avatar.[38]

In a brief and rather unexplained use of the documentary hypothesis in *Genèse*, Ellul argues that the use of YHWH in the second so-called "Yahwist" creation account marks this emphasis on *history over and against nature*. Indeed, Ellul takes YHWH to mean "Je suis," "I am," meaning that God reveals himself as the One always present throughout all history.[39] This sovereignty or freedom of God within history is for Ellul the revelation which founded Israel in the exodus from Egypt, a revelation which then founds Israel's doctrine of creation by the Word. "Speech is the expression of freedom, supposes freedom, and calls the interlocutor to assert themself as free in the act of speaking. God is the liberator. We must not cease to recall that the God of Israel manifests himself for the first time in the Exodus."[40]

It is thus no surprise that the Creator is presented as a Victor in the creation account. Moreover in the original setting of the Babylonian exile, creation by the Word of God alone had a polemical intent over and against contemporary polytheism: it represented a refusal of the idea of a celestial power-struggle between hostile forces, a struggle out of which nature and culture are born. In the *Enuma Elish*, the powers of Babylon have their rationale in the conquest of chaos by the Babylonian god Marduk.[41] In contrast, Genesis 1 is in an *anti-theodicy* for it presents creation not as a mighty effort,

---

37. *Parole*, 61. Ellul's account is primarily theological. He does not mean to critique scientific accounts of the simultaneous creation of space-time, but to offer a theological interpretation. "['God says'] leads us immediately to God's absolutely infinite greatness and power. Astronomers probe pulsars and quasars, speaking of billions of light-years, billions of degrees centigrade, billions of megawatts, and unimaginable explosions of energy. All this, encompassed in reality within the 'God says,' gives us an idea of the distance between the creator and us."

38. *Parole*, 62.

39. *Genèse*, 108–110. There follows a somewhat confusing comment in *Genèse*, 110, about the possibility of knowing Elohim from nature but YHWH only from this revelation.

40. *Parole*, 65.

41. Ellul alludes to other ancient Near Eastern accounts of creation (*Genèse*, 30).

but as a simple divine fiat: "There is no fight, no-one gets killed, there is God, that's all. . . . This well demonstrates the total lack of effort on God's part."[42]

However, in a substantial discussion of the phrase *tohu wa bohu* (Gen 1:2) in *Genèse*, drawing on the Talmud, Ellul contends that the Hebrew Bible in a significant move retains the primeval waters of the Babylonian account. Why is this so? At one level, Ellul here flirts with dualism by bringing in the *chaoskampf* motif: the waters express the threat that creation might degenerate into chaos. However, the use of *tohu wa bohu* is essentially polemical, for whereas the waters are divine in the Babylonian account, in Genesis they are the power of nothingness: "an annihilating power."[43] In Genesis, it is precisely over these waters that the Spirit swoops to conquer. Creation is only achieved against this threat but this does not imply any substantial matter pre-existent to God's creative word.

With Barth, Ellul wishes to make clear that Genesis presents an original *No* implied in the Creator's *Yes*, a victory over *tohu wa bohu*.[44] This again is desacralization. The fact that humanity receives the power of the Word is a sign that humanity is called to exercise a godlike sovereignty, the power of the Word, over the threat of chaos. Earth's blessing is threatened if humanity does not play its part.

As I have established in the previous two chapters, there is limited reward in asking ontological questions of Ellul. However, his characteristically idiosyncratic revision of the classical *creatio ex nihilo* formulation of the later Western tradition bears brief examination, if only to highlight his purposes and to flag up some problems. Indeed, Ellul claims to be lining himself up with a new, even "modern" way of thinking about creation, in terms of separation and difference. "God . . . separates things from each other. This is fundamental, and I believe it is an acquisition of modern theological thought: we now understand that creation cannot be thought of as *from nothing-to-something*, but as a separation between confused things that will become distinct, and thereby take on their existence."[45]

Significantly, Ellul has in mind a way of reading Genesis which can resonate today, hence the title, *La Genèse aujourd'hui*.[46] Indeed, despite the symbolic and non-scientific character of Genesis, and despite his dislike of de Chardin's scheme, Ellul suggests that there are some "verisimilitudes" between Genesis and evolution, conjecturing that the creation of plants

42. *Genèse*, 31.
43. *Genèse*, 30.
44. Barth, *CD* 3/3:50.
45. *Genèse*, 34.
46. *Genèse*, 34–35.

and animals "for the purpose of their species" (as he translates verses 12 and 21, "according to their kinds") implies that the text indicates an open-endedness in creation.[47] To some degree, Ellul does seem happy to offer *ad hominem* arguments to contemporary scientific readers of the text, and yet ultimately, he argues for the pointlessness of reading the symbolic brevity of Genesis scientifically.[48]

Genesis is ultimately a book about hope. In fact, in his earlier book *Hope*, in a section headed "And in the Beginning Was Hope," Ellul had already begun to develop this argument:

> So here we are right back at the beginning of things, back at the first day for man and for the creation. We must remember that the act of creation does not graft itself onto an absence, a nothing, a nonbeing. It is not a matter of *creatio ex nihilo*. It is the affirmation of the hope of God against the aggressive threat of non-being, against the invasion of that which normally would win.[49]

Despite the difficulty of interpreting Ellul's somewhat elusive language here, his point, as he develops it from here, is that for Christians, the theology of creation is a theology of hope. Ellul does not speak of creation as if we have access to a pristine order. To say we believe in creation is, rather, an apocalyptic statement about the future coming towards us, because it is to say that the Creator will one day win a final victory over disorder and chaos.

And yet again, we see in *Hope* that Ellul sees the account of the Creator's desacralization of matter as a model for our desacralization of matter in the activity we might call Technique. If things are things, to be used, this does not imply they should be exploited. Rather we are to *rightly use* created things,

47. *Genèse*, 68–69.

48. We concede that much more can and has since been said about Genesis and scientific knowledge. The scientist-theologian Keith Ward, for example, wants to hold to the Bible's account of *tohu wa bohu* in a more tightly logical sense than Ellul does. He asks: can one find in Genesis 1 a primeval chaos without acknowledging its prior creation by God? Either there was a pre-existent matter incorporated into creation for its own ultimate good, or God in fact created both positive and negative potentialities. Moreover, in a move that has garnered much support in recent scientific theology, Ward finds a potentially fruitful theology hidden in this second possibility. "This is the mystery, that God creates something . . . which has the capacity to frustrate God's purpose. If the Great Deep . . . is created by God, why should God create what frustrates the very purpose of creation? Does this point, in some way, to the fact that conflict and destruction is in some way essential to development and creation, even in a universe that is 'very good'?" (Ward, *What the Bible Really Teaches*, 69). Ward goes on to suggest that this interpretation fits well with both modern thermodynamics and evolutionary biology. Clearly at issue here is a question of theological method, and as a dialectical theologian, neither Ellul's logic is as tight as Ward's nor is his scientific knowledge as reliable.

49. *Hope*, 229.

that is, *for the glory of God.* "Hope leads us to seize upon these desacralized things, not to make them sacred again . . . but in order that they might manifest the glory of God, which is their true, if not only purpose."[50]

Moreover, we can then even bring our own technological creations to his glory: for outside of his glory, they will be consigned to nothingness.[51]

Summary: Ellul the "Irregular" Theologian

It should be clear by now that Ellul's account of chaos and cosmos marks out his creation theology as apocalyptic. Yet despite the power of Ellul's polemic, we note two potential problems for its reception today.

First is the question of its coherence. Ellul argues that chaos has a real power and yet at the same time, he denies it any ontological grounding. As we began to explore in chapter 3, to allow the possibility of a threat to the goodness of creation while denying there are actual created powers which turned hostile is troubling to many orthodox Christians. Anabaptist theologian Greg Boyd provides a more coherent, if controversial, account of chaos and cosmos by arguing that:

> Genesis 1 is not so much an account of creation as it is an account of God's restoration of the world that had previously been rendered formless, futile, empty and engulfed by chaos. According to this view . . . which I prefer to call the restoration theory, the cosmos that had been created in verse 1 had been embattled, corrupted, judged and brought to the nearly destroyed state we find it in verse 2.[52]

As Boyd puts it, if one accepts the admittedly speculative notion of an angelic fall, this suggests a logically temporal dualism, if not an ultimately metaphysical dualism. Indeed, despite the influence of Augustine's "meontic" account, Boyd claims that this restoration theory has both greater claim to the tradition and greater explanatory power today.[53] However, given his suspicion of theodicy, Ellul does not seek to offer a coherent account of natural evil—whether scientific or demonic.

Indeed, if one were to push back against Boyd's warfare motif here, from Ellul's perspective, what this speculative "fall of angels" could be seen to imply is an act of original divine violence in their expulsion from

---

50. *Hope,* 233.

51. *Hope,* 236.

52. Boyd, *God at War,* 104. See also Angel and Wright, *Playing with Dragons,* 27–30.

53. Angel and Wright, *Playing with Dragons,* 105–113.

heaven. For his part, Ellul affirms that creation over against chaos is not an act of violence but of the word alone.[54] And this makes a statement about the character of God's original and ultimate power; it is the power of the mere word which creates order against chaos, a non-violent power.[55] Moreover, Ellul affirms that it is only in the non violent life, death and resurrection of Jesus that the "Satan"—the powers of opposition and accusation—is expelled from heaven.[56]

Secondly, from a rather different perspective, is the more general question of Ellul's use of tradition. If one grants that the *chaoskampf* in Genesis has a demythologizing intent, in effect marking out the ability of the Creator to overcome the power of chaos by the mere word, it seems odd on Ellul's part to deny that that is what the tradition meant by formulating the *creatio ex nihilo* in the first place. For ecological theologian Michael Northcott, *creatio ex nihilo* makes just this essential contribution to a contemporary theology of creation, upholding precisely the ideas of power and dominion that Ellul is seeking to promote. For Northcott, *the ex nihilo* formulation, emerging late in Jewish history, becomes central to Christian understanding:

> In this doctrine Christians affirm that God's relation to the world is not one of complete identity nor one of controlling or instrumental dominion . . . this representation of creation as the free utterance of God in summoning being from nothing means that the act of creation is not well expressed in the language of power or control or management, but is rather an act in which intrinsic worth is created in divine freedom and generosity . . . creation is not power, because it is not exercised on anything.[57]

This, Northcott claims, also establishes humanity's working relationship of dependence upon and attentiveness to the material creation, a dependence undermined by technological progress.

---

54. *Parole*, 60. Girard clearly holds this view: "The later insertion of Satan's expulsion into the creation narrative may be the result of a 'sacrificial reading' of the Hebrew Scriptures via a sacrificial reading of the Gospels—the work of Christian exegetes who fundamentally misunderstood the Gospel revelation" (Pattillo, "Violence, Anarchy, and Scripture," 16, citing Girard).

55. Gerhard von Rad, whose influence on Ellul is patent, argues that the Hebrew verb used in Genesis 1:1—*bara*—"contains the very idea of complete effortlessness and creatio ex nihilo, since it is never connected with any statement of the material" (*Genesis*, 47). He therefore goes on to summarize the insight of this formulation: "The theological thought of chapter 1 does not so much move between the poles of nothingness and creation as between chaos and cosmos" (*Genesis*, 49).

56. *Subversion*, chapter 9.

57. Northcott, *Moral Climate*, 77–78, makes this pithy defense of *creatio ex nihilo*.

In probing Ellul in this way, it becomes clear that he plays slightly fast and loose with the tradition as with his other sources. In short, Ellul is himself an exponent of what Karl Barth liked to call "irregular dogmatics." We now turn to another example of such creative and irregular dogmatics: Ellul's reading of the Sabbath. Here too we find the interrelationship of creation and eternity.

The Creator's Work and the Creator's Rest

Ellul takes the close of the priestly creation account (Gen 2:1–3), the seventh day of the divine rest, as the "crowning" of the entire account. In *Genèse*, Ellul argues that the seventh day signifies both God's rest after the completion of his work and his continuing blessing over all time.[58] In his characteristically polemical vein, Ellul intends here to engage with two elements in contemporary doctrines of creation.

Firstly, Ellul engages with the idea of continuous creation, the so-called *creatio continua*. As fully blessed, creation is now complete, and in no need of additional work, although this does not imply it is unchanging. Rather, in a perhaps intended echo of the words of Frederick Temple's famous theological gloss on evolutionary theory, "God did not make the things, we may say, but he made them make themselves,"[59] Ellul argues that "each piece of work is successfully completed, and continues itself."[60] Creation has its own relative freedom as "a space for the unfolding of life in the many convergences . . . in evolutionary history."[61]

Secondly, and more importantly within Ellul's overall trajectory, this reading of God's Sabbath rest enables a redefinition of the classical doctrine of providence, which appears in somewhat disguised form in his earlier writings in terms of the "order of preservation." However, by the time of *Genèse* and especially *Ce que je crois*,[62] Ellul argues that there is no particular order that God sustains. The Creator is not a cause of all that is, for God freely limits himself by entering into his rest. History is therefore not simply His Story, for it is humanity that makes history. "And I believe this is indeed the essence of biblical thought: God ceases to act so as not to interfere in the action . . . and

58. Blocher defends this interpretation of the Sabbath and locates it in Augustine. Among modern commentators, he lines up Von Rad and Westermann in agreement (Blocher, *In the Beginning*, 56).

59. Peacocke discusses this concept in Polkinghorne, *Science and Theology*, 23.

60. *Genèse*, 41.

61. Northcott, *Moral Climate*, 78.

62. See *Ce que je crois*, chapter 12.

work of humanity. God respects his creature to the point of no longer acting, in order to give us freedom. And after the rupture . . . it is not quite freedom in the sense that God wanted it, but it is independence."[63]

Yet as God of love, this rest does not imply God's absence or indifference, and indeed in blessing the seventh day of creation, God's blessing remains upon all human history. Indeed, the continuing freedom of humanity to create history, although twisted by the rupture towards independence and autonomy, is still grounded in God's continued blessing.[64] In *Ce que je crois*, Ellul constructs upon this base the idea of all human history as an eschatological adventure. We are created in order to enter into God's eternal rest, into a love relationship with the Creator, and even to direct all creation towards God's rest. In a sense, God does continue to work by responding to and blessing our works, yet still respecting the freedom we and all created things have been given. It is worth citing at length his interpretation of Genesis 2:1–3, in which he notes the ambiguity present in the claim that in resting, God "finished" the work of creation which he had already completed:

> Everything is complete by the seventh day, but it seems that there was still something to do, for we are told that God finished his work on the seventh day. If everything was finished, what need was there to say this? There is indeed duality here, for on the seventh day, the same formula being used in each case, we read that he both finished his work and rested from it. Everything is complete, yet God still did something. God enters into his rest, but he still has something to do. We can understand the contradiction if we accept the contingent action of God whereby he lovingly continues his work (not a work of creation, for creation is not continuous) even though he has entered into his rest. The two facts revealed here are both true. God is no longer the Creator doing new works of creation, but he is always attentive to the doings of the exceptional creature that is called human and that he is able to sanctify. It is precisely because he is resting that he may seem distant (he is present only in Jesus Christ) and silent and perhaps even absent. It looks as if he has abandoned the world, as if there is dereliction.[65]

We see here perhaps the significant place of the development of the Sabbath in Ellul's theological trajectory. Over and against his early argument for God's providential preservation of the world, Ellul now argues

63. *Genèse*, 81–82.
64. *Ce que je crois*, 205.
65. *Ce que je crois*, 214–15.

that we are radically free, to the point where we may even provoke a situation in which we enter into the experience of God's absence. The theme of God's silence in what Ellul saw as the closed world governed by Technique is elaborated in a number of his darker writings, such as *Espérance* and *Trahison*, in which he asks the question which bothers him most: "how can we understand the presence of God in a world where human beings rely more on Technique than his Word revealed in Jesus Christ?" However, in this later treatment of the seventh day, Ellul seems to respond to his own doubt and despair with this understanding of God's overarching blessing, from a distance, as it were. Creation was destined for God's Sabbath rest and although we constantly trouble God's rest, Ellul argues that nothing can finally threaten it.

Indeed, God does enter history at a specific point to work towards the end for which he created in the first place, our entry into God's rest. It is in this context that *Ce que je crois* relates the work of Christ to the work of creation. In commenting on Jesus' saying in John 5:17–21 that "the Father is working until now" (a teaching given precisely in the aftermath of a healing work on the Sabbath), Ellul argues that Jesus here teaches that the Father has never given up on the rest for which creation was intended. John's presentation here does not fund a general notion of divine providence, but rather offers a view of creation in which the Son plays a role with the Father. "Undoubtedly when he says that 'my Father is working still' with regard to a single healing, he is not saying that his Father is the supreme cause. He is saying that God works in human hearts and seeks reconciliation, which is achieved in Jesus Christ."[66]

The climax of the work of God in history therefore is the punctiliar work of Jesus in one time and in one place, which alone guarantees that we will enter into the rest which has always been God's intention for us.[67] And this work is carried on by the Holy Spirit in all places and especially in those who "assume" the work of Jesus. "But the work has still to go on with the action of Jesus Christ through those who take up this action and carry it forward and with the action of the Holy Spirit, who constantly begins again what we tear down. We are already in the seventh day, but if everything has already been accomplished, everything has not yet been consummated."[68]

As we make the transition from considering Ellul's theology to his anthropology, we note that Ellul's libertarian theology gives a meaning to the works of human history lacking in predestinarian accounts. And yet at

66. *Ce que je crois*, 215.

67. *Genèse*, 84.

68. *Ce que je crois*, 215.

the same time, because this rest is God's initiative, human works have no salvific power outside of Jesus Christ. At the end of his theological trajectory, through his meditation on the Sabbath, Ellul arrives at a confidence that although we trouble God's rest and we sense that God has abandoned us, God has not stopped blessing creation, or else all would cease to be. Moreover, here he seems to show greater confidence in the presence and work of the Holy Spirit in the world to bring about the reconciliation God desires. In Jesus and through the Spirit, all creation will ultimately enter the rest for which it was created, but history goes on, and we have not yet entered its rest. To understand our role in the present time, we will return to the Sabbath theme, as we explore the part we have to play in the corresponding section below. We move now from Ellul's theology to the anthropology which emerges from it.

Humanity the Creature

Ellul's anthropology flows directly from his theology for the simple reason that humanity alone is made in the image of God. The creation of humanity in the image places humanity to some degree on the truth side of the truth-reality dialectic, whereas the rest of creation lies on the reality side. Echoing Ellul's description of God as the "wholly other," humanity has "a wholly other role" to the rest of creation.[69] However, Ellul's anthropology is based on the notion of a rupture in creation which is our doing. "The Bible repeatedly tells us that this is not creation as God gave it. And, for example, we know from Romans 8 that creation has completely 'fallen' as a result of Adam's break from God; that violence and destruction have entered in, that creation became both enslaved and fragmented, awaiting with suffering the moment of its reintegration."[70]

However, Ellul's concern, as we have seen, is not to engage scientific accounts or to explain natural evil. *Genèse* was written against the backdrop, at least for Ellul, of an ecological crisis unleashed by the "technical phenomenon." In *Genèse* and in numerous other texts, especially in his sociological writings, the established "reality" Ellul turns to is the consensus that we are in an age of unprecedented threat. In this light we will now consider what Ellul has to say about the human vocation—relational, functional and eschatological—in a ruptured world.[71]

69. *Genèse*, 68.

70. *Théologie et Technique*, 142.

71. Bookless argues on the one hand that "the shattering effects of sin and fall include a breakdown . . . in the relationship between God and the created order"

Created for Relationship

In the second exposition of *Genèse*, Ellul takes as his text Genesis 1:24–31 to 2:1–3, with the title, "Genesis of the free and loving human being." In parallel to his theology, in his anthropology, Ellul says that creation in the image of God paradoxically refers to the gift of the word.[72] There is a fundamental and unique relationship between the divine Word and the gift of speech, the word, to humanity.[73] Ellul sees the creation of humanity in the image of God as the call to enter freely into communion, relationship with God. Humans are created in the image of a speaking God and therefore we have a unique capacity to hear God's voice and to respond. "God creates human beings as speaking beings. Perhaps this is one of the meanings of the image of God: one who responds and is responsible; a counterpart who will dialogue. . . . Speech constitutes human specificity, just as it constitutes the specificity of this God when compared with all other gods."[74]

Evidently, our freedom is not God's absolute freedom. Indeed, for Ellul, the concept of image implies an original divine limit for humanity, for the Hebrew translated "in the image of" implies, for Ellul, "in the shadow of." This implies that humanity is *only* image: humanity has no intrinsic nature beyond this calling to communion with God. There can be no abstract definition of humanity beyond this call, no rational or moral definition. Ellul puts this in characteristically dialectical terms. "Man has no aseity. He is therefore both autonomous and not autonomous . . . both perfect and imperfect. . . . He is indeterminate. He contains good and bad. He is not fixed in goodness: he can be something else and he can do something else."[75]

This understanding has clear implications for how Ellul understands our relationship with God now. In writings only recently published together in *Théologie*, Ellul asserts again that the image of God implies not an essence, but rather an open-ended vocation within God's purposes. The characteristic terms Ellul turns to in order to describe this becoming are "artifice" and "symbol," and in this Ellul claims to find a fundamental similarity between the Bible's portrayal of our vocation and what social anthropology reveals:

(*Planetwise*, 38), including death. Yet on the other, he concedes that there are positive ecological consequences of natural death in the present age.

72. *Parole*, 63–64.

73. However, citing Barth, Ellul is clear that the divine word is superior to the human word in that it alone implies a decisive and immediate power (*Parole*, 57).

74. *Parole*, 71.

75. *Genèse*, 72–73. He claims such a view is implied in the fact that there is no declaration of creational goodness after the creation of humanity.

What we have tried to describe above about man as indeterminate, unsettled etc. seems to me to correspond exactly to the creative will of the biblical God, who in no way establishes an order for the human being . . . but institutes a freedom, a truly free being, with all the uncertainty that this supposes   And it is exactly to the extent that human beings respond to this vocation that they become and makes themselves human, though they can also refuse to do so! In other words, the human being lives only through what is artificial. Our animal "nature" is transcended through the the symbolic order of the imagination, and our human being is realized only as we produce this artificial world.[76]

Ellul clearly argues therefore that to speak of a Human Nature is fundamentally mistaken. Moreover, it is misguided to make appeals to a Natural Law in ethical discussions of the limits of human action.[77] "This being who is artificial because human, who has in some sense made themselves who they are, has no external reference point to know what is permitted or not."[78] There is therefore nothing dangerous about artifice in itself—indeed, it is mandated in a biblical understanding of desacralized creation, the closest Ellul comes to a "cultural mandate" for science and technology.

This perhaps surprising celebration of artificiality does not however mean that the given material form of our lives has no meaning. We cannot make nature sacred in order to protect it, but we need rather to hear the summons to relationship issued by the Creator, first of all in the form of our embodiment. For Ellul, this relationality is reflected in the biological dimorphism of male and female: an otherness within the image mirroring the love relationships within God: "This love relationship between man and woman is an image of the relationship that exists within God."[79] Our creation in the divine image reflects and expands the communion of love within God. However, Ellul notes that human beings are also "in the lineage of animals," for the creation of humanity is located just after a brief repetition of the creation of the other animals (Gen 1:25). For this reason, we share with all animal life a limited lifespan ended by bodily death.[80]

However, all of these creaturely limits take on a new significance after the events encoded in Genesis 3 and 4. As we have seen, God is wholly other

76. *Théologie et Technique*, 136.

77. *Théologie et Technique*, 136–38.

78. *Théologie et Technique*, 138.

79. *Genèse*, 71.

80. Ellul notes in his account of the creation of animals that since God addresses the animals with a blessing, this is what both sets them apart from other created things, and gives them most affinity with humanity (*Genèse*, 41).

to us, but this implies relationship, not separation. However, this otherness takes on a new meaning, and what was intended in creation for blessing, now becomes alienation. This is the significance of the narrative of Adam and Eve and its account of eating from the Tree of the Knowledge of Good and Evil (Gen 3). Drawing on Philippians 2, Ellul describes the man's decision to eat the fruit as an act of claiming autonomy from God. He claims Genesis intends to place a divine prohibition upon human decision about the good, for the good is simply what God says and gives. Therefore, for Ellul, eating from the tree connotes the act of deciding for oneself, rather than responding to God: "But to assert that the good is nothing other than what God decides (i.e., his commandment) means that the good is not for human decision, nor is it a mere possibility. For this good has an independent reality. The good is given . . . and it is forbidden for the man to discover it by himself. We can only act well when we hear the Word of God."[81]

That sin is in essence a grasping at divine power is most clearly revealed, for Ellul, in the axiomatic and summarizing final command of the Decalogue, the proscription of covetousness. Covetousness establishes a clear link between sight and the desire for power and possession; "covetousness" and "the spirit of power" are indeed near-synonyms in Ellul.[82] For him, the judgment of Genesis 3:6–7, which speaks of the fruit as "pleasing to the eye" and of Adam and Eve having their "eyes opened" by eating, re-echoes into the modern world, where we have given the power of decision over to the "evidence" of the scientific method and its technological achievements.[83]

Quite simply, instead of listening for the Word of God, we now trust ourselves to sight. The image in Ellul's register always implies Technique, since they share a commonality, a "connaturality."[84] Moreover, according to Ellul, the symbol of the Tree of Knowledge in Genesis connotes "the

81. *Vouloir*, 10.

82. In *Parole*, Ellul identifies the spirit of power with covetousness. See Goddard's account of "la convoitise," 79–80.

83. We recall the characteristically strident statement, "Evidence is the absolute evil" (*Parole*, 108). Keith Ward's approach to original sin both chimes and yet clashes sharply with Ellul here. Ward wants to see the Fall of Humanity in terms of Irenaeus's scheme: a fall from naivety and innocence, and as such a fall away from God into brute nature, although ultimately a fall from which we must rise *upwards*. Yet in contrast to Ellul, he starts with the prior evidence of evolutionary science: "The sinful nature is that nature which evolutionary history has left us with. We are lustful, aggressive and hostile. . . . It is quite natural for us to have those propensities and no blame attaches to us for that. . . . The story of eating of the fruit from the tree of knowledge is a symbol for the failure of humanity to accept the divine-human unity that would have made possible the transformation [from 'natural human affections' to 'love and vitality']" (Ward, *What the Bible Really Teaches*, 85–86).

84. *Parole*, 168.

beginnings of morality," the way we decide for ourselves what is right and what is wrong.[85] It is therefore not surprising that, despite the burgeoning ethical business of "Technology Assessment," we find it curiously difficult to limit and regulate what we can see, grasp and manipulate.[86] Despite our best intentions, without discerning the divine Word we cannot stand over and against Technique. And yet, we retain a thirst for good, which at one and the same time serves as an indication of our original good creation in God's image and of our now-constant desire to justify our own decisions in terms of the good.[87]

Genesis records that death results from this broken communion with the Creator who alone gives life. "To break communication with the one who gives the breath, the *Ruach*, means thus losing one's very life."[88] As a result, God's otherness now becomes a source not of invisible communion but of simple alienation. And the fact of death is now all-encompassing, becoming the Death that Ellul writes of in his account of Revelation: Ellul now defines humanity as a being "destined to," and trapped by death.[89]

However, none of this is meant to imply that the divine image is "effaced" from humanity and our dominion revoked. Rather, by the very fact of our dominion, we now have the power to spread Death into creation, as we shall now explore.

Created for Dominion within Relationship

We have already noted that Ellul does not deny humanity powers (*pouvoirs*) gifted to us by virtue of our creation in the image of God. However, to see dominion in terms of scientific and technological progress is an *a posteriori* justification of the will to power which has come to dominate the Western world, under the guise of "natural theology."[90] We find the clearest theological statement of this position in *La Technique et les premiers chapitres de la Genèse* published in *Foi et Vie* (1960) and recently integrated into *Théologie et Technique*:

> Because Technique is a great human achievement, it is necessary
> to legitimize it somehow. . . . And indeed we have now clearly

85. *Genèse*, 113. There are echoes of Girard's account of morality, and once again, we see Ellul's dismissal of natural law.

86. See Brock, *Technological Age*, 10–20, on "Technology Assessment."

87. See *Ce que je crois*, chapter 6, concluding with Romans 7:15, 25.

88. *Genèse*, 117.

89. *Ethique*, 79.

90. *Subversion*, 19.

got to the point where theologians are vying with one another
to legitimate technique and work. We find . . . the idea that
humanity has a demiurgic, godlike function, that he completes
creation, that he creates in some way alongside God. . . . And all
this, taken from these two verses of Genesis [Gen 1:28; 2:15]. . . .
And, of course, when we say work we mean Technique . . . Adam
is said to be an inventor and technician in Eden. This set of ideas
seems to me gravely to misunderstand what the Bible tells us
about creation before the fall.[91]

This, Ellul argues, is the theology of Francis Bacon: that in submitting
to the laws of nature, humanity is able to rule them, as God rules, even to
alleviate the Fall. Yet, he argues, this was not the rule intended by God *ab
initio*. The creational rule intended for humanity was purely a work of the
word, the means of God's creative power over matter. Ellul's thoroughgoing
anthropocentrism is significantly controlled by his interpretation of the command to exercise dominion over creation in terms of the love with which God
governs creation. Adam's loving naming of the animals (Gen 2:19–20) is the
essential act of dominion. "In his sovereign power and perfect initiative Adam
reveals himself to be free before God. . . . Human sovereignty is due more to
our language than to our techniques and instruments of war."[92]

The human word shares the power and efficacy of the divine word in that
it offers a purchase over reality. But it is not by "techniques" but by language
that humanity reigns. In "the gratuitousness and artificiality of language," God
and humanity are called to encounter each other.[93] God does not determine
what we are to say in response to the call to name the life that exists around us,
but awaits and responds to our response.[94] There is thus no God-given "natural language," or "order of things." Humanity was intended to be radically free
to shape language and therefore to shape the world itself.

In Ellul's hermeneutical strategy, the "spiritual mastery" of Genesis
2:19–20, centered on the power of the word, reinterprets the other dominion texts, both Genesis 1:28 and 2:15, which speaks of "tilling and keeping"
the land. Moreover, to use these texts to legitimate Technique is to fail to
follow the order of the canonical text which places Genesis 4 after the first

91. *Théologie et Technique*, 304. The original French article (1960) was translated
into English in Mitcham and Grote, *Theology and Technology*. It went on to become a
commonplace of American Ellul scholarship. Marva Dawn comments, misleadingly,
that this key article "outlines Ellul's biblical foundations for his opposition to technique"
(*Sources and Trajectories*, 164).

92. *Parole*, 59.

93. *Parole*, 74, citing Paul Beauchamp.

94. *Genèse*, 119. Ellul refers to this as "a curious mission."

creation covenant, before adding a key but often neglected covenant, the covenant given to Noah in Genesis 9. "Between the two texts (Gen 1:28–29; 9:1–7), we have the Fall (human autonomy), the establishment of the disorder of powers, and the invention of Technique, expressly attributed to Cain (Gen 4.17–22). It is no longer a question of words but of hands. . . . Technique finds its legitimacy at this point and not in the first covenant, in which the word was the only power."[95]

Technique has therefore some biblical legitimacy in this Noachide covenant with "all flesh," and Ellul reads this intervening ordinance as a reconfiguration of Genesis 1:28, noting that it gives permissions for and imposes limits upon the power of the hands, and therefore by extension upon the tool and Technique.[96]

In *Théologie*, drawing upon earlier work, Ellul explains why Technique, as he understands it, cannot be posited as an original cultural mandate. Beginning with a compressed account of the communion and immediacy of relationships within creation such we have sketched above, Ellul goes on to argue that because there was no division intended for creation, the ends and means of human life were to be one and the same. "There was no distinction between ends and means. The living Adam was in communion with his only possible end, and he had no means to exercise. I have tried to show [in *Présence*] how in Jesus Christ . . . the means are reunited with the end. Yet in creation, the distinction was not yet established."[97]

However, whereas means and ends were to be united, in reality they are divided, and Ellul speaks of creation as a shattered mirror.[98] Positing that work was to have been non-instrumental, no mere means to an end, in a circular argument, Ellul therefore contends that Technique, as nothing but mediation—a collection of means—would have been superfluous. Adam "had no method to follow, no Technique to apply, because he had no constraint to exercise, no need to fill, no need to overcome."[99]

---

95. *Parole*, 76–77.

96. "God blessed Noah and his sons, and said to them, 'Be fruitful and multiply, and fill the earth. The fear and dread of you shall rest on every animal of the earth . . . into your hand they are delivered. Only, you shall not eat flesh with its life, that is, its blood. For your own lifeblood I will surely require a reckoning: from every animal I will require it and from human beings, each one for the blood of another, I will require a reckoning for human life'" (Gen 9:1–5a). These limits apply to all flesh, for indeed the very concept of covenant implies limit. See *Théologie et Technique*, 210.

97. *Théologie et Technique*, 150.

98. The image of the mirror is most likely drawn from Calvin. However, Ellul allows that creation may even still be a mirror of God, see Goddard, *Living the Word*, 67.

99. *Théologie et Technique*, 150.

Work in creation was pure word-work, for only the word has a power which directs while leaving the other intact, oriented towards "communion, participation, love." The covenant with Noah clearly marks this fall from grace, now mandating the power of means, tools, Techniques, but only as concession: "On the one hand, there's the word, on the other, there are the hands: it is really here that we see where Technique is introduced."[100]

Genesis 1 and 2 unveil the fact that the present order of the world is not a revelation of the Creator's will. Ellul reads Genesis 1 and 2 as describing a kind of divine and human dominion by means of the Word, without power or violence. That is, this text announces "an ontology of peace."[101] What does Ellul then achieve by claiming that in Christ we recover a unity of ends and means? This is not meant to imply a return to Eden, as we have seen that is not the direction of apocalyptic theology. Rather, it marks that the Gospel does not make sense without Genesis 1 and 2: In Christ we find a new and livable story, but this was what God had intended for us from the beginning.

Summary: The Ellulian "Cultural Mandate"

Is there then a universal cultural mandate? We have already glimpsed that desacralization renders created goods as "things" for to use. However, lest we misunderstand him here, Ellul outlines a Noachide rather than an Adamic dominion for all flesh, a limited mandate still in force today. The Flood narrative is on his reading concerned with the second conquest of the chaos unleashed by the disorder of powers. The covenant or promise introduces not just hope but concrete limits. This covenant is thus as much about limit as promise.

Michael Northcott, who engages Ellul at points in his earlier writings, argues that Christians need to recover Noah's dominion in the face of an ecological crisis, for Noah is the model "climate steward" for our day.[102] Granted, Christians may reclaim their dominion through Christ, but this dominion reveals, "like the ark of Noah, a creator who works in, not against our limits . . . a creator who, as the one who calls forth being from nothing, gives without dominating."[103] Northcott thus interrogates influential movements within global Christianity which take the

100. *Théologie et Technique*, 153.

101. See Milbank's use of Augustine in Milbank, *Theology and Social Theory*.

102. Northcott, *Moral Climate*, 71–80. He contrasts Noah with the command and control approach of Joseph.

103. Northcott, *Moral Climate*, 79.

story of Noah as an assurance that human dominion cannot fatally harm creation, and take redemption in Christ as a blank check for exploiting natural resources in the name of national economic progress. "Conservative Christians, particularly in North America, are misled by the claim that humanity recovers its rightful dominion after the coming of Christ, and cannot imagine that the planet could be in danger of running out of control, as the global warming scenario suggests."[104]

Such Christians especially need to recover the note of warning inherent in the story of Noah, and turn away from "theological and technological hubris," being willing to "change direction in response to the clear signs of impending danger."[105] In a similar vein, but addressing an essentially agnostic interlocutor, Ellul holds together both the threat and the promise in the account of Noah. God will not let creation return utterly to chaos, and yet there is a call to faith and acceptance of revealed limits that he sees it as his responsibility to put across. Indeed, this is what motivates his own writing:

> I'm not saying: "Convert to save nature or, if you want, to save creation." Not at all. I am saying . . . "To radically change lifestyle, it takes a very deep motivation. I know of no deeper motivation than faith in God . . . who is only described as being love. . . . This God cannot bear that this creation should be brought back to nothing. . . . Faith in this God must therefore lead us to change our technological behavior as we accept a whole set of limits." This is what I have to say.[106]

The need for faith is crucial therefore. Whereas the Noachide covenant sets a pattern for all humanity, the commands of Torah in the Siniatic covenant embed detailed limits and permissions, in one particular community of faith, Israel, which thereby offers a model of human freedom and responsibility which still pertain after the coming of Christ.[107] The summary tenth commandment against "covetousness-power" is worked out in a series of limits determining which means or methods are acceptable. Ellul cites limits proscribing the mixing of different kinds of substances; limits regulating the killing of animals; the limits on the use of trees for construction of weapons;

104. Northcott, *Moral Climate*, 79. He is concerned here that the Noah account could be misused to imply that the earth will not again come under such judgment (77–79).

105. Northcott, *Moral Climate*, 79.

106. *Théologie et Technique*, 215. This whole section in *Théologie* (210–15) is a re-publication of an earlier article, "Le rapport de l'homme à la création dans la Bible," first published in French in 1974. In the intervening period it was published in English translation in Mitcham and Grote, *Theology and Technology*.

107. *Théologie et Technique*, 204–214.

and paradigmatically, limits on work established in the Sabbath and limits on exploitation of the land, the accumulation of wealth and the alienation of workers established in the Jubilee. Our dominion is thus set within a set of limits, without which contemporary appeals to "stewardship" will simply be captive to covetousness-power, Ellul claims.[108] We have already noted that the commandment which Ellul highlights as most prophetic for our times is the Sabbath, and it is to this that we now turn.

Created for the Eternal Sabbath

Sabbath is a creation command, related to an original creation ordering.[109] The direct relationship between Sabbath and work in the Bible is a reminder that our work is not a work of self-salvation, but must be placed within the framework of gratitude for what God provides. Indeed, it is in being limited by the Sabbath command that work finds legitimacy. "It is with the creation of the Sabbath that it is said that it is after all legitimate to work—nowhere else. It is by setting the limit to work that it is stated that it is even good for the human being to work."[110]

Quite simply, in Ellul's words, what we say about work applies to Technique.[111] Therefore, Sabbath is at one and the same time the "suppression" and "validation" of Technique.[112] The fuller implications of Sabbath are worked out in the Jubilee legislation. Indeed, Leviticus 25 suggests that freedom from work/Technique is to be enjoyed not just by humanity but also by the earth, allowing it thus to express God's glory. Indeed, it is because this creation ordering is lost that the Sabbath and Jubilee Year serve a special, indeed evangelistic purpose in a fallen world.[113]

It is within the wider framework that we now return to the key text of Genesis 2:15, which mandates that humanity "till and keep" the garden. Although this verse is commonly interpreted in mainstream theology as mandating tool-making, and by extension technology, Ellul dissents here

108. *Théologie et Technique*, 210. For an account of OT law and stewardship, see Wright, *God's People in God's Land*.

109. *Théologie et Technique*, 206.

110. *Théologie et Technique*, 209. Compare Brock's account of Luther's account of Sabbath (Brock, *Technological Age*, 296–97).

111. *Théologie et Technique*, 209.

112. *Théologie et Technique*, 207, 209.

113. *Théologie et Technique*, 212. Volf comments that "the Jubilee presupposes the normative ideal that all individuals . . . should take care of their needs by working with their own resources, and that they should control production themselves rather than being dominated by others" (*Work in the Spirit*, 173).

from the modern tradition. He bases his argument upon his interpretation of the key Hebrew word *avodah* (Gen 2:15): "We cannot, therefore, trace to a text like this the fact of necessity, the law of work. . . . The Hebrew will help us here, for the word used is the word *avodah*, which means at the same time both work and worship. . . . In other words, [this activity] serves no purpose, but I do it simply because God said so."[114]

In a similar vein in *Théologie*, Ellul sees the charge "to till and to guard" as a work of free worship and an act of play. All is abundantly given; the earth produces of itself; nothing needs improvement. "The human being works in this creation without completing it, without causing it to flourish, without bringing forth the new, living only within this perfection itself. Complete, the human being has nothing to invent . . . nothing to start, nothing to gain, nothing to develop: there's no progress in the sense of improvement but yes, there's clearly progress in the sense of movement, in the humblest sense of the term."[115]

There were no weeds to root out, no threats to guard against, no productivity to seek, no utility to serve. The role of steward or guardian was hence a free, spiritual dominion granted by God. "It is not by a technique that the human being cultivates, keeps, dominates, it is by the word alone, in accordance with God's creation, not by technological means but by his word. . . . The word is the expression of spiritual superiority, of the direction that leaves the other intact and free even in its decision (which the Technique never does)."[116]

Just as God does not labor by the hand or the tool, so humanity was not to labor, Ellul claims. Moreover, as he argues, in the Creator's intention, human dominion was not meant to coerce creation but to direct its worship, and to lead it to glorify God. And here, drawing upon the entire biblical narrative, in a move we are by now familiar with, Ellul draws a significant parallel between this original vision and the vision of the tribute and glory of the nations in the closing chapters of Revelation. These chapters do not limit worship to endless prayer and praise, but re-present worship as works gathered into the New Jerusalem.[117]

It is resurrection which ties the knot, so to speak, between the creational Sabbath and the eschatological Sabbath. In *Ce que je crois*, drawing on the account of Sabbath in Hebrews 4, Ellul argues that the Sabbath announces the reconciliation which God prepared from the beginning and achieved for all

114. *Genèse*, 118.
115. *Théologie et Technique*, 147.
116. *Théologie et Technique*, 153.
117. *Genèse*, 118–19.

time through the resurrection of Jesus. Sabbath is a promise of rest made to all creation but to be anticipated through faith in the resurrection. Sabbath and the LORD's Day, Sunday, therefore belong together:

> We need to live the Sabbath in its fullness of meaning. For I believe that the Sabbath is not annulled by the resurrection. The two days are essential to each other: the ending of work and the beginning of life. But to stay with the Sabbath, we must live it by finding our own forms of life, provided we keep its threefold symbolic meaning: first, it tells us that the condemnation represented by the constraint of work is lifted for one day, until it is lifted for all eternity. We are no longer condemned. Secondly, it is the promise that we will enter the rest of God, when at the end of time and when the LORD decides, the story ends. But at the heart of our history is this sign: rest is for us and awaits us. Thirdly, it is the sign of the reconciliation promised and accomplished in Jesus Christ.[118]

This promise of reconciliation is what we celebrate in Sabbath and on the LORD's Day, in the eyes of a world which does not yet believe it. The Sabbath, as the continuing seventh day, is for Ellul not only a creational order but an eschatological order also. It represents thus an essential continuity between God's original ordering of the creation, inaccessible to us, and the world after the rupture. On his account, Genesis 1 and 2 present the human vocation not in terms of a call to develop or improve creation, but to live within its perfection, freely. We cannot reclaim this way of life in history through our own efforts but this is the kind of life that we anticipate in keeping the Sabbath. But Sabbath is above all for Ellul God's initiative, signifying the blessing and reconciling action of God over all creation, even over the works of progress which we strive for after the fall. The Creator will judge, sift and reconcile the works we do in the course of history to his ultimate purpose.

The Apocalypse of Creation: Creation in Christ

We have glimpsed above in *Ce que je crois* a christological account of creation, which is not a feature of *Genèse,* since it is a work in which Ellul strives to keep within the bounds of the Hebrew text. However, Jesus Christ is axiomatic to Ellul's theology of creation, for it is only in the light of the New Testament's interpretation of Genesis that we find a fully Christian doctrine of creation, as key Ellul texts make clear. *Subversion* states baldly

118. *Ce que je crois,* 219.

that Genesis 1 and 2 play a more central role in primitive Christianity than in Jewish thought.[119] And *Ethique* and *Parole* contain sustained treatments of apocalyptic texts about creation from within the Pauline corpus, albeit in unsystematic fashion.

Ellul dwells a number of times in *Ethique* and *Parole* upon perhaps the key text for him, Colossians 1:15–16, in which the Apostle establishes the relationship between Christ and creation. It is only after his vision of the resurrected Jesus that the Apostle can see the invisible person of Christ at the head of creation, and not the impersonal but visibly enacted principle of the law. Colossians 1:15–16 affirms that all things *were* created "in," "through" and "for" Christ, as the firstborn of creation.[120] "Once again it's only *afterwards* that Paul can say: 'He *was* God present in our midst; Jesus *was* the eternal Christ,' 'the glory of Christ who is the image of God,' or 'as the firstborn of creation, all things were created in him,' etc. He is 'the image of the invisible God.' But these things are said precisely *when he is no longer seen!*"[121]

The Resurrection enables us to say that nothing in all creation is more elemental or powerful than Christ.[122] However, the invisibility of Christ now, except to the eye of faith, is crucial. The Ascension suggests that in the present time we do not seek an understanding of God's ordering of the world by looking back to Genesis or looking at the world around us, which everywhere reveals Cain's order, as Ellul puts it. Instead, we look up, where Christ is set at the right hand of God, and the present time marks for Ellul a contrast between "a religion of sight," relying on evidence, and a proclamation of the Word, which leads to understanding and obedience.[123]

What Is a Theology of Creation?

We began by asking whether Ellul has a theology of creation. We begin our conclusion by noting that it depends what is meant by a "theology of creation." As Douglas Harink notes, "Usually that [a "theology of creation"] means a

119. *Subversion*, 73.

120. As Harink rightly states, "Paul is arguing that God's relationship to all creation is established through Jesus Christ and not through Torah" (*Paul among the Postliberals*, 92). Ellul is not particularly interested to situate this proclamation within its historical context. However, he does offer a fascinating discussion of the Pauline term *stoicheia* (Col 2:20). He interprets "the system" in the modern world to mean the working of "impersonal structures" and "abstract organization" in human society (*Ethique*, 177–78).

121. *Parole*, 94.

122. For example, Rom 8:37–38; Eph 1:18–23.

123. *Parole*, 94.

theological account of what can and cannot be said about humanity before the fall into sin and redemption through Christ and 'in general' apart from the appearance of Jesus Christ. Typically, it involves paying a great deal of attention to Genesis 1–2 and on that basis developing statements about the status, structures, relationships and orders of creation and creatures in relation to God and to one another."[124] As Harink continues, in such an approach, "typical in much Christian theology," the person and work of Jesus Christ receive subsequent treatment, detailing how we are redeemed from the fall.

We have found that on closer examination, Ellul did indeed have rather a lot to say about Genesis 1 and 2. However, what Ellul characteristically offers is an apocalyptic and christological vision of the destiny of creation. This christological emphasis bears the influence of Barth.[125] Following Barth, Ellul surmises, good theology should fund a recovery of good anthropology, for the God who will become incarnate creates humans in his image.[126] As we have seen, Ellul's theology of creation is not *systematically* christological, in obvious contrast to Barth's account of the interior and exterior bases of the covenant. Yet Ellul shares Barth's basic denial of natural theology in severing any legitimating connection between human culture as we know it and an original cultural mandate.

For Ellul, Genesis 3 and 4 intervene, and therefore Ellul's contribution, though fine-grained, is not the kind theology of creation some are looking for. To critics, Ellul's apocalyptic account appears sectarian. However, as we have seen, Ellul argues for a universal recapitulation of all things, not a return to Eden for a blessed few. Moreover, crucially, Ellul does not seek to isolate his account from insights from beyond the Bible. What he offers, perhaps surprisingly to his critics, is an interdisciplinary biblical theology of creation: a dialogue between scripture and a broad range of historical and sociological insights about the origins of human culture.

124. Harink, *Paul among the Postliberals*, 97.

125. Ellul argues from John 1 and Colossians 1, citing Barth, that "the incarnation is an integral part of God's creative work from the beginning." The incarnation moreover is the meaning of the word which establishes the relationality of which we have been speaking in this chapter. "The human Jesus in God is the expression of God's turning towards humanity as it is being created" (*On Freedom, Love, and Power*, 217).

126. Barth scholar Colin Brown aptly summarizes the significance of this: "Underlying this whole train of thought is the theological axiom that all God's dealings with men are effected in and through the person of Jesus Christ. Hence creation and the doctrine of God are just as much the concern of Christology as reconciliation and redemption. Protestant theology goes wrong, [Barth] argues, when it teaches that the Incarnation was an ad hoc counter-measure necessitated by sin" ("Karl Barth's Doctrine of the Creation," 100). So Ellul writes: "The creation of Adam in the image of God was an echo of Jesus who was that image in God" (*On Freedom, Love, and Power*, 216).

As I noted in my opening two chapters, it is this interrelationship between the canonical account of the world (the divine story) and dominant cultural accounts (human stories) that Ellul sets out to explore in what I have called his sociological-theological works. This attempt is far from theoretical; it is polemical and indeed, to put it bluntly, as *Présence* does, evangelistic. Ellul explores the workings of covetousness-power in human culture, as unveiled by the Bible but explored in social analysis, not in order to berate but in order to save. Moreover, he is not blindly opposing the theological tradition, but actually seeking engagement.

In this respect, it will be suggestive to note interesting parallels between Ellul and the work of the Roman Catholic theologian and Girardian, James Alison. Alison sets out to take Catholic theology beyond naive applications of the Thomist principle of analogy. Under the evident influence of Girard's theory of mimetic desire, Alison refuses to erase Cain in his account of culture, but rather sees the narrative of Cain and Abel as the Bible's account of the founding narrative of all civilizations. Following Girard, he reads it as the Bible's demythologization of the idea that coercion and violence are necessary for the sake of order and progress.[127] All human culture is founded on this murderous lie, this false order of things. What the "eschatological imagination" of the New Testament shows is a God "pruned of violence," on the side of Abel, the remarkable account of a God who offers himself in sacrifice in our place, to end our sacrificial systems.[128]

Working from the insight that the Bible is a fundamentally "demythologizing" and "desacralizing" text, Alison symphonizes his theology in a way that strikes one Ellulian note after another, especially in terms of creation.[129] Arguing that "the human perception of God as Creator is something which, itself, has a history and is by no means a simple concept," he notes that Genesis records a contrast to the theologies of creation of the Ancient Near East, which tied the order of the world to the god(s).[130] Even then, Jesus does not leave the Jewish doctrine of creation where he found it but filters it through the prism of his "eschatological imagination."

127. Alison, *Living in the End Times*, 23.

128. For his part, Alison argues that Jesus subverts the violent dualisms of the "apocalyptic imagination," and hence he prefers the term "eschatological."

129. The claim here is evidently not that Ellul exerts some influence on Alison, or even that Girard is a common denominator. It is rather than the NT's account of creation in Christ is accessible to two theologians from contrasting and indeed apparently opposing traditions. Moreover, the perhaps surprising consonance between them may suggest that Ellul is worthy of a hearing in circles where he is not usually heard.

130. Alison, *Living in the End Times*, 52.

Jesus' person and work is in this sense pictured as completing the work of creation. The New Testament, Alison says, redefines our understanding of the creation from a past act to a reality present in Jesus. Above all, it is the resurrection which "*separates* God from the ordering of the world," for until the resurrection, creation was incomplete.[131] However, Alison states, Jesus himself witnesses to this self-understanding, perhaps most clearly in his actions and teachings concerning the Sabbath, especially as interpreted by John.

Alison focuses sharply on John 5:17, arguing boldly, and beyond Ellul, that "Jesus is formally denying that God is resting on the Sabbath, a solemn contradiction of Genesis."[132] On this account, Sabbath was not intended to be a statement about God's withdrawal, nor first and foremost a commandment for humanity, but rather "a symbol of creation yet to be completed and still needing its fullness. So Jesus also works . . . brings creation to its proper fulfillment, making people whole on the Sabbath."[133]

Hence, Alison states, John's Jesus speaks the final word *tetelestai* on the cross, which for Alison signifies "it has been brought to fulfilment." The resurrection happens on the first day of the week, as a sign that creation has been completed by the overcoming of death and separation.[134] Creation begins fully, in a new way, in and through Jesus, on the first day of the new week. Any truly catholic and apostolic theology of creation must therefore be a theology of creation in Christ, which is the meaning of texts such as Colossians 1:15–16, which we considered above. However, this does not amount to what Alison caricatures as "the somewhat mythic-sounding notion that Jesus was involved in creation," read back into or tacked on to a flat reading of Genesis 1.[135]

What this means is that the Creator was working through Jesus to reveal what creation truly aims for, a life beyond death and separation—and Jesus was "in on it from the beginning," as Alison characteristically states.[136] Moving beyond a "creation-fall-redemption" ordering, we now see that: "The redemption reveals creation by opening up its fulfillment in heaven and it reveals at the same time the fall as that which we are in the process of leaving behind."[137]

131. Alison, *Living in the End Times*, 52.

132. Alison, *Living in the End Times*, 72.

133. Alison, *Living in the End Times*, 72–73.

134. Alison, *Living in the End Times*, 74.

135. Alison, *Living in the End Times*, 55.

136. Alison, *Living in the End Times*, 55–56.

137. Alison, *Living in the End Times*, 56.

Conclusion

This brief engagement with Alison is intended to confirm that engaging with Ellul is rewarding and reinvigorating to the degree that it shows that reading Ellul today is far from an academic exercise. In a world where chaos threatens, as in Ellul so in Alison do we see that only by faith in a God who is "wholly other" to the world's progress can we find a hope that another, better world is possible. We are invited not to hope in ourselves, and in our powers, but to hope in a Creator who raises the dead.[138] Creation has come to fulfilment in the Apocalypse of Jesus Christ *Now*, within history, but we still await Apocalypse *Then*. How then shall we live in the light of this revelation? What place now for human power and human action?

138. Alison, *Living in the End Times*, 170.

6

Hearing the Word

Confronting Technology, Confronting Ellul

IN THE PREVIOUS FOUR chapters, I have offered a broadly sympathetic exposition of Ellul's apocalyptic theology through engagement with key texts, namely *Sans feu; Apocalypse; Si Tu es le Fils de Dieu;* and *Genèse.* I have attempted to argue that all of Ellul's theological texts carry, as Rognon states, an implicit "internal dialectic" between theology and sociology. In other words, Ellul's theology carries on a dialogue, though often not much more than snatched conversations, with his sociological writings on Technique. However, as I stated at the outset, this dialogue between theology and sociology becomes explicit in what Rognon calls "exceptional texts," which have been interwoven into this discussion, *Présence, Nouveaux Possédés, Parole* and *Changer.*

The recent appearance of a posthumously published text under the telling rubric, *Théologie et Technique,* reveals Ellul's hand, delineating Ellul's theological confrontation with Technique. This closing chapter will draw together the threads of my argument so far, engaging at some length with *Théologie* for the first time in English-language scholarship. There are of course other places one could look for theological ethics in Ellul's corpus: not least his methodological text *Le Vouloir et le Faire,* and his three-volume work, *Ethique de la Liberté.* The claim made here is that *Théologie* marks a major landmark in understanding Ellul for two particular reasons.

Firstly, as the title bears witness, unlike the other texts we have considered, which range widely, it is essentially devoted to a theological account of Technique.[1] Secondly, what Ellul does here, in a more systematic way than anywhere else, is bring his work on the powers, the city and work into direct relation with contemporary questions around technology. This is indeed what, perhaps uniquely, a text such as *Théologie* offers—a series of what we might now call interdisciplinary conversations. In short, here Ellul pays up,

---

1. Ellul bluntly states that he is concerned here with "the theological status of technique" (*Théologie et Technique,* 96).

and offers some ethical currency impressed with his theology. However, before we proceed, I need to offer a couple of caveats. Although *Théologie* represents a major new resource, my concern here is not to expound it, but rather to present it as an effective summation of Ellul's theological confrontation with technology. Moreover, in a perhaps more discriminating vein, I will now attempt to interrogate Ellul's ethics by subjecting them to critiques from a variety of sources, in order to construct the foundations of a Christian ethics in a technological age through, and beyond, Ellul.[2]

Discerning the Spirits

In keeping with his theological trajectory, in three interrelated chapters, Ellul explores the resources the Christian ethicist brings to confronting technology.[3] Technique, he claims, is not rooted in a creation order, nor does it ensure our progress towards the final eschaton. It is strictly a phenomenon of human history, unmasked by the myth of Cain, but open nonetheless to God's final recapitulation of all human works. What is required for the Christian ethical task therefore is to situate technology where it belongs, "between two poles . . . Cain and the Apocalypse":

> Technique does not affect the origin or the final end [of creation]. . . . It is as a result circumscribed within human history. . . . And in the closure that it can cause, Technique is incapable of offering a way out of this closure. . . . The only way out of the shutdown of history is God's assumption of human works, as all things are recapitulated in Christ[4]

Three clear implications emerge. Firstly, Ellul argues that a Christian "ethical orientation" towards Technique must ultimately offer a hope for all history. Secondly, however, because the technological system is so pervasive that it has colonized the human person, meaningful action begins with persons, before structures: in his words, a social ethic only emerges from an individual ethic. Thirdly, Christian ethics is an arena of battle: in the terms we considered above, it is concerned with the powers which operate in human

---

2. The main dialogue partners here will be Roman Catholic (*Caritas in Veritate*), Reformed (Miroslav Volf, Jeremy Kidwell, Marva Dawn, and Brian Brock), and Anglican (Michael Northcott and Oliver O'Donovan).

3. "Technique et Eschatologie" (chapter 4), "La Médiation Ethique" (chapter 5), and "Les Prolongements Ethiques" (chapter 6).

4. *Théologie et Technique*, 258.

history. It is therefore not a leisured, privatized and academic activity, but a fight for all our futures.[5]

In turning then towards Technique, Ellul argues that the Christian ethical task is the discernment of spirits, a task he sees outlined in the New Testament in 1 John 4.[6] "What is the Spirit animating Technique . . . if we want to know the truth about a human phenomenon, we must proceed with the discernment of spirits . . . this discernment is not an abstract matter. It means engaging in a practice, creating a form of behaviour."[7]

This reading is confirmed by his designation of the two spirits he wishes to confront as "the spirt of power" and "the spirit of lies."[8] The former appears to be what 1 John 4:3 refers to as the "spirit of the antichrist," whereas the latter is what 1 John 4:6 calls the "spirit of error." The anti-Christian spirit of power must be confronted by a Christ-like non-power and the spirit of lies must be confronted by iconoclasm.[9] As early as *Présence*, Ellul had argued that Technique is that which turns us away from the Incarnation. However, this judgment is not intended to condemn technology; rather, he is offering a diagnosis corroborated through the dialogue with sociology and theology, a negative diagnosis with a positive intention:

> Thus Technique is the manifestation of the spirit of power and the spirit of lies. It is their most complete form; it is entirely inspired by these spirits. I do not formulate this as a judgment against Technique: it is simply a matter of getting to its heart. I arrive here by bringing together a biblical reading, that is to say a theological reading, with a sociological reading.[10]

What Ellul seeking is a breakthrough into human history by the working of apocalyptic hope; this is the fundamental purpose of the prophetic

5. This is an effective summary of *Théologie et Technique*, 264–72. In *Ethique* he makes the same basic claims. See Goddard's detailed discussion of Ellul's individual ethic and social ethic (*Living the Word*, 101–114).

6. "Beloved, do not believe every spirit, but test the spirits to see whether they are from God; for many false prophets have gone out into the world. By this you know the Spirit of God: every spirit that confesses that Jesus Christ has come in the flesh is from God, and every spirit that does not confess Jesus is not from God" (1 John 4:1–3a).

7. *Théologie et Technique*, 272.

8. *Théologie et Technique*, 272–73.

9. Ellul speaks first of the ethics of rupture but I will refer to iconoclasm, which is what he states is its outworking (*Théologie et Technique*, 330), and the term "desacralization" is what this amounts to (*Théologie et Technique*, 333). We see again that here "rupture" can have the positive sense of an apocalyptic "breaking-in."

10. *Théologie et Technique*, 297.

word.[11] I will follow this tripartite framework in three short explorations of the Spirit of Power, the Spirit of Lies and the Ethics of Hope, before proceeding to a closing discursus on the Word and the Number.

The Spirit of Power and the Ethics of Non-power

The first spirit Ellul discerns in Technique is the "spirit of power." He has in mind the dominance of means over ends, indeed the replacement of ends by means, by the fact of power itself: "The Means is by itself both meaning and end."[12] The expressions Ellul explores in *Théologie* will come as no surprise to his seasoned readers: "This trinity of efficiency, dominion and utilisation fully encompasses the spirit of power."[13]

In practice, unbridled efficiency translates into a constant breaking of limits, domination requires a constant growth—of quantity, consumption, speed and distance—and utilization seeks constantly to exploit and profit from every available resource.[14] This focus on the means is nothing less than a concern for literally endless power, for powerful means inevitably become ends in themselves. Ellul is here suspicious of attempts to reform the technological system, by offering so-called "technologies douces," what we might now call sustainable technologies.[15] Rather, he wishes to argue for a "spiritual subversion," a turning upside down of the world's judgments about the means and the end.

The language of ends and means is of great importance to Ellul's understanding of Technique. In chapter 1, we noted Ellul's intellectual debt to both Marx and Kierkegaard in this respect. We have seen that in his theology of creation, Ellul argues that all human work was indeed originally intended to be a free and playful activity in which means and ends were united. One might go further to argue that here Ellul (re) theologizes sociological insights he gains from Marx, employing Marx's concern for freedom and self-directedness in work and reading it back into Genesis 1–2. Moreover, just as Marx reads the Bible as pointing to the fallen reality of alienated, industrial labor, as opposed to the original

---

11. *Théologie et Technique*, 351.

12. *Théologie et Technique*, 275. Marva Dawn notes that the Greek word translated "schemes" in Ephesians 6:11 is in fact *methodia* (Dawn et al., *Unnecessary Pastor*, 95)!

13. *Théologie et Technique*, 277. In modern French, "efficacité," effectiveness, judged against varying criteria, is often contrasted with "efficience," which implies a basically mathematical calculation of cost-effectiveness.

14. *Théologie et Technique*, 280–82.

15. *Théologie et Technique*, 281.

vision of Genesis 1, so Ellul severs Technique from creation.[16] Marx also saw the Bible's account of Cain as marking it out as essentially hostile to technology,[17] a position Ellul clearly espouses.

The essential difference between Ellul and Marx is on the question of teleology. Whereas Marx believed that technology could now become a means to the end of humankind's redemption, making the world a workers' paradise within the time of history, Ellul follows Kierkegaard in insisting that the means and the end are indivisible: Technique cannot save us. Citing Kierkegaard in *Les Combats de la liberté*, citing Kierkegaard *verbatim* in his own argument, Ellul notes: "The judgment on end and means is exactly the opposite in the world and in faith. In the temporal sense, the end is more important than the means. 'For eternity, the relation between the means and the end is in fact reversed.' . . . We human beings are absolutely responsible for the means we employ."[18]

For Ellul, as we see most clearly in *Présence*, it is only in Christ that ends and means are reunited.[19] For Christians, in Ellul's terms, the end is already given: the Eternal Word has become flesh. We propose no other end than Christ, and no other means to that end but the way of Christ. What this means in ethical practice is that Christians are to be God's only means, his flesh and blood instruments.

In *Théologie*, he reprises this argument, proposing that Christian ethics starts from the imitation of Christ in his rejection of powerful means. "If there is an imitation of Jesus we must accept, it is strictly here [non-power] that we find it."[20] Whereas many scholars take Jesus' non-violent confrontation with the Roman Imperium as a model for political theology, Ellul's perhaps novel proposal in *Théologie* is that Christian ethics must take Jesus' example seriously with regard to technological power. Today it is precisely *the rejection of powerful means* which constitutes the imitation of Christ for the Christian disciple.[21]

---

16. Michael Northcott claims that the influence of Marx led to such a "Protestant misreading" of Genesis, seeing labor as "brutish and demeaning" (*Moral Climate*, 129).

17. Volf, *Work in the Spirit*, 181.

18. Ellul citing Kierkegaard, *Upbuilding Discourses in Various Spirits*, in Rognon, *Pensée*, 196.

19. *Présence* in *Défi*, chapter 3.

20. *Théologie et Technique*, 315.

21. Greenman et al., *Understanding Jacques Ellul*, 72. With a hint of agreement, see Elaine Graham's "Embodying Technology, Becoming Our Tools: Discussing the Post/human," in Baxter, *Wounds That Heal*, 125–48. "Is it really the case that to be made in the image of God involves the emulation of such qualities of omnipotence, immortality and invulnerability?" (139).

Ellul thus takes issue with all so-called Christian ethics which assume that technology represents eschatological progress, or a further revelation. Ellul argues that such ethics, which claim that technological means can now best achieve purportedly Christian ends such as maximizing equality, liberating workers, ending suffering or furthering community, tend to displace Christ's work and example: "We do not have to ask ourselves about the end. . . . The end is already given, already present in the kingdom. . . . The only question is: how do we live in the light of this end given us by grace? It is therefore a question of the means."[22]

The modern multiplication of powerful technologies therefore presents Christians with an arena of great temptation to deny the Incarnation by unthinkingly using these new means. And this is why Ellul has drawn upon 1 John: for the first test proposed by the writer is discerning the spirit of antichrist who denies that "Jesus Christ has come in the flesh" (1 John 4:2–3).

Despite the potential for a helpful corrective here, there are some troubling aspects to Ellul's advocacy of non-power, resting as it does on an essentially suspicious and anarchistic reading of power, political and technological. Yet, to nuance his view, we note that non-power is not a mere powerlessness, a justification of being on the wrong end of history. It assumes the act of discerning what kinds of power one should employ, and what kinds one should eschew. Ellul here offers two brief examples. Firstly, non-power must imply total non-violence, arguing moreover that the very concept of non-violence needs to be governed by non-power, lest it become merely the first weapon used in a war, discarded if it proves ineffective.[23] Secondly, non-power is definitely not quietism or passivity, but rather a systematic pursuit.[24] It is the active choice to abandon power in the guise of dominion, and even in the guise of efficiency: "Non-power is refusing to what one is able to do. . . . Choosing not to exercise dominion or efficiency; choosing not to go all out for success. It is to lay down one's power."[25]

What Ellul establishes in his account of the temptations in various texts, briefly recapitulated in *Théologie*, is that Jesus entrusts himself entirely to the

22. *Théologie et Technique*, 321. By way of example, a recent work of Christian ethics falls foul of Ellul's critique. Celia Deane-Drummond argues that the technological revolution must be understood "as a revelation" of a kind, fulfilling the Christian ethic of the "precedence of love over law" (Deane-Drummond, *Re-ordering Nature*, 318).

23. *Théologie et Technique*, 319. Although Ellul does envisage the possibility that Christians may be involved in sabotaging the technological system, he rules out the kind of violence that the Unabomber employed. Goddard outlines Ellul's approach to violence in *Living the Word*, 171–79.

24. *Théologie et Technique*, 317.

25. *Théologie et Technique*, 315

will and power of his Father, over and against the spirit of power. Jesus is powerful, but not as the world knows it. Non-power means imitating Jesus in his absolute insistence on using the right means, in his total renunciation to the Almighty God who alone could give him success. "There is no middle way between power, the spirit of power, the will to power, actualized today exclusively by Technique, and the choice of non-power which is how we imitate Jesus' faithfulness, his faithfulness to his Father almighty!"[26]

For Ellul, only when our power is voluntarily laid down do we leave space for God's power. Therefore, Christian ethics must not be firstly concerned with effectiveness in this age, but with faithfulness. By refusing to respond to the powers on their own terms, Christ reveals the secret of history, which is that God's power is made perfect in human weakness. Therefore, as Fasching rightly notes, Ellul does not decry effectiveness, but points rather to God's power, his alternative efficacy, working through his frail and imperfect human means.[27] As God's servants, we are responsible for the means we employ, not their final result, for it is not our task to manufacture the end.[28]

However, in the final analysis, though we accept the danger of christening technologies too quickly, Ellulian non-power lacks practical outworking. If we ask, what means we are to employ, here as in *Vouloir*, Ellul points quite simply to "faith, hope, and love."[29] Our contemporary task is to embody these means. The ethic of non-power can thus best be summed up as a "critical lifestyle."[30] Articulating what "non-power" might look like in a technological society, Ellul argues that we imitate Jesus by modeling in the place of growth, efficiency, domination and maximization, a lifestyle of "conviviality, service, transparency, friendship, and generosity."[31]

However, and this marks an interesting contribution, Ellul discerns the spirit of power not only in blatant attempts to control the future through the technological imperative, but even in radical movements which tend to reject technology outright. Ellul's sociological writings attract welcome interest from movements for "sustainability" and "de-growth,"[32] and some have noted the similarity of many of Ellul's concrete ethical proposals in his

26. *Théologie et Technique*, 328.

27. Fasching, *Thought of Jacques Ellul*, 98.

28. *Théologie et Technique*, 322.

29. *Théologie et Technique*, 322.

30. *Théologie et Technique*, 322.

31. *Théologie et Technique*, 319.

32. See, for example, the work of "Ellulian" economist Serge Latouche on "frugal abundance" (Chastenet, *Être Ellulien aux XXIe Siècle*, 321–44). A presentation of a similar model is offered in Jackson, *Prosperity without Growth*.

sociological texts to the now popular "precautionary principle."[33] Indeed, Ellul himself was open to working jointly on initiatives with those who did not share his theological convictions. However, Ellul detects a disguised form of power, as well as a distorted view of apocalypse, in the scaremongering of technophobes: "Provoking fear and panic, faced with the extent of the threats, but isn't this still a spirit of power?"[34] Indeed, elsewhere he goes as far as to state that such responses share a common fear of loss and are thus the perverse forms of the "spirit of power" that technological societies have created. In this respect, Ellul notes that the radical novelty of our age is to have invented an endemic anxiety and sense of scarcity, a form of testing the incarnate Son did not know.[35]

To conclude, Ellul's rejection of technological power lies squarely within the tradition O'Donovan refers to as the modern "practice of suspicion."[36] I now intend to interrogate Ellul's account of power, especially in its critical application in *Théologie* to technological power. I will review briefly two types of evidence: firstly, his interpretation of human power and work in Genesis 1 and 2 and secondly, his neglect of texts which speak of divine-human co-working in material form, paradigmatically, the account of the construction of the Tabernacle/Temple.

Genesis and the Material World

To Till and to Keep

Ellul's interpretation of Genesis 2 is in the final analysis unwarranted. The Ellulian logic of God's transcendence and our difference-in-relation might suggest that in describing God's creative power as word-work, Genesis means to *relativize* all human work in comparison with *creatio ex nihilo*.

---

33. As early as *Technique*, but most clearly in *Bluff*, chapter 2. See Porquet, *Jacques Ellul*, chapter 5.

34. *Théologie et Technique*, 283. See Northcott, *Moral Climate*, 279, commenting on some of James Lovelock's work, on cinematic portrayals of climate apocalypse and the politics of fear.

35. "He [Jesus] did not suffer from the disease that afflicts us today, one of the most widespread in developed nations: the fear of tomorrow, the fear of 'not having enough' (not enough money, not enough nature, not enough work). In a word, anxiety, often purely psychological" (*Si* in *Défi*, 980). For a similar analysis of the "genealogy of late capitalist desire," see Wannenwetsch's analysis of insatiable desire and the fear of loss in Barton, *Idolatry*. He comments that a Christian critique of capitalism should increasingly focus on its "destructive power among the system's winners" (327).

36. O'Donovan, *Desire of the Nations*, chapter 1. The late Anglican theologian Stephen Sykes terms it "the rejection of power" in his book, *Power and Christian Theology*.

This is indeed what Blocher argues: "The instrumentality of the word, by replacing that of the hand or the tool, proclaims the absolute liberty of the Creator, the radical difference that distinguishes his 'making' from all the 'making' done by humankind."[37]

In stark contrast, Ellul argues that the naming of the animals (Gen 2:19) defines our dominion as word-work, arguing that the vocation "to till and to keep" the garden (Gen 2:15), is an aspect of this word-work. However, these verbs, though cultic, do suggest labor, placing the use of the hand and the tool within the context of worship. The recent Roman Catholic encyclical of Pope Benedict XVI, *Caritas in veritate*, while noting the ambivalence of technology, argues that Genesis 2:15 mandates technology as an expression of human dominion:

> Technology enables us to exercise dominion over matter, to reduce risks, to save labor, to improve our conditions of life. It touches the heart of the vocation of human labor: in technology, seen as the product of his genius, man recognizes himself and forges his own humanity. . . . For this reason, technology is never merely technology. It reveals man and his aspirations towards development, it expresses the inner tension that impels him gradually to overcome material limitations. *Technology, in this sense, is a response to God's command to till and to keep the land (cf. Gen 2:15) that he has entrusted to humanity, and it must serve to reinforce the covenant between human beings and the environment, a covenant that should mirror God's creative love.*[38]

Corroborating this reading, Ellul's account of the impossibility of working to improve the earth, is surely struck down by the opening verses of the second creation account, Genesis 2:5–7, a text which anticipates 2:15, but which Ellul neglects:

> In the day that the LORD God made the earth and the heavens, when no plant of the field was yet in the earth and no herb of the field had yet sprung up—*for the LORD God had not caused it to rain upon the earth, and there was no one to till the ground;*

37. Blocher, *In the Beginning*, 67. Moreover, Blocher notes the distinctive creation verb *bara*, in contrast to *asa* used of divine making.

38. Benedict XVI, "Caritas in Veritate" 69 (my italics). It makes, moreover, a clear link between technology and human purpose: "The idea of a world without development indicates a lack of trust in man and in God. It is therefore a serious mistake to undervalue human capacity to exercise control over the deviations of development or to overlook the fact that man is constitutionally oriented towards 'being more'" (14). Exploring the different emphases between *Caritas* and the more recent *Laudato Si'* lies beyond my scope here.

but a stream would rise from the earth, and water the whole face of the ground—then the LORD God formed man from the dust of the ground.

These verses imply a covenant between humanity and the land, given for the fruitfulness of the earth.[39] As Miroslav Volf comments: "There is a mutual dependence between God and human beings in the task of the preservation of creation. . . . God the Creator chooses to become 'dependent' on the human helping hand and makes human work a means of accomplishing his work."[40]

Although Volf clearly privileges an "eschatological" account of work over a "protological" account, he claims that every human worker responds to the call to preserve creation, even if unawares and even after the fall, for on his account Genesis 1–2 offers us an enduring pattern. Volf goes on to argue that if we are mistaken about the "protological" framework that scripture sets up, "eschatological" frameworks will be liable to error.[41] In drawing these frameworks together in conclusion, Volf argues that in the light of Genesis 2:5 and 2:15, "work cannot only be a means to life which exists fully in something outside work, but must be considered *an aspect of the purpose of life itself.*"[42] We were created with work to do, and despite the Fall, we must still seek that purpose in our work.

The Image and the Body

As we have seen, Ellul does not deny the goodness of creation. However, at times he does tend to intellectualize and dematerialize the biblical picture. Take for example Ellul's reading of the *Imago Dei* as signifying essentially Word, which is explicated as speech and relationship. The body, for Ellul, is not part of the divine image, for the body, and its functions, implies finitude. The body implies a limit, and death is for Ellul the very condition of being a finite creature. "That human beings have bodies, that is to say we are limited in space, conditioned to certain functions, for example, having to eat, that is finitude. That human beings are placed in nature to work is also a function of our being created."[43]

39. See Wenham, *Genesis*, 59.
40. Volf, *Work in the Spirit*, 99.
41. Volf, *Work in the Spirit*, 95–98.
42. Volf, *Work in the Spirit*, 197.
43. *Ethique*, 48.

Work too is a necessity, implied by our need to eat, by our having a body. These are *ab origine* simply aspects of our creatureliness, our difference-in-relation to God.

In contrast, Volf argues that "we have to maintain that human beings do not have a body; they *are* also a body."[44] And moving far beyond Ellul, Volf looks towards the common presence of the divine Spirit in human beings *and in nature*, as a biblical insight essential to a theology of human power and work. This does not imply that creation has an "inherent sanctity," however. Rather it suggests that the Christian worker needs to be inspired by the Spirit of God in order to develop and perfect the material world according to God's purposes and his promised reconciliation.

Volf's account of the Spirit-filled worker draws, moreover, upon OT accounts of the building of the Tabernacle and Temple, suggesting his "theological basis" of *Work in the Spirit*. For Volf, although these are particular accounts which distinguish ordinary from extraordinary tasks, they exemplify a more general principle:

> We can read these passages from the perspective of the new covenant in which all God's people are gifted and called to various tasks by the Spirit. . . . *All human work* is made possible by the operation of the Spirit of God in the working person; *all work* whose nature and results reflects the values of the new creation is accomplished under the instruction and inspiration of the Spirit.[45]

Volf's use of the Tabernacle/Temple motif is suggestive for a fully material account of human power and work as cooperation with God. However, his main concern quickly turns to how this theological basis can be extended to *all human work*: "Can this theology be applied to the work of non-Christians or is it a theology of work only for a Christian subculture?"[46] This, I contend,

44. Volf, *Work in the Spirit*, 96. The late Evangelical spiritual writer and phenomenologist Dallas Willard, seeking to overturn a traditional Protestant reticence about the body as fallen, argues too that the body is itself part of the image of God: "The human body is part of the *imago Dei*, for it is the vehicle through which we can effectively acquire the limited self-subsistent power we must have to be truly in the image and likeness of God. . . . This explains, in theological terms, why we have a body at all. *That body is our primary area of power, freedom, and—therefore—responsibility*" (Willard, *Spirit of the Disciplines*, 53).

45. Volf, *Work in the Spirit*, 114, citing Exod 35:2–3; 1 Chr 28:1–11; Isa 28:24–29. Paul Stevens observes that Volf makes Bezalel the "patron saint of work" (*Abolition of the Laity*, 122)!

46. Volf, *Work in the Spirit*, 113. It is clear that Volf wishes to drive towards a more inclusive conclusion. "To the extent that non-Christians are open to the prompting of the Spirit, their work, too, is the cooperation with God in anticipation of the

tends to take him away from a distinctive *Christian* account of human work and human power in the Spirit. To pursue a reading of the Tabernacle/Temple texts within a fully canonical framework that considers how Jesus Christ relates to Tabernacle/Temple, we need to look elsewhere.

The Ethics of Power: Rediscovering the Lost Tabernacle?

We have considered at some length in this study Ellul's reading of work and power in Genesis 1 and 2. Ellul dates the text to the Babylonian exile, and reads it within that context, and yet he perhaps neglects to fully explore the intertextual referents here. Following the work of Joseph Blenkinsopp, many recent accounts see in these chapters the genre of the Temple dedication ceremony common in Ancient Near Eastern literature.[47] What this genre suggests is a fundamental affinity between the early chapters of Genesis and the liturgical performance of the text in the post-exilic Israelite Temple.

The account of work in Genesis 1 and 2 should, on this account, be read in dialogue with the rest of the Pentateuch and its instructions for worship in particular. I do not intend to give a detailed account of this new perspective here. The emerging scholarly consensus is well summarized by Jeremy Kidwell:

> In relative contrast to Genesis, the Tabernacle account in Exodus is concerned not exclusively with the work of God, but with the work of God's people. Of course, these two are intimately related, as is suggested by the connections between the Genesis creation account and the Tabernacle account and Temple. There is strong intertextual warrant to suggest that *the Tabernacle account sets a standard by which well-explicated worship construction narratives are morally explicable.* It is important to note that there are references to a variety of different kinds of work and workers across the text of Scripture, but it is my contention in this dissertation that the account of work detailed in the making of the Tabernacle is uniquely paradigmatic. The paradigmatic status of this account is emphasized by the literary resonances between Exodus and Genesis.[48]

eschatological transformation of the world, even though they may not be aware of it" (*Work in the Spirit*, 119). Willard likewise offers an account of our bodily engagement with the material world, and how human beings "mesh the relatively little power resident in their own bodies with the power inherent in the Rule of God" (*Spirit of the Disciplines*, 54).

47. Blenkinsopp, *Prophecy and Canon*.

48. Kidwell, 25. Kidwell's recent book, *A Theology of Craft*, is an expansion of his

Taking issue with Volf's assertion that "the explicit biblical statements about work are, for instance, more or less irrelevant to fundamental contemporary questions,"[49] he argues that the divinely mandated building of the Tabernacle in no less than thirteen chapters of Exodus marks a covenant context within which we need to understand free, Spirit-filled work:

> On a symbolic level, the Tabernacle as it is described in Exodus resonates with the construction by YHWH of Eden, a narrative of divine Temple construction. Along these lines, it can be said that the events which follow Israel's deliverance from Egyptian slavery narrate a recapitulation of the creation account in Genesis. The elaborately described construction project presents a re-creation of the people of Israel, marking their first free labor since delivery from Egypt.[50]

The account ends with Moses blessing the people, in a recapitulation of the Sabbath blessing. In contrast to other Ancient Near Eastern accounts, the Israelites were not to work as slaves of the gods; work was not to be slavery. The people of God were called to work as free people working in God's Temple of creation: and in the liturgical cessation from work on the Sabbath, centered on the tabernacle/temple, work is framed *within* the context of worship.

This discovery evidently has significant implications for understanding human work and human power in collaboration with God. Kidwell's thesis finds support in Michael Northcott's account of the OT's concern for "the construction and design of material artifacts" in three paradigmatic moments of building: Noah's ark, the Tabernacle and the Temple, all objects rich in numerological and cosmological significance. The rich symbolism of the Tabernacle/Temple narrative clearly designates it as a microcosm of the universe, a theme corroborated in a number of texts.[51] What this establishes, in short (we shall explore further below) is an analogy between human work and the work of the Master builder in creating the universe. At least two key insights about the exercise of human powers in good work flow from this.[52]

---

doctoral thesis, "Drawn into Worship." Quotations will be drawn from the original thesis.

49. Kidwell, "Drawn into Worship," 8, citing Volf, *Work in the Spirit*, 77

50. Kidwell, "Drawn into Worship," 26 (following Blenkinsopp closely).

51. See, e.g., Exod 26; Wis 9:8: "You have given command to build a temple on your holy mountain, and an altar in the city of your habitation, a copy of the holy tent that you prepared from the beginning." For corroboration in NT, see, e.g., Heb 8:5.

52. Northcott, *Moral Climate*, 205–6, in a section headed, "The Building and Microcosm." Northcott was Kidwell's doctoral supervisor.

Firstly, the covenant setting implies that good work must be done in humble obedience to God. Within the canon, it is clear that the "imperial project" of Solomon's Temple is morally ambiguous, for, as Northcott states, the implication appears to be that "good building, good work, requires persons of moral character to carry it out."[53] Christians should be wary of claiming that humanity simply "recovers its rightful dominion after Christ's coming," without attending to the character implicit in their work.[54]

Secondly, good work is, as Northcott claims Karl Marx intuited, and as Volf argues, an essential part of what it means to be human. Good work by definition enables a participation of the worker in the product of her labor. As Northcott puts it:

> In the [biblical] analogy between divine work and human construction, we discern that work in Jewish and Christian traditions is not simply the way to get to something else: creative leisure, enjoyable holidays, secure wealth, contented retirement. Work is not instrumental but intrinsic to the vocation of the human creature; the human being finds fulfillment in the ability ... to mirror the work of the Creator.[55]

It would perhaps be unwise and unfruitful to judge Ellul for not engaging with a theme in historical scholarship which was only emerging later in his own career. Indeed, Ellul shows a perhaps prescient awareness of the significance of the Tabernacle and the Temple in his work. *Sans feu* discusses at some length the building of the First Temple as a model of divine-human collaboration, and it exhibits a passing interest in the symbolism of the Temple as macrocosm of the universe: "The spiritual history of the Temple implies ... the symbolism of the Temple as a sign of the architecture of the universe."[56]

However, in *Parole*, as we have seen in chapter 4, Ellul takes his cue from the narrative of the Golden Calf. More significantly, drawing on Jesus' indisputable critique of the Second Temple, *Sans feu* revolves around what Ellul calls Jesus' desacralization of the Temple, and his "fulfillment and substitution" of its role and function.[57] This is, as we have seen, of crucial

---

53. Northcott, *Moral Climate*, 206. He develops on this basis a critique of late capitalist construction and making as "bad work."

54. Northcott, *Moral Climate*, 79.

55. Northcott, *Moral Climate*, 208

56. *Sans feu*, 182, citing Visscher. Moreover, see Ellul's fascinating exploration of the connections between the High Priest's clothing (Exod 28; 39) and the New Jerusalem (Rev 22) (*Sans feu*, 353–55).

57. *Sans feu*, 249.

significance for understanding Ellul's entire theology. Jesus' statements, indebted as they are to the OT prophetic critique of the First Temple, make sense, as Greg Beale and others have shown, when we understand that the symbolism of the Temple designated it not only a microcosm of the universe, but also a macrocosm of the human body.[58]

Jesus implies his body is a new Temple.[59] Therefore, the NT witness offers finally a vision of a last-days Temple "not made with human hands," but instead formed by God as the body of Christ.[60] Kidwell summarizes the relationship between the testaments with regard to the renewed significance of these Temple texts: "As a growing group of scholars—including Margaret Barker, Crispin Fletcher-Louis, Greg Beale, and Nick Perrin—have begun to observe over the past several decades, the Temple actually gains strength over the remaining course of the canonical text of the Bible as a metaphor for the restoration of the people of God."[61]

We now turn to an Ellul scholar who has developed Ellul's work on non-power precisely in dialogue with the theme of the Tabernacle, Marva Dawn.

"Drawn into Worship"

In her book *Powers, Weakness, and the Tabernacling of God*, Dawn generates ethics for a technological age from Ellul, developing a theology of the "Tabernacling" presence of God.[62] There can be no detailed account here. My purpose here, as I round off this appraisal of Ellul's work on non-power, is simply to point to the direction of travel Dawn heads off in, having gained

---

58. "Early Judaism clearly understood the high priest's clothing to be a microcosm of the whole universe. The most likely reason for this is that they also believed the priestly attire was a microcosm of the Temple itself, which was also a small model of the entire cosmos" (Beale, *Temple and the Church's Mission*, 48).

59. See John 2:21 for a statement of the Temple as body: "Jesus answered them, 'Destroy this temple, and in three days I will raise it up.' The Jews then said, 'This temple has been under construction for forty-six years, and will you raise it up in three days?' But he was speaking of the temple of his body." See also Mark 14:58–59; Beale, *Temple and the Church's Mission*, esp. 192–200, "Jesus as the temple of the new creation in John."

60. For example, Eph 2:14–21; 1 Pet 2:4–6.

61. Kidwell, "Drawn into Worship," 85.

62. Dawn, *Tabernacling of God*, 80. "My concerns parallel those of Ellul . . . [which are] remarkably timely for our purposes as we note the ways in which churches act as fallen powers." Dawn was an early interpreter of Ellul's technology criticism, although she falls into a trap it is hard to avoid: restating Ellul's sometimes cryptic analyses and stitching them onto contemporary issues.

momentum from Ellul, and to highlight a number of questions one encounters if one chooses to take the same road.

Dawn begins with an account of NT occurrences of cognates of the noun σκηνή derived from the Hebrew root *shkn* and alluding to God's dwelling, or *shekinah*, in the Tabernacle/Temple in Exodus/1 Kings, respectively. Having outlined these OT and NT connections, she states that the Tabernacle/Temple is a "sublime theme interlocking the entire meta-narrative" of scripture.[63] For Dawn, however, a theme that in the OT seems to be associated with physical place loses this connotation "because of developments in the Hebrew faith," and ends up being used "figuratively" in the NT.[64] Indeed, she perceives a significant NT reinterpretation of the *shekinah*, with God's power now present primarily in human weakness, what she sees in terms of "Tabernacling and Ending of power."[65] The key text here is 2 Corinthians 12:9.[66]

Based on her account of how the LORD "tabernacles" in the human Jesus, she offers an account of how he "tabernacles" in his people, the church, primarily in the mode of weakness, which for Dawn, implies "infirmities, dependency and humility."[67] Turning to Ellul's writing on the true and false presence of God,[68] she suggests that churches reject the "tabernacling of God" by "adopting the means the world employs," for example in politics, economics, scientific inquiry and professional life.[69] In a closing chapter on the church entitled *Images of Weakness*, she offers a number of Ellulian applications, touching on the church's use of power, decrying especially its pursuit of effectiveness, its use of business models and its communication strategies.[70] As Dawn sees it, the Tabernacle/ Temple motif in the NT marks not a place of divine and human collaboration, but rather a work from God's side. What we are to bring to the table is not our "skills, pedigree, background, training or power," but our weakness.[71]

If we step back and consider the Ellulian background here, we remember that Ellul tends both to emphasize the exclusive and hidden presence

63. Dawn, *Tabernacling of God*, 44.

64. Dawn, *Tabernacling of God*, 43

65. Dawn, *Tabernacling of God*, 45–49.

66. Dawn offers this translation: "[The LORD] said to me 'My grace is sufficient for you, for your [Paul's] power has been brought to its end in weakness.' . . . All the more gladly then will I boast in my weakness that the power of Christ (not mine!) may tabernacle on me" (*Tabernacling of God*, 41).

67. Dawn, *Tabernacling of God*, 49.

68. The most commonly cited texts are *Présence*; *Fausse*; *Subversion*; *Parole*.

69. Dawn, *Tabernacling of God*, 80–82.

70. Dawn, *Tabernacling of God*, 123–64.

71. Dawn, *Tabernacling of God*, 49.

of God in Christ and to de-emphasize the power motif in Jesus' ministry, stressing rather his suffering non-power, also downplaying his power and presence in the church. We may be entitled to ask therefore: can Ellul's ethics of non-power assist the public discipleship of the church, especially in the daily professional lives of its people? Of course, we are aware, with Dawn, of Ellul's eschatological hope that the New Jerusalem will one day be built at God's initiative, but recapitulating those works of ours which survive the judgment. But the potential problem here is this: does Ellul help us to generate a positive account of our empowerment by and co-working with God *here and now*?

We can do little more at this stage in our research than point to the need to explore further the significance of the Tabernacle/Temple as microcosm of the universe and macrocosm of the body. Simply put, if all creation is God's great Temple, surely human work within creation has no other ultimate meaning than to be drawn into worship. And if the human body is God's small Temple, there is to be no ultimate competition between human power and God's power in the body of Jesus of Nazareth or indeed, in the bodies which constitute the one Body of Christ. In his careful account of the relationship between the Testaments, Kidwell contends that the reframing of Tabernacle/Temple language in terms of the Body of Christ is not some unexpected discontinuity within the biblical narrative. "It is important to affirm, then, that the true juxtaposition in the NT is between work which results in the making of idols and work which can re-construct God's Temple. Only the latter is exercised under divine superintendence."[72] The intention is not to exclude human agency but to point to God's empowerment of human work. "To argue a position of absolute discontinuity [between the Jerusalem Temple and the Body of Christ] would require that one assume the declaration by Jesus that the new Temple would not be built by human hands, meant by extension that the work inaugurated at Jesus' resurrection would not involve human participants."[73]

Therefore, he suggests that the "Temple not built of human hands," the Body of Christ, should in its accounts of good work have "recourse to the same notion of craftsmanship" clearly outlined in OT Tabernacle/Temple texts.[74] *Work is drawn into worship* precisely at the point of offering the fruits of the people's labor in the paradigmatic "tabernacling" of God in the

72. Kidwell, "Drawn into Worship," 131.

73. Kidwell, "Drawn into Worship," 133.

74. Kidwell, "Drawn into Worship," 135. "[In the gospels] one finds an account of construction of a new ecclesial Temple which carries through hints at a shared coherence between the work being done by the disciples and the ordinary work of the people."

gathering of the church, the Eucharist. Kidwell's purpose is to highlight how such work contrasts sharply with bad work:

> It is my hope that this study might provide a basic context for contemporary worshippers to consider a renewal of offertory practice. In terms of the practices of the church, this offers a promising site for a renewal of this ancient dynamic where worship is drawn into work and brought into a theologically construed moral context. Such a renewal might provide a more robust basis for contemporary Christians to resist those secular theologies which have caused modern worshippers to sustain and collude with modern forms of work and work organization which destroy humans, other creatures, and put the whole created order at risk.[75]

What further exploration promises here would be to assist Christians to discover and practice alternative patterns of collaborating with God, drawing even technologies into worship. In the biblical account of Tabernacle/Temple, we find that God invites us to build a workspace wherein his blessing can dwell. Yet, the tabernacle marks a challenge as much as a promise. The Tabernacle/Temple is "a paradigmatic example of human building as a response to God's designs," a work carried out in gratitude and leading to plenitude and satisfaction, in stark contrast to the work demanded by the "technological worldview."[76]

We have raised here a number of problems with Ellul's application of non-power to technology which deserve further exploration. Do similar problems arise in his ethics of iconoclasm?

The Spirit of Lies

The Spirit of Lies and the Ethics of Iconoclasm

The second spirit Ellul discerns in Technique is "the spirit of lies," the spirit identified in 1 John 4:5–6. This has to do with the incarnation again, more precisely with not believing the testimony of the Spirit of Truth. This rejection takes myriad forms in the technological society, claims Ellul, and once again, he locates this spirit in a trinity of phenomena present in a technological

75. Kidwell, "Drawn into Worship," 230. In contrast, Dawn's account of the unseen presence of God in the Eucharist points away from the present, with "time and space abolished" (*Tabernacling of God*, 49, citing von Schenk).

76. Brock, *Technological Age*, 228.

society: "counterfeiting," "manifestation" and "myth-making." We will offer a brief account of *Théologie et Technique* at the outset.

What does he mean by the process of "counterfeiting"? The technological "counterfeit" is not a question of the "legitimate and healthy" artificiality which is intrinsic to our humanity.[77] The "counterfeit" has to do with the way Technique normalizes, as "second nature," needs, behaviors and habits which are illusory, purely artificial, technologically manufactured.[78] These counterfeit norms lead to the prevailing feeling of psychological anomie in technological societies, as the inability to satisfy one's perceived needs, which are constantly stimulated, goes hand in hand with the imposition of tighter and tighter technical habits and behaviors.[79] As a result, what was once the domain of traditional, relational norms—learning a trade, making friends, bringing up children, producing art, even playing sport—are now mediated via "the screen of Technique."[80]

The spirit of lies operates secondly through manifestation. What El-lul is essentially concerned with here is the sacred character of Technique. Ellul notes that Technique is sacred because it has a visible power, needing no proof other than itself. "Manifestation is indeed the very essence of Technique. . . . Technique is the manifestation of its own power, its own structure, its own meaning."[81] What he has in view is the self-legitimation of technical progress. Technique is "scientific," therefore it is true.[82] Ellul offers not the rejection of science, but of scientism. "Of course, I'm not talking about the rejection of science as such, but only Science in its exclusive claim. . . . When science, which is only an image, entirely based on images, translating everything into images, claims to integrate the whole of the world, and particularly when it becomes Myth.[83]

---

77. Ellul's 1980 article, "Technique, Nature, and Artificiality," which enters into a dialogue between sociological and theological anthropology, is reproduced in *Théologie et Technique*, 187–201.

78. *Théologie et Technique*, 286. There is some parallel with Herman and Chomsky, *Manufacturing Consent*.

79. *Théologie et Technique*, 288. Ellul here references his predecessor at Bordeaux, Emile Durkheim. For an interesting contemporary treatment of "anomie," see James, *Affluenza*.

80. *Théologie et Technique*, 288–89. Brock's approach to technology is also similarly anthropological, attentive to technological habits and observed practices (drawing on Foucault).

81. *Théologie et Technique*, 290–91. Here Ellul references *Nouveaux possédés*.

82. *Théologie et Technique*, 332.

83. *Parole*, 286. This kind of critique has been variously pursued in the work of Mary Midgley.

Thirdly (and we glimpse this concern above), Ellul argues that as sacred, Technique becomes a creator of meaning by populating our language and imagination with potent symbols—since it is the stuff our myths are made of, it is the stuff our future itself will be made of. The "spirit of lies" is positive and positivist: always pointing to Technique's positive effects, ever in denial about any negatives. Its modern guise is advertising.[84] In the end, Technique will have to solve all our problems, especially those it has created, because there is nothing else we can think or dream of. Even critics such as himself, Ellul concedes, worry that anything else would spell chaos: "If there is a conceivable future, if there is a way out of chaos, it's through more Technique."[85]

The point of iconoclasm is of course not negative. What is required is a decisive desacralization of Technique, which can lead to its reconciliation within God's purposes. We will be familiar by now with this basic dialectical shape to Ellul's apocalyptic theology: the apocalypse breaks into the present time in two modes: judgment and recapitulation. As I have explored at length, the final judgment dawns now in the work of "desacralization" and the final recapitulation dawns now in the work of reconciliation.

I hope I have demonstrated thus far not only that Ellul's theology is interestingly and coherently apocalyptic but also that the very purpose of his theological enterprise was to engage with present ethics, indeed with everyday life, *tout court*. Ellul's purpose was not to construct a perfect architectonic structure. We have noted along the way, as many others have, numerous cracks and missing bits as well as over-rendering and repetition; none of which, I hope, makes his work a house of cards.

However, Ellul was a professional historian of institutions,[86] and he believed that Christians needed to find their bearings by finding out about their forebears, discovering the mysterious working of the "spirit of lies" in history. Indeed, Ellul's work seems to be precisely what is in mind when Oliver O'Donovan writes: "Modernity criticism has taken the form of sweeping intellectual and cultural history, which has it in view to notice the fateful

---

84. *Théologie et Technique*, 285. *Parole* speaks of "the lying language of advertising" (*Parole*, 292). Ellul authored a famous sociological study of propaganda (*Propagandes*) along these lines as well as a polemic against popular slogans or "commonplaces" (*Lieux Communs*). See also *Bluff*, chapters 14–19, including prescient chapters on gadgets, games, and advertising. For an arresting contemporary analysis, see Alexander et al., *Think of Me as Evil?*

85. *Théologie et Technique*, 335.

86. Witness Ellul's five-volume work, *Histoire des institutions*.

turns, the points of departure, the paths not taken, which have built modernity up into the 'necessity' that now surrounds us."[87]

Perhaps a better metaphor for Ellul's work is that of a vast tableau. Although there is an abundance of fine detail within Ellul's sweeping historical vistas, often reworked, for good measure, over a career of fifty years, the basic shape on the canvas is drawn in confident dark swathes. I will seek below to offer both an appreciation and a critique of Ellul's modernity criticism; this will also serve to demonstrate the degree to which his theology and sociology are increasingly overlaid as his career goes on.

Ellul's Somber Apocalyptic Tableau

As we have begun to see in earlier chapters, in *Les Nouveaux Possédés, Ethique and Subversion*, Ellul argues that Christians bear a historical responsibility for the West, and indeed, especially its technological development. Yet Ellul had not always believed this, and in these texts he argues explicitly against positions he had once held. In the first book of the so-called "technological trilogy," *Technique* (1954), in a significant section entitled "Christianity and Technique,"[88] Ellul had openly denied that Christianity had encouraged technical development. The early church was ambivalent towards imperial technologies like the military and transport; a desacralized nature, he claims here, implied Christians should refuse to practice the dark arts of Technique.[89] He plays down the impact of the abolition of slavery by the medieval church in the tenth century, claiming that no significant technological progress took place for seven hundred years after the ending of serfdom.[90] The only techniques that the medieval church fostered from the tenth to the fourteenth century, Ellul claims, were the ponderous intellectual techniques of scholasticism.[91]

By the time of *Subversion*, he has made a volte-face, arguing that the Gospel gave birth to science and Technique by desacralizing creation. "The origins of science and technology are often traced back to this event: since things are only things, nothing more, there is no divinity hidden

---

87. O'Donovan, *Desire of the Nations*, 228.

88. *Technique*, 29–31.

89. "The depiction of a nature inhabited by the gods was, on the contrary, a powerful actor in favour of techniques. Over against this, Christianity deprives it of this justification" (*Technique*, 34).

90. *Technique*, 33.

91. *Technique*, 33.

within, no mysterious power, *we can attempt to know them completely and use them without limit.*"[92]

As we will see Ellul will refute this over-interpretation—denying that the Word mandates a *limitless* utilization of things—and the impersonal construction admits of a certain distance. However, it is clear that at this point in his career Ellul no longer distances the Gospel from scientific and technological development.[93]

Already in the intervening text, *Nouveaux*, he had linked the ending of slavery and the beginnings of modern technologies together. He now he agrees with a developing consensus that the church led the way: "For, in the final analysis, we must also recall the degree to which the action of the church and the organization of Christendom were beneficial to humanity. And first of all through the ending of slavery. After a century when it was quietly asserted that this came about through Christianity, it was fashionable from 1930 to declare that Christianity had nothing to do with it."[94]

The once-fashionable materialism is false, now untenable by any serious historian, Ellul claims. Theologically driven social change led directly to technological change: new techniques such as water and wind mills, mining, metallurgy and weaving, as well as the production of paper and glass. "The decisive fact is the transformation of people's mindset through Christianity. If technical progress came about, it came as a result of the ending of slavery, to deal with the sudden loss of manpower."[95]

In conclusion, Ellul now posits that the ending of slavery in Western Christendom launched it upon a path to technical development.[96]

92. *Subversion*, 75 (my italics).

93. "It is not for nothing that freedom is a creation of the Judeo-Christian world, and it's by virtue of this fact that we were immersed in this scientific and technological adventure" (*Parole*, 293).

94. *Nouveaux possédés*, 28. In a footnote in the later 1980 edition of *Technique*, 32, Ellul admits he was wrong, simply following an earlier consensus in the 1960 edition.

95. *Nouveaux possédés*, 33. As well as abolition, Ellul argues that Christendom fostered the peace-building institutions of the Leagues of Peace and the Truce of God, economic structures such as the just price and the ban on usury, as well as institutional structures to defend the victim and the weak. Ellul argues that the slide back into the slavery represented by the trans-Atlantic slave trade was caused by the corrupting influence of the Arab slave trade (see chapter 5, "The Influence of Islam"). Ellul's writings on Islam are a highly controversial aspect of his legacy in France. See his posthumous work *Islam et judéo-christianisme* (published in English translation in 2015).

96. Ellul references Lynn White at various points, with agreement. Ellul's early instinct had been to play down the importance of explicitly theological reasons for technology, preferring to focus on economic drivers. Ellul's later account of Christian history in *Nouveaux* and *Subversion* equates Christendom's abolition of slavery with the rise of technology—and it is absurd to continue to argue to the contrary, he claims (*Subversion*, 130).

If the early medieval church achieved this liberation, the Reformation, on Ellul's account, marked another great moment of liberation from the bonds of nature and culture, which led to an even freer use of technology. However, once again, Ellul arrives late at this conclusion. In *Technique,* Ellul had argued that the Reformation merely caught up with the economic and political circumstances.[97] However, in *Nouveaux* he revises his position, arguing that the Reformers not only responded to circumstances, they shaped them. By severing nature from grace, the use of nature, rather than nature itself, became the new sacred, fostering economic development. Work was now given a theological justification denied it for hundreds of years: the Protestant understanding of vocation and a corresponding work-ethic were born.[98] Of course, the Reformers, Ellul concedes, were not economic or political thinkers masquerading as theologians—they were above all "men of the Word."[99]

In an earlier and significant article entitled "The Contemporary Significance of the Reformation" published first in 1959 (and translated by Marva Dawn),[100] Ellul had already begun to elaborate this position, but with an ambivalence which will come to mark his later assessments. Ellul claims that the achievements of the Reformers included the secularization of the state and the ending of a hierarchical order, a new awareness of the person over and against society along with a new work ethic, the development of mechanical skills and "the great adventure of technology."[101] Yet at the same time, in more critical vein, he names as the "worm-eaten fruits" of the Reformation, the bourgeois spirit, the rise of capitalism and the unfettering of the will to power in Enlightenment Technique, and ultimately, at the end of this direction of travel, an ecological crisis.[102]

Although he had at first insulated the church from the critique that it had created the modern West, as his sociology and theology become more integrated in dialogic texts, Ellul came to argue that neither the church nor the West are understandable without one another. Yet Technique, which was indeed the fruit of Christian desacralization, had been sacralized, and the church bore a particular responsibility to continually desacralize and control it. As Rognon puts it, for Ellul, Judeo-Christianity had been the

97. *Technique,* 34. Moreover, Ellul insisted that the economic impact of the Reformation had been singularly overstated.

98. The critique of scholasticism is perhaps the safest ground, for many critics have noted the estrangement from economic life which led inevitably to the Reformation.

99. *Nouveaux possédés,* 93–99.

100. *Sources and Trajectories,* chapter 6.

101. *Sources and Trajectories,* 141.

102. *Sources and Trajectories,* 138–39.

poison, but must also be the antidote, "the cause of the planet's devastation and its only cure."[103]

Indeed, Ellul's given task in *Subversion*, in his own words, is to track how the Gospel has produced a civilization so opposed to its Founder:

> Thus the question arises: "How is it that the development of a Christian society and of the Church has given birth to a society, a civilization, a culture which is in every way contrary to what we read in the Bible, of what is the indisputable text of the Torah, the prophets, Jesus and Paul?" . . . There is not only drift here, there is radical contradiction, a veritable subversion.[104]

For all time, Christ has invaded time and space, unsettling the sacred politico-religious order of the Greco-Roman world. With the sacred canopy removed, everything is secular, and there are no intrinsic limits. The only limits are extrinsically given, received in listening to the Word of God. There is both danger and opportunity here: the options are love or nothing. Yet Christian desacralization does not aim at a dangerous vacuum or a secularist wilderness.[105]

In other words, an ethics of iconoclasm requires an ethics of attentiveness to the divine Word, which I shall explicate below as an ethics of holiness. As Fasching rightly notes, for Ellul: "Secularization is not a permanent accomplishment. The world can remain secular only through the constant iconoclasm of the holy. Without that constant subversion of the sacred by the holy, the secular itself becomes a new sacred order."[106]

The Ethics of Holiness: Sabbath

Creation by the Word, we recall, marks both separation and relationship. Human beings are uniquely called to hear, to respond and to bear witness

---

103. Rognon, in his preface to *Théologie et Technique*, 22–23.

104. *Subversion*, 1.

105. For an account of the parallels between Patrick Berger and Ellul, see chapter 16, "Social Intolerabilty of the Christian Revelation," in Jeronimo, *Jacques Ellul*. Ellul's critique overlaps in interesting ways with the works of a more recent theologian and modernity critic, David Bentley-Hart (see Clausen, "Love or Nothing?"). There are parallels also with Girard's account of the opportunity and threat posed by the incarnation: "To make the revelation wholly good and not threatening at all, humans have only to adopt the behaviour recommended by Christ: abstain completely from retaliation and renounce the escalation to extremes. For if that escalation continues, it will lead straight to the extinction of all life on the planet" (Girard and Chantre, *Battling to the End*, 18).

106. Fasching, "Sacred, the Secular, and the Holy," 7.

to the Word of God, in the hope of final reconciliation. This is Ellul's account of holiness.

Holiness results from relationship with God, and it is embodied in covenants God makes with his people: to respond to Him and to live within given limits. Holiness destroys sacred limits, for there is no longer quasi-divine power invested in any particular natural order or law.[107] But it offers covenant limits, limits within time and history, in their place, paradigmatically for our purposes here the limits of Sabbath and Jubilee.

In *Théologie*, Ellul claims it is just these limits that Christians are called to model today.[108] Indeed, we have seen that Sabbath finally becomes the motif of Ellul's entire theology. It is taken to imply God's blessing over separated and thus created forms, and the promise of eternity within and over all human history. The temporal Sabbath, as we have seen, points to an eternal Sabbath, God's final act of reconciliation, anticipated by Jesus' resurrection from the dead. Moreover, it is within the framework of Sabbath that Ellul finds both a limit upon work and also an announcement of the final eschatological reconciliation of human works.[109]

Ellul dissents from naive theologies of creation in accounts of work[110] and Sabbath is part of his armory here, for he reads it as a sharp demarcation between Technique and worship:

> The Sabbath is also a suppression of Technique in time. . . . A limit to Technique is thus established as regards to its duration and as regards to its meaning. In other words, if we have an attitude of adoration, of veneration towards Technique, we cannot draw the line. . . . But theologically, this attitude of veneration is that expressed in the theories to which we have alluded: Technique expresses the co-creative nature of human beings; Technique makes us co-workers with God in his creation.[111]

Moreover, he claims that eschatological accounts which assume, in popular parlance, that "technology is the future," cut the nerve of a

---

107. Ellul argues that we will never be able to regulate technology through moral boundaries; what can be done will be done. See also Brock, *Technological Age*, 189.

108. *Théologie et Technique*, 325. For an account of Sabbath, heavily influenced by Ellul, see Dawn, *Keeping the Sabbath Wholly*.

109. See chapter 5, section 2.3, above.

110. "Ellul will have no truck with theologians who want to ground the meaning of work in our being created in the image of God or commissioned to serve as co-creators with God" (Gill, "Business Ethics," 9–10).

111. *Théologie et Technique*, 207.

vital Christian practice of discernment.[112] Ellul finds the "spirit of lies" in modern secular theology, hence his bitterest critiques are directed at theologians who celebrate the technological society uncritically, un-dialectically.[113] This polemic is expressed with particular force in *L'Espérance oubliée* (1973), a critical appraisal of the increasing connections between technology and eschatology within modern theology. Most controversially of all, here and in *Trahision de l'Occident*, Ellul offers a theological judgment that the Word of God is falling silent in a technological age, as the West enters an exile, analogous to the experience of Israel in the intertestamental period. This is, in effect, Ellul's response to the then-popular secular theology and "Death of God" movements.[114]

In my introduction, I set out to show that the uncritical celebration of technology in much modern theology has consequences. In Ellul's account of Sabbath, the seventh day recalls us to finitude, to given, creaturely limits. Sabbath is what separates mundane, necessary work from worship. "You must of course, of necessity, use Technique, you can do no other, for without it you will revert to an animal state, or you will simply be unable to live. But learn to see it as but a hard and painful necessity, do not make it your joy, your hope, your value, your truth, your strength or your security. . . . That's exactly what the institution of the Sabbath is about."[115]

Moreover, Sabbath is a command for a particular community. It is then no surprise that in closing *Théologie*, Ellul calls for Christians to make a personal decision to live differently towards work and technology. This implies, in a reiteration of *Nouveaux*, *using* technological *things*, but not taking them too seriously. By beginning with our own behavior and attitudes towards actual devices, we will proceed to *turn away* from the ideologies of production and consumption, modelling rather than condemning:

> If this radical questioning takes place . . . of the sacred character of Technique, this will then have repercussions on these things themselves, producing a refusal, a conscientious objection to devoting one's life to producing these wonderful devices and to

112. For agreement, see Talbott, *Future Does Not Compute*.

113. We have already noted Ellul's ire against de Chardin. In *Nouveaux possédés*, he takes aim at the then famous work of Baptist theologian Harvey Cox, *The Secular City*. "Given that I fully agree with him on his three themes: Creation—disenchantment of Nature—Exodus, desacralization of politics—Covenant—desacralization of values . . . it's a shame he doesn't apply them effectively" (61).

114. Goddard discusses this point (*Living the Word*, 159–60) with reference to *Hope* and to *Betrayal of the West*. See *Betrayal*, 78–79, on late modern Western history as a betrayal and a re-crucifixion of Jesus.

115. *Théologie et Technique*, 209.

finding one's joy in their consumption. There is no point in putting forward prohibitions.[116]

This is a helpful and realistic perspective. However, is it correct to imply that the call to holiness on the Sabbath is essentially concerned with desisting and ceasing? At this point, we run up against real problems in appropriating Ellul's understanding of Sabbath today. For biblically, Sabbath is not merely a rest from the necessity of work; Ellul scholar David Gill straightforwardly argues against Ellul at this point:[117]

> One reason not to follow Ellul [on work] is The Decalogue, which is given in two forms. In the Deuteronomy version both work and Sabbath are grounded, Ellul-style, in liberation from work as slavery in Egypt. But in the Exodus version, *Sabbath and work are grounded in God's example of both in creation.* So taken as a whole, work and rest are both viewed within a dialectic of good creative work and fallen necessary work.[118]

It is perhaps incorrect to frame Ellul's position entirely in terms of the fall: he can move between seeing work as a necessary, creaturely activity and seeing it as a curse. However, Gill rightly argues that the continuing goodness of work is surely biblically established.

For this reason, Gill disputes too Ellul's interpretation of *avodah*—which Ellul claims connects work and worship only in the freedom, the playfulness of non-technical work. For if both our rest and our weekly work are explicitly compared to God's paradigmatic "six days of work" and "holy day," if this is the weekly liturgy of the "royal priesthood,"[119] then free work cannot be reduced to what we do in contemplative activity, leisure or in volunteering, outside of the necessity of paid employment, although this is what Ellul adamantly argued of vocation in a technological age.[120]

---

116. *Théologie et Technique*, 334. We perhaps find some unexpected support for this reading in the work of Jonathan Sacks, the former Chief Rabbi of the United Kingdom, who suggests not a rejection but rather a mere lack of interest in the Hebrew Bible in the activities of human making. He comments that the Bible is "simply uninterested in Homo Faber, the tool-making, environment-changing life-form. It is interested exclusively in homo religiosus, the first humans to hear and to respond to the Divine voice" (Sacks, *Great Partnership*, 229).

117. "His attempt to make work in any form a result of the fall involves him in a twisted interpretation of the Genesis story" (Gill, *Word of God*, 122).

118. Gill, "Business Ethics," 15–16.

119. See Stevens's discussion of what he calls the Jewish vision of the "clericalization of the laity" (*Abolition of the Laity*, 34).

120. "If it is not in work that we can unify our lives, or even incarnate our Christian vocation, if the society of technique brings us back to the hard condition of relative

This is surely something of a counsel of despair—indeed Ellul him-self does not offer it gladly.[121] Granted, in the final analysis, Ellul points towards the final recapitulation of technological products, for the new creation will entail God's work of glorifying creaturely artifacts as they pass through the fires of judgment. Yet despite this, as Gill asks, is not his account of Technique too estranged from the material world in this in-between time in which we live now?[122] Is it not possible to draw even our working week into worship?

> The opportunity for human kindness and care, for creativity, for meaning and even redemptive impact on others can present itself in business organizations, not just in the volunteer sec-tor. Not all businesses, all the time, crush out human freedom, relationship, and creativity. In fact the best businesses promote such things. It is just not an either/or situation where work is all crushing necessity and external vocation is all freedom and meaning. Ellul actually hints as much (and told me as much in personal conversation).[123]

If there are hints in Ellul's published writings, they are hard to find. Ellul's account of Sabbath does not offer a particularly embodied account of holiness.

Reuniting Work and Worship: Beyond Ellul

What might it mean to move beyond Ellul at this point? The moral theolo-gian Brian Brock argues cogently that Sabbath is not only a limit to work, but the orientation of all our work towards worship.[124]

He begins with a brief historical sketch to show how we have come to a point where work is too often separated from worship, with an appre-ciative discussion of how the Rule of Saint Benedict offered an integrated vision to early monasticism. Labor is good based on its bodily goodness, the

---

work, without ultimate value and significance, then it is obvious that we *must* discover a form of activity which expresses our Christian calling, which implies an incarna-tion of faith" (*Freedom*, 507). Many of Ellul's articles on work have been collected and republished in *Pour qui, pour quoi travaillons-nous?*

121. *Freedom*, 508.

122. If the New Creation does indeed break into the present, "We can make judgments about what conforms with God's will . . . because 'God's will for the city-as-co-humanity' is not visible only at the End, although it is clearest there" (Gill, *Word of God*, 176).

123. Gill, "Business Ethics," 20.

124. Brock, *Technological Age*, 289–302.

discipline provided and the satisfaction gained, rather than because of the value it produces. Gathering for worship interrupts work, not to demarcate it from worship but to interject a critical impulse into it. Worship is never to cease: the community is oriented toward the question of what it means to render Christ's love to the world in every form of work, most concretely in its hospitality to the neighbor.[125]

However, as Brock argues, later monasticism degenerated from this high calling, and came to display a marked lack of theological interest in questions of work. "By the tenth century, however, this mutually defining relationship of work and worship had begun to fray. Monks now began to set work and worship into conflict, giving up work in favor of worship, obscuring its function as a necessary crucible for the formation of faith."[126]

It was the formal scholasticism of the thirteenth century which made the division of work and worship explicit, as monasticism evolved into an "urban academic discipline," defining worship "as spiritual in *opposition* to the bodily, rather than as bodily *and* spiritual."[127] For Brock, it was the scholastic split "between a spiritual component, worship, and a physical component, work which began the estrangement of the church from many areas of modern economic life."[128]

Recovering a unified vision and suggesting a practical Christian ethics for a technological society, he argues that the biblical vision of communal, reflective and playful work can be recovered in the modern technological workplace.

Communal work implies work which is woven into the fabric of social life, which includes place, family and neighborhood.[129] Yet this social location is often obscured by eschatological accounts, Brock contends, and this is why he dissents from Volf's account of good work:[130]

> By paying attention to the demands of created materiality . . . we
> are alerted to the tendency to overemphasize the eschatological

125. Brock, *Technological Age*, 301. See MacCulloch, *History of Christianity*, 312–19, on early monasticism. See Jamison, *Finding Sanctuary*, for an accessible account of Benedict's rule for today.

126. Brock, *Technological Age*, 305.

127. Brock, *Technological Age*, 305. For Peter Scott, it is Duns Scotus's severing of nature and grace in late nominalism that is decisive.

128. Brock, *Technological Age*, 326.

129. Brock goes on to offer marriage as a model for thinking about what it means to be embodied (*Technological Age*, 328).

130. He characterizes Volf's view of the aim of good work as "creating products that will endure the fires of judgment. . . . The criterion of its goodness is its eschatological purity" (Brock, *Technological Age*, 297).

or pneumatological basis of work to capitulate to the ideology of mobility. This is the primary danger of theologies of work like Volf's, which unquestioningly baptize modern ideologies of mobility without considering the many associated problems they engender such as deskilling, outsourcing, poor provision for retraining and health care, and so on.[131]

This "relentlessly and voluntaristically optimistic view" tends, he argues, to be "deaf to the limitations that the finite and particular conditions of the material world place upon social change."[132]

Reflective work seeks to involve workers in the product of their labor, although Brock concedes it is a daunting task to challenge the strict division of labor and the desensitizing of workers from the end products of their labor.[133] Work can be *playful* not only extrinsically, with respect to the quality of perks a company might provide, or the purchasing power a salary offers, but intrinsically so through challenging work practices which are efficient and time-saving, but which sap creativity, risk and skill acquisition.[134]

Although Ellul would no doubt argue that these are counsels of perfection, given the influence Christian ethics can exercise upon contemporary society,[135] his particular tendency to turn away from Technique, at best a protest against the technocratic spirit, offers little resource for practical Christian discernment. And herein, perhaps, lies a rather significant problem for appropriating Ellul today: it is not that he is solely focused on the fall, but that he tends to remove creaturely, bodily labor in the material world from the context of worship. If we return to the apocalyptic tableau we observed earlier, it is possible to see that some of Ellul's ethical positions are new renderings of historic but misguided views of worship and work.[136] Indeed, despite his critique of Scholasticism, and his thoroughgoing engagement with the affairs of the world, Ellul's theological severing of body and image, as well as of work and worship, can at times appear to veer towards neo-Scholasticism.

---

131. Brock, *Technological Age*, 308. He cites the level of support for part-time work as a sign that other social values have their place.

132. Brock, *Technological Age*, 308.

133. Brock, *Technological Age*, 311. He cites the arms industry as particularly challenging here. This research has been completed in one of the cradles of the British arms industry, Farnborough, and I can bear witness to the challenge of raising ethical questions with those employed within the "military-industrial complex."

134. Brock, *Technological Age*, 318.

135. *Freedom*, 510.

136. As far as I can see, there is a complete silence in Ellul's writing on work on the Rule of Saint Benedict.

In the final analysis, this would perhaps be too harsh a judgment, for there are signs of Ellul's concern for embodiment in *Théologie*, along with warnings against technophobia. Ellul states in *Théologie* that this kind of iconoclasm requires the embodied Word as a witness to the truth.[137] Indeed, in many places in his writing, he claims that the Spirit-empowered, prophetic witness is the only truly revolutionary force in the world.[138] This finally is what we explore below as we turn to his ethics of hope.

The Ethics of Hope

Written within a short space in time, *Parole* (1981) and *Changer* (1982) represent different moments, despite sharing a common concern with the prophetic word and the information revolution. In the first, *Parole*, the note of desacralization is loudest, and Ellul argues for the prophetic power of the spoken word and the embodied witness. In *Changer*, he proposes a revolutionary role for new information technologies, once desacralized and chastened by the prophetic word.

Embodying the Word

Let us briefly recapitulate the logic of the dialectic of the word and the image in *Parole*, and the prophetic judgments Ellul infers from it, which are visible in their sociological form in *Le Bluff Technologique*.

In a phenomenological opening passage of *Parole*, Ellul argues that the spoken word is the essential medium of non-power—non-coercive, ambiguous and connotative.[139] It is a living presence, requiring two persons in relationship in time: "The spoken word is essentially presence. It is a living thing. Never an object."[140] It is in dialogue and distance that we discover "the same-other and the other-same."[141] Theologically this marries with

137. *Théologie et Technique*, 335.

138. In the final chapter of *Subversion*, chapter 10, "Eppur se muove," he contrasts the Communist language of revolution with the revolution produced by the Roman Catholic Solidarity movement under labor activist Lech Walesa in Poland. The faith of the people and the courageous witness of leading clergy made this possible. There is a positive mention also of Liberation theology, which Ellul had often critiqued.

139. *Parole*, 24.

140. *Parole*, 20. Only when written does it become an object, requiring focused attention, rather than the "overview" that spoken language enables. Ellul's treatment alludes, often in disagreement, to the seminal work of Marshall McLuhan (see, e.g., 31n1).

141. *Parole*, 21. This happens paradigmatically for Ellul in the relationship of male and female, who together make the image of God.

first creation account, which speaks of Adam's naming of the woman: "The dissimilar similar one. . . . Discourse begins again and again because the distance between us remains."[142]

In this distance between speaker and listener, between the moment of speech and the moment of reception are born symbol, metaphor, and analogy.[143] Almost each time Ellul speaks of *metaphor*, there is a trace of its etymology—"carrying beyond."[144] Ellul sees spoken communication through the musical image of a symphony.[145] Communication is the achievement of the word's basic musicality. The word offers communion with one another: by a *polyphony* of *overtones*, a *symphony of shared echoes* is established, which creates a *concordance*, never static but a movement in time.[146] Yet it also offers communion with the "wholly other," for it has a capacity to reach beyond words, beyond reality, to create another universe, what he calls the order of truth. "The word is not bound to reality, but to its capacity to create this different universe, which you can call surreal, meta-real, or metaphysical. For the sake of convenience we will call it the order of truth."[147] The word is concerned with ends.

The image on the other hand is concerned with means, and therefore power.[148] Sight functions in space and collapses time into a single moment. It prefers focused attention to whole attention, taking snap shots of the world, viewing it in small parts, to see how they work, and then putting them back together again. After all, objects are there to be used, and indeed, Ellul contends that the eye and the hand are closely coordinated.[149] This part-wise observation leads to manipulation, enabling rational and efficient *techniques*. If the Word is dialectically opposed to the image, so it is to Technique: "We must become basically aware of the fact that the word is strictly contradictory to Technique in every way."[150]

Ellul claims that in modernity sight has become dominant, as exemplified by Descartes, the speculative philosopher looking out of his window.[151]

142. *Parole*, 22.

143. *Parole*, 24.

144. See, e.g., *Parole*, 26–27, 37, 77–78 (in brief dialogue with Paul Ricoeur), 119, 181.

145. *Parole*, 22. The other image Ellul uses is that of a spider's web.

146. *Parole*, 24–25.

147. *Parole*, 27.

148. *Parole*, 14–15.

149. *Parole*, 15.

150. *Parole*, 177.

151. *Parole*, 43. Ellul credits Kierkegaard for this critique, citing Viallaneix, *Kierkegaard.*

From that perspective, the world becomes a "world-for-me," making me a subject and all else an object. Drawing on a study by the late French paleoanthropologist André Leroi-Gourhan, Ellul argues that there are two languages: the language of hearing, and the language of sight.[152] The language of sight thinks in terms of subjectivity-objectivity, non-contradiction and binary logic. It cannot hear the word. It wants to see it. Creation even speaks, Ellul goes as far as to say, but instead of listening, we want to *see* its secret.[153]

The dialectical thought so intrinsic to humanity is increasingly submitted to binary mathematical logic.[154] The metaphoric and poetic word over time loses its power, as the average person's language is now drawn from an impoverished stock of technologically generated symbols, diminishing critical faculties and the intellectual process: "The conversation with a computer becomes the model for all conversation."[155]

Ubiquitous *audio-visual* devices, Ellul claims in *Parole*, attempt to reconcile the word and the image prematurely: "They claim to mend what was broken and to restore unity of being through the precise relationship they foster between sight and hearing, thanks to increasingly sophisticated gadgets. But in reality they signify the final exclusion of truth, or else its reduction to some secondary, accessory use. Such methods empty the word of its value and reduce truth to efficacious, usable reality."[156] They offer an alluring but false transcendence and false communion. "No device, however ingenious, will enable humanity to discover the meaning of life. . . . Nor can a device enable us to recover a relationship of communion with other men and women."[157] They offer the illusion that we are well informed and connected, when in fact we may be overwhelmed and permanently distracted.[158]

This admixture of the word and the image not only affects us at a personal level but also at a political level. Politics develops a cult of spectacle as well as its own liturgy. Graphs and statistics replace words in forming judgments.[159] *Bluff* offers a more concertedly sociological exploration

---

152. *Parole*, 48.

153. *Parole*, 215. At one level, Ellul concedes that this is a perennial human problem, as old as Cain, though he sees it as an acute problem in modernity (*Parole*, 218).

154. *Parole*, 146–47.

155. *Parole*, 178–79. For a riposte to Ellul, see Christian, *Most Human Human*. Christian argues that the ability of artificial intelligence to mimic human conversation (the purpose of the famous Turing test) challenges human beings to be more, not less human.

156. *Parole*, 255.

157. *Parole*, 255.

158. *Parole*, 284–87.

159. In *Parole*, Ellul berates us for believing something because a computer generates it: "The computer can never be the ultimate reason" (286).

of the effect of Technique upon language, turning upon what "algebraic rationality" does to reasoning, politics, economics and culture. Decision-making becomes technical, held in fewer hands, and further from the people it will affect.[160] Indeed, in a neat example of Ellul's prescience in *Bluff* (see chapter 13, "The Costs"), he predicts the collapse of financial markets as "real accounts" will catch up with the speed and illusion of computer-based transactions.[161]

Parole is central to Jacques Ellul's legacy, replete as it is with eerie phrases which strike the reader as ahead of their time. As I outlined in chapters 1 and 2, *Parole* is an incarnational text, constantly aiming to re-embody the word in an age of Technique. As Greenman, et al., argue, here we see that Ellul's "considerations about a major issue in the modern world are grounded in his Christian view of what it means to be a human being."[162]

It is this theological horizon which leads him to argue that Christians have a particular responsibility to restore the word. As well as recovering the dialectical reasoning it enables, this means insisting on its clarity and trust-worthiness: "We have at length insisted on the fluent, moving, ambiguous character of speech, but mark that the word of the witness must be clear."[163] This too is a work of holiness breaking in, for ultimately it is only the presence of the Holy Spirit who gives power. The Spirit makes the written witness of scripture the spoken word of God in the adventure of preaching.[164] More-over, the one who bears witness that God still speaks restores the power of every human word. Yet Ellul does not have in mind here only the preacher, for every word spoken originates in the gift of the speaking God and only in seeking to point to that source can language find its true purpose. "[The witness] must have the courage, audacity, enthusiasm, and presumption to declare, despite his deep humility: 'What I say expresses the Word of God. My word projects the Word of God.' This is inconceivable and must surely be paranoia. Yet only thus can all human language gather strength and find

---

160. *Bluff*, 30. "The technocrats have a strange blindness to the complex reality of the world and to the lessons of common sense."

161. See French financier Bruno Gizard's use of Ellul to interpret the impact of algorithmically-generated transactions on the 2008 global financial crisis (*Être Ellulien au XXIe Siècle*, 44–67). Gizard begins by citing *Bluff*, 451, but goes on to offer a series of proposals centered on Ellul's advocacy of regulation on the basis of the recovery of face to face trading and the "precautionary principle" (67).

162. Greenman et al., *Understanding Jacques Ellul*, 46.

163. *Parole*, 120.

164. *Parole*, 122. As we have seen, for Ellul, Scripture itself is a metaphor for the Word of God, not its presence, and Scripture must be embodied by the Spirit-led wit-ness, for the Word of God to be "carried over" to us.

a new beginning."[165] The word is the gateway of a transcendent God into the world, "this presence of the Wholly Other," embodied in the immanent human witness who speaks.[166]

Ellul closes *Parole* with a theological hope for the final reconciliation between the word and the image. But this process of contradiction creates "a living hope here and now, which can change the situation." This is the task not only of preachers, Ellul states, but of ecologists, scientists, journalists, teachers, artists and poets, all workers of symbol and metaphor, creating an open language, helping us touch both truth, and reality, again.[167]

But Does Theology Mislead Sociology?

Perhaps more than on any other topic, Ellul is worth engaging with on the topic of language, communication and attention, although this will require critical and creative reappropriation. Moreover, Ellul's account of the image (glimpsed in part 1 above) is troubling to some. Indeed, Jolyon Mitchell, in his book *Visually Speaking*, argues that Ellul's simple dialectic of word and image is bad theology and therefore bad sociology. He summarizes what he sees as a nub of the issue: "Ellul places in dialectical separation reality and truth, linking them with image and word respectively. Thus natural theology is critiqued by a logocentric revealed theology which resonates with the

---

165. *Parole*, 122. See 1 Pet 3:11. On "communication versus information management," see Brock, *Technological Age*, 265–70.

166. *Parole*, 123.

167. *Parole*, 293. For a parallel account of the power of the spoken, metaphorical word, see McGilchrist, *Master and His Emissary*. Drawing on recent studies, McGilchrist argues that metaphor is a most bodily form of communication: reminding us that the word itself has its roots in the gesture and rhythm of the body (see chapter 3, "Language, Truth, and Music," and his account of "musilanguage"). There are hints of this connection of metaphor to the body in *Parole*, e.g., 22, 72, 73n1 (citing Beauchamp on Ps 139), 185n1, 285. However, three notes of caution must be added before making Ellul an enthusiast for the body. Firstly, this line of argument is not developed in any sense scientifically, and Ellul dismisses talk of "body language" as a symptom of excessive visualization (175). Secondly, in a discussion of the medieval church, Ellul folds the idea of the corporeal nature of medieval worship into the increasing visualization of the age (207). This second point is part of a wider argument that it was indeed the medieval church that sowed the seeds of modernity's fixation on the image. Ellul therefore finds the modern protest against Christianity's supposed suppression of the body to be simply a restatement of medieval Christian themes (207). Thirdly, and most significantly, for Ellul the human body is subject to Ellul's dialectical schema: it is real, created, but as a bearer of the image, the human body has a vocation for truth. This means that our relationship with God is experienced *both in and out of the body* (see 86–87, in the context of a discussion of "theophanies").

work of Barth. . . . *For Ellul the image can only deal with surface 'realities' and appearances, it is unable to communicate truth.*"[168]

Mitchell argues that this oversimplified distinction leads Ellul to offer rash assertions about audiovisual technologies in place of substantiated sociological arguments.[169] Moreover, he goes on to argue Ellul's theology is "reductionist" and "unbiblical." It is reductionist, Mitchell contends, because Ellul tries to reduce every theophany to the concept of word, claiming that the OT denies that God can be seen or sensed. It is unbiblical, because, for Mitchell, Ellul's summary of Jesus' ministry as essentially word-based makes short shrift of much of the NT evidence, especially the parabolic imagery and the extremely visual miraculous "works of power" of the Synoptics. Moreover, it downplays the fleshly emphasis of the Johannine literature (particularly and interestingly in this connection, 1 John) in implying that in Jesus, the word of God is a verbal, rather than a multisensory revelation.[170] Mitchell concedes that pointing up the dangers of the image may be an understandable suspicion of its excesses. Yet he concludes that Ellul's preoccupation with defending the spoken word at the expense of other senses leaves a rather "muted version and colourless form of Christianity."[171]

This trenchant criticism is one example of attacking the way Ellul's understanding of the Incarnation prejudices his choice and use of material in putting together his "global sociology." Although the image is the presenting issue in *Parole*, elsewhere Ellul's understanding of Jesus' earthly ministry as expressing non-power presses its ethical claims. For the miracles of Jesus, within the framework we explored in chapters 3 and 4, are not to be celebrated as acts of power over natural and supernatural powers, but rather over the concentrations of power that falsely hold sway over human life: "Argent, Etat, Technique" (and within the framework of *Si*, we might add "Religion").

We have offered an essentially sympathetic account of this exousiology until now. However, it is important to note that we might see Ellulian non-power as an outworking of what O'Donovan denotes as the modern Western practice of suspicion. This leads, he claims, to a misreading of

---

168. Mitchell, *Visually Speaking*, 215n29.

169. He cites sociologist Michael Real, "as a generalist, Ellul sometimes lacks familiarity with specialised studies, opinions muscle aside evidence and unfounded generalisations result about the role and effect of a particular medium or research method" (Mitchell, *Visually Speaking*, 207). These tendencies account perhaps for the limited interest in Ellul in communications theory or history.

170. Mitchell cites Heinz: "Revelation culminates in the incarnation which is the highest degree of plurisensoriality" (*Visually Speaking*, 210).

171. Mitchell, *Visually Speaking*, 211.

non-Western societies, with deleterious effects on Western engagement with them. "It is a Western conceit to imagine that all problems arise from the abuse of power or over-concentration of power; and this is why we are so bad at understanding problems of power that come from a lack of power or its excessive diffusion."[172]

In other words, in many non-Western contexts (he cites Somalia), overheating economies, a bureaucratic state, and advanced technologies are not the presenting "powers." Here, "disease and famine" may more likely be the "chief enemies," producing depoliticization, preventing people from living in communities, working together, and maintaining justice and security.

Arguing that political power is founded in part on power over nature, O'Donovan makes a strong and potentially positive connection between technological power and healthy political and social organization. "If the ink in the dictator's pen won't flow when he wants to sign the decree . . . if the military jeep won't start or the radio fails to broadcast then his dictatorship will come to a humiliating end. *But the power the tyrant depends upon is that which all political organisation depends upon.*"[173]

Outlining a positive account of power based upon Jesus' *dunameis or* works of power, O'Donovan argues that Jesus confronts the powers—however we understand the demonic forces of the Gospel accounts—time and again, precisely, with power. "His own intervention by miracle could not have been effective unless it represented the intervention of a superior and coordinated power which was capable of sweeping the predatory power of demons before it."[174]

And Jesus' intervention has political implications—not in the sense that he confronted Roman oppression directly, as if power always operates in a zero-sum game, but in that he demonstrated a new power in Israel's midst. On this reading, Jesus' recreative works of power and healing provide a positive account of power over nature. Moreover, O'Donovan implies, this positive account can furnish a positive Christian account of both political and technological power.[175]

In this brief use of O'Donovan, I intend essentially to question Ellul's claim to a "global sociology" along with his sweeping analyses of the "Third

172. O'Donovan, *Desire of the Nations*, 94.

173. O'Donovan, *Desire of the Nations*, 94 (my italics).

174. O'Donovan, *Desire of the Nations*, 94, citing Luke 10:20. He grants that the Gospels are reserved about Jesus' acts of power but claims that "idealist" interpretations make too much of this reserve.

175. For an ambitious attempt to outline a Christian "ecology of power," with reference to public and global leadership in politics, business and Christian ministry, see Walker, *Undefended Leader.*

World," which are a feature of a number of his books, including both *Parole* and *Bluff*.[176] This is of no little importance given the shifting centers of World Christianity, and the increasing, rather than diminishing importance of exousiology.[177] From O'Donovan's critique, we might surmise that Ellulian non-power too easily assumes a suspicious Western perspective about power and powers.[178]

Despite the theological weaknesses at points, *Parole* marks an important chapter—a moment of contradiction, of desacralization in the hope of reconciliation. When and how might that happen? We turn to a work published just one year later, *Changer de ré*volution to find possible answers. For indeed we find here an argument that seems to imply that technological power and political liberation can be positively correlated.

Changing Revolution: New Tools, New Rules

One of Ellul's most enigmatic books is his *Changer de révolution* (1982), an attempt to reinterpret Marx's account of the alienated worker in the technological society, hence its subtitle, *l'inéluctable prolétariat*. We highlighted in chapter 2 that this too is an exceptional text within the overall corpus, as a text largely concerned with social analysis, but ending with a theological tour de force. However, in its concern with revolution, it is right at the heart of Ellul's integrated vision, and was the third of a trilogy of books on the topic of revolution.[179]

Although it has recently been republished in an annotated form (2015), *Changer* belongs to a particular moment in time: the transition to a post-industrial, information age.[180] Ellul begins on familiar territory in arguing

176. Others include *Trahison* as well as his writings on Islam. One of Ellul's successors at Bordeaux University, political scientist and Africanist Daniel Compagnon notes that Ellul's writings on Apartheid were especially ill-informed, arguing that any claim to a "global sociology" must be balanced by conceding his provincialism (Rognon, *Générations Ellul*, 94). Rognon notes that Ellul's greatest followings are in the advanced technological societies of the West and the Far East.

177. Witness Prather, *Christ, Power, and Mammon*. See my discussion in chapter 3, part 3.

178. However, at the same time, O'Donovan does acknowledge that Ellul calls for a discerning attitude towards technology in the late-modern West. What is at stake in Ellul is not technical achievement in and of itself but the mutation of practical reasoning into Technique (*Desire of the Nations*, 274).

179. It was preceded by *Autopsie de la révolution* (1969) and *De la révolution aux révoltes* (1972). Rognon addresses its place within his treatment of revolution (*Pensée*, 58).

180. The latter term belongs to Manuel Castells, but it has become the accepted way of describing the transformation. See Castells, *Rise of the Network Society*.

that industrial Technique has been the basic driver of a mass proletarization. This is both local and global, for he is concerned with "the sinking of the Third World into a proletarian situation," as well as two forms of proletariat in the developed West: both the continuing existence of Marx's "miserable proletariat" (now largely among immigrant communities) alongside "a new proletariat" of semi-permanent unemployment, low social mobility and unsustainable welfare dependency in a technologically-driven, consumer society of rampant inequality.

However, Ellul also reissues Marx's call, but calling for a new kind of revolution. Somewhat unexpectedly, Ellul perceives an unprecedented potential in what he calls "microtechnique" as the way forward. The word "micro" here is everything: new tools make new rules, and since there has been a "change in capacities," a miniaturization, there can now be " a genuine change in the entire direction of society."[181] What socialism has failed to do all over the globe—create a free, fair and just society—new technologies might just make possible. In short, "computerization makes *Small is Beautiful* a real possibility."[182]

Drawing on Schumacher, Ellul argues that "a freedom-based socialism" is possible only through the means of a total and rapid informatisation of the economy and society at the local level.[183] Previous revolutionary attempts have had the will but not the means to succeed. Now, the means are available, but where is the political will, asks Ellul?[184] Observing that the situation is enormously fluid, he calls for urgent action to fundamentally reorient society in the direction of a five-point program of liberation.

Productive power is to be turned over to the "Third World" freely as aid; Western governments are to make the deliberate choice for non-power, putting an end to the centralized state; larger entities should be broken up and diversified, replaced by small self-governing companies with staff of no more than 100 people; most radically, working hours should be cut to as little as two hours a day, to allow more time for leisure, rest, creativity, and culture, enabling the fundamental questions of meaning and purpose to be asked. Finally, the wealth produced by automation and information technology should be shared out fairly through a program of economic planning that will impose some frugality, as well as generosity to the poorest.[185]

---

181. *Changer*, 257.
182. *Changer*, 260.
183. *Changer*, 260.
184. *Changer*, 243.
185. For this programme, see *Changer*, 247–50.

This necessarily brief summary is enough to beg two key questions. Has not Ellul here contradicted a whole set of previous positions he has taken with vehemence over many years, not least only a year or so previously? And have not such optimistic projections, common at the time, about the impact of technologies on the distribution of power as well as patterns of work and leisure proven tragically misguided?

Let us consider each question in turn.

Firstly, on the question of internal consistency, the movement from *Parole* to *Changer* demonstrates clearly the pattern of desacralization and reconciliation intrinsic to prophecy. *Changer* perceives a narrow way ahead and in the closing chapter, Ellul turns explicitly to theology to plead for an information-driven socialist revolution, drawing on the Christian cultural and spiritual heritage of the West. He offers a theological program for this information revolution: the desacralization of idols (especially "the sacred number"),[186] the love that denies oneself for others, the non-power that chooses not to use means to dominate others, the hope that enables risk, the change that the Holy Spirit brings, the realism that renounces illusions, the justice that comes with peace, and the truth that outworks itself in love and the freedom given by the God of Abraham, Isaac and Jacob, the God and Father of the LORD Jesus Christ.[187]

Changer provides enough evidence to suggest that Ellul believed that when desacralized, Technique could lead to a freer and fairer society. But this was a conviction he had always held, he claims, for it was not Technique he opposed but the sacralization of Technique.[188] Although Porquet places his account of *Changer* in a prominent position in his summary of the contemporary power of Ellul's thought, especially amongst "altermondialistes," this is no new Ellul we find here.[189] The novelty was in the circumstances.[190]

Unlike *Parole*, *Changer* has never been translated into English, and is therefore a lesser known text within Anglophone Ellul scholarship. Yet, this is not the only reason for its marginality. For, secondly, although *Changer* demonstrates Ellul's prophetic openness, his hope for revolution died an

186. "The sacred number, the value of truth" (*Changer*, 287).

187. *Changer*, 290.

188. For Ellul's defense of his judgment, see *Changer*, 288.

189. See chapter 20 in Porquet, *Jacques Ellul*, on working two hours a day only! He states that Ellul saw automation as both threat and opportunity (Porquet, *Jacques Ellul*, 211).

190. "I don't believe absolutely that *micro-informatique* is the solution. It is a possibility that exists now and that didn't exist before. . . . The microprocessor is an instrument that can help to find a solution. I don't see any other" (Ellul, "New Hope").

early death. By the publication of *Bluff* in 1986, Ellul admitted that for him at least, the tide of history had by that point decisively turned:

> [People] say that [in *Changer de révolution*] I changed my view of technique because some new techniques serve the cause of decentralization and offer more free time. But I never denied this. The trouble is that they ignore half my argument. Some techniques can have positive effects so long as there is at the same time a change in society: the coming to power of a revolutionary socialism of liberty, which has nothing whatever to do with modern socialism or communism. . . . Also demanded is a basic socioeconomic upheaval (e.g., in remuneration and distribution). Previously, there was no way to do this, but new techniques make it possible, though naturally they do not bring it about automatically. . . . We have lost a decisive opportunity in human history.[191]

Indeed, in his own final accounting of the book in 1994, with typical irony, he considered it to be "the most pessimistic of my books," because in measuring what a revolution might look like, he realized "the infinitely minute possibility" that it might come about.[192]

Changer is an important corrective to views of Ellul as a "technological determinist," as well as a key piece of evidence for the case this thesis has made for the theological vision in dialogue with Ellul's sociological writings. However, it also marks two problematic aspects of Ellul's thought.

The first is this: his obsession with revolution. *Changer* bears the hallmarks of Ellul's first love of Marx, never completely repudiated, in assuming that social change can be programmatic and total. To this, perhaps, the Christian realism of *Présence* is to be preferred, with its acknowledgement of "orders of preservation," lest the language of revolution becomes "an evasion, a tyrannical and yet despairing belief that all can be remade at once."[193]

---

191. *Bluff*, viii. In *Théologie et Technique*, 282, Ellul had argued that, without disruption, information technology reinforces centralized and hierarchical power bases. For an early exploration of Ellul's contribution to debates about a "digital divide," see Andre Vitalis in Chastenet, *Sur Jacques Ellul*. Pattillo, drawing on Ellul, writes: "Recent years have witnessed the rise and fall of the 'Information Age,' with its promise of decentralized power and freedom for individuals through the supposed egalitarianism of the Internet. The vastly increased technical power of the State to house and reference information on the lives of individual citizens, the rabid proliferation of electronic surveillance and identification systems since the early nineties, to name just a couple of recent 'advances,' have made such short work of this craze that it was scarcely uttered before it was dead in the water" ("Violence, Anarchy, and Scripture," 12).

192. Ellul in Porquet, *Jacques Ellul*, 214.

193. Brock, *Technological Age*, 384, drawing here upon Yoder.

Moreover, secondly, there is a nagging assumption in *Changer* about work, regardless of how Ellul's reading of "micro-technique" turned out. It is the same problem we noted above. For Ellul, these new tools, when reduced to their rightful place, could offer a disenchanted efficiency and utility: reducing the number of hours we have to work to the bare minimum, making our lives more free, so that we might commit ourselves to the really important aspects of human life: leisure, rest and the spiritual life. In this vision, we are freed *from labor*, but we are in no real sense freed *for good work*. Indeed, one could argue that it is this misguided anthropology which is at the root of the ambivalent history of "labor-saving" devices.[194]

The significant question for any attempt to articulate ethics beyond Ellul today, simply put, is this: is it not possible that Ellulian Technique tends to elide what God has created good? I have in mind here his severing of the body from the Image of God, work from worship and moreover, the number from the Word. Indeed, is it not the case that his polemic, while a helpful challenge to our long-established capitulation to statistics and newly acquired dependence on algorithms, lacks an substantive account of how we might not only desacralize mathematical rationality, but explore its potential as an agent of God's reconciling work?

The Word and the Number: Beyond Ellul

Desacralizing the Sacred Number?

As mathematician and theologian Virginia Landgraf point outs in her account of *Changer*, Ellul was no blind Luddite or technophobe.[195] As we have seen above, for Ellul Technique should not be shunned but should be rendered useful, ordinary: neither more nor less.[196] However, she makes

194. See, for example, James Martin's brief account, 326–29: "Perversely, the greater the automation in a society, the more overworked people seemed to be." See also Brock, *Technological Age*, 386–87, on the "myth of labor-saving."

195. She discusses her thesis, "Abstract Power and the God of Love," completed in 2003, with Rognon, *Générations Ellul*, 211–13.

196. Peter Scott, whose pioneering theological interest in technology we touched upon above, rejects Ellul's "reification" of Technique (capital T), working from the starting point that technologies should be treated as simply ordinary. "For technology is neither solely an instrument nor a reified force but instead should be interpreted as ordinary, located in the practices of everyday life." See Scott in Deane-Drummond, *Reordering Nature*, 275–92. At the end of this theological account of Ellul, we see that this is precisely what Ellul's distinctive concept of the desacralization of Technique seeks to make possible—taking away the capital T—although clearly Scott thinks that all people should be able to operate in this way towards technologies.

a significant claim in contending that Ellul wrongly fears an intrinsic threat in technology implicit in its mathematical processes by assuming that its processes "yield unequivocal results." This, she suggests, is a logical mistake, for it is not mathematics, which is most often open to "multiple results," but the deciding criteria one brings to it that carry the threat. It is worth citing her at length:

> The introduction of deciding criteria between multiple results of a mathematical calculation requires a will to exclusiveness going beyond the first problem and its solutions . . . what matters is that the answer is defined, fixed and therefore controllable. This kind of reaction towards mathematical solutions is a subset of the will to grasp reality—in theological terms, covetousness— that Ellul believes is inherent in fallen human beings. . . . We want answers that can be immediately possessed and controlled, and mathematical calculation seems to provide these.[197]

She cites *Technique*[198] as early evidence for Ellul's view of technical autonomy from the word as rooted in the "one best way" of mathematical calculation. At the end of his career, Ellul sees this same threat in the rise of digitalism:

> Technocrats, too, have their own language. They do not have to spell things out to each other. . . . The language that technicians speak among themselves is not just algebraic; it is digital. This transposition from multiform information, transmitted by an analogical method, to uniform information, in the elementary form of "bits," this omnipresence of numerical logic, means that the language no longer has the same consistency.[199]

Instances of this contrarian approach to numbers are widespread in the technological trilogy, as well as in many of Ellul's theological texts (notably *Parole*) which oppose revealed truth with the purportedly undialectical reality of mathematical processes. However, Landgraf argues persuasively, in posing the problem of mathematics in this way, Ellul misses that it is not "mathematical results but our will to control them [which] forestalls waiting for questions from the realm of truth."[200] At the deepest theological level, she argues, Ellulian technique rests upon a theological conviction about human sinfulness, with which she concurs. However, she argues that the

197. Landgraf in Jeronimo, *Jacques Ellul*, 215.
198. Citing *Technique*, 74. See also my treatment of this on 15–18 above.
199. *Bluff*, 27.
200. Landgraf in Jeronimo, *Jacques Ellul*, 215.

"lacuna in Ellul's logic," about mathematics underpins the concept of technical autonomy he applies to critique technologies. But it does not have to be this way, Landgraf argues. The problem with divorcing Technique from the word is reductionism, not mathematical rationality itself.[201]

In his book *L'Homme artifice*, Roman Catholic philosopher Dominique Bourg had already advanced a similar critique of Ellul, arguing that he wrongly severed language from Technique. Bringing Ellul in from the margins of French academic life, he recognized his work as a pioneering attempt to come to terms with the ecological crisis of a late technological era.[202] Yet Bourg argues that Ellul's bald opposition of Technique and language is an essentially theological imposition on the complex reality of technology.

Sociologically, he dismisses the idea that modern Technique exhibits a new and dangerous autonomy, which places it above language.[203] Modern Technique is essentially no different to ancient Technique.[204] Technique, he argues, always has a *relative* autonomy as it has a *mathematical basis in the given natural laws of physics*: "Their foundation is constituted by the laws of physics."[205] Yet, technologies are never *purely* mathematical, for techniques require a "double writing" in word and number: "The mathematical formalism of Techniques gives them only a relative autonomy with respect to language … technology depends as much on language as on tools."[206]

In terms of anthropology, there can be no humanity without artifice, and therefore no humanity without Technique. Humanity, and even language, comes into being through Technique, the work of human hands, the *manipulation* of the world: "Human beings formed themselves and their language by manipulating objects, and in return technology is dependent upon language."[207] Indeed, Bourg claims that speech and tool-making are

201. Ellul is aware of a potentially unhelpful dualism in his work, a challenge he tries to forestall. He opens *Parole* by admitting that his work is unscientific: "I do not claim to be a scientist, but I write as an ordinary person, without scientific pretensions, talking about what we all experience, I feel, listen, and look" (5). Theologically, he claims that word and image, truth and reality are not hostile to one another in creation (*Parole*, 107).

202. *L'Homme artifice* was perhaps the first mainstream commentary on Ellul's technology criticism in French.

203. Bourg, *L'Homme artifice*, 106.

204. He explicitly refutes the spectre of modern Technique as an all-encompassing milieu, arguing instead for an essential continuity with past Techniques (Bourg, *L'Homme artifice*, 124).

205. Bourg, *L'Homme artifice*, 225.

206. Bourg, *L'Homme artifice*, 124.

207. Porquet, *Jacques Ellul*, 224, cites Bourg's argument for "a parallel evolution of the tool and language."

closely bound in evolutionary perspective: "The ability of the first humans to manipulate their environment, would, at the end of a process of evolution, lead them out of their silence, to develop articulated language."[208]

In Bourg's theological reading, grace and nature are not opposed, and indeed, Genesis offers a view of the creator God as an artificer, shaping creation from nothing. It is this which legitimates a view of humans as, in his words, co-creators with God, refuting a naive view of nature opposed to artifice.[209]

Although Bourg probes Ellul helpfully, there are two problems here. Firstly, Bourg assumes there is an essential, unchanging thing called technology, and therefore misses the socio-historical perspective Ellul offers. Secondly, starting from an evolutionary perspective, Bourg's Thomist natural theology lacks a biblical theological account of creation by the Word or, for that matter, of the fall.[210]

Landgraf and Bourg have suggested that Ellul misunderstands mathematical reason; it is not mathematics proper, but the idolatrous abuse of mathematics which creates technical autonomy. Jake Rollison's fascinating recent work *Revolution of Necessity*, interacting with *Parole* and *Bluff* for the most part, suggests that this was indeed the direction of Ellul's critique:

> It is also important to note that for Ellul, the linguistic wager neither excludes nor abolishes mathematics, though his style of writing certainly lends itself to this misinterpretation. I would argue that a good summary of Ellul's position is that everything matters and is good in its place, and in tension with everything else; but nothing is where it belongs. . . . In the binary world, where anything mathematically expressible, anything conforming to the laws of non-contradiction is so easily replaceable by anything else, so simply reproduced a trillion times, sizes, places, where time and distance have been so silenced . . . Ellul proposes an ambiguous, difficult, and ascetic way that relies on the paradox of a language which does not conform to the exchangeability of mathematics, which attempts its desacralization (but not its abandonment).[211]

208. Bourg, *L'Homme artifice*, 159.

209. Bourg, *L'Homme artifice*, 318–20.

210. For an attempt to outline an argument for a basic, original musicality to the word, prior to manipulation, drawing on the work of Iain McGilchrist, see Prior, "Technique, Language." This was first published in French as "La technique et le cerveau: un dialogue entre Jacques Ellul et la neuropsychologie," in Chastenet, *Être Ellulien au XXIe Siècle*, 191–208.

211. Rollison, 135, of a manuscript sent to me by the author, later published as Rollison, *Revolution of Necessity*.

Basing myself on this suggestive starting point, I now turn to the work of Brian Brock to explore what attending to the Word in an age of Technique might entail.

Attending to the Word in an Age of Technique

In *Christian Ethics in a Technological Age*, Brock operates a dialogue between Heideggerian technology criticism and Barthian theology. Brock shares to that degree a common heritage with Ellul, though he interacts sparsely with him. For the most part he reads Ellul through the lens of one of his lesser known North American interpreters, George Grant. Indeed, Brock records that Grant turned his attention from Ellul to Martin Heidegger because of Ellul's lack of engagement with traditional metaphysics.[212]

This dense discussion offers precisely a treatment of the question of the proper place of the *mathematical method* and the status of the *mathematical truths* (e.g., the laws of physics) we learn through it: "mathematics proper (geometry, etc.) relies on a deep experience of reality, an experience that may be learned. . . . The term 'mathematics' has two meanings: what we learn through this manner of enquiry and the way we learn it."[213]

Indeed, where Brock's treatment differs most from Ellul's is in allowing the status of truth to mathematical reason. Yet in the medieval concept, he records, this kind of truth was held in dialectical tension with the truth revealed in the Incarnation. Following Heidegger, Brock traces modern Technique to Descartes's deductive method which "must begin not with stories, metaphors or images but with the simplest propositions."[214]

Rejecting the Ellulian notion of the radical transcendence of truth implicit in the truth-reality dialectic, what he calls "the right God in the wrong form," he seeks to outline a Christian theology of creation in terms of attending to materiality. Drawing on Heidegger's concept of an ontologically grounded "earth-world," a "house of being," Brock argues for the recovery of attention to a created material order, "the many layers of atomic, molecular and macro structures that make up the material world."[215] This order may be intelligible, unveiled to us, through "the fantastically close attention . . . paid by scientists to [these] given properties." And yet

---

212. Brock, *Technological Age*, 67. This led Ellul, according to Grant, to a philosophically thin account of the power of mathematical rationality in the modern world, the argument we have explored above.

213. Brock, *Technological Age*, 42.

214. Brock, *Technological Age*, 46. For his account of Heidegger's concept, see 45.

215. Brock, *Technological Age*, 322.

in Brock's dense discussion, he interprets Heidegger to say that although manipulating or enframing is our human vocation,[216] it must be dialectically constrained by the given limits of earth and being to which we attend. The given exerts a moral claim, that is to say, it is not mere brute material for manipulation. This recognition of creation as gift best serves to deny the reality-truth distinction dominant since the European Enlightenment: the dangerous attempt to propose the autonomy of scientific enquiry and its applications from revealed truth.

However, interacting with Roman Catholic teaching on technology in *Caritas in Veritate*, Brock is clear that the recognition of created material order as gift and claim does not mean returning to a Thomistic natural theology. It is worth quoting him at length at this point:

> Yet if we believe that with sufficient study materiality will deliver to us a clear set of moral rules and ignore the central role of interpretation in our understanding of the moral claim of material orders, we remain technological activists. The alternative to this activism is not passivity, nor throwing up our hands to say all is interpretation, but the openness Heidegger has brought to our attention, an attitude of waiting for "nothing," as it were.[217]

This act of attending, the opposite of sheer instrumentalism, is the first step in a theology of creation.[218] However, commenting that in practice Heidegger's "overly idealized" account floated free of material order,[219] and that he displayed a "remarkable inability to generate concrete moral recommendations,"[220] Brock's concern does not end there. The Christian ethical task is to recruit mathematical reason as an ally in the campaign for a recovery of wonder and gift, over and against the myth of total neutrality and manipulability. However, we do this rightly only when we do not deny the brokenness of creation revealed in scripture. Drawing on Barth, Brock captures well the theological basis of Ellul's technology criticism when he writes: "Christian theology has always taken [the curse on the ground (Gen 3:17)] as a real, objective disordering of created materiality.... But this punishment is also promise ... (Rom 8:20). This is a crucial distinction when analyzing

216. The modern attempt to know and shape material order is what Heidegger calls Gestell, or Enframing.

217. Brock, *Technological Age*, 62.

218. See chapter 4 for "an ethos of listening to God's word": "Properly creaturely life is characterized by a specific form of alertness" (*Technological Age*, 171). For an interesting parallel, see Vanstone, *Stature of Waiting*.

219. Brock, *Technological Age*, 321.

220. Brock, *Technological Age*, 61.

work in a technological age. That God cursed the ground is gospel in releasing humanity from the aspiration to total control."[221]

Thus, in Ellulian mode, Brock argues that the Christian ethical task in a technological society begins by naming the powers at work. "What the technological imperative offers society fits the classic description of that offered by a god, principality or power."[222] For the acute question is this: what do we do about the encroachment, the totalization of mathematical rationality in a technological society, if it is to the detriment of the truth revealed in the incarnation? Indeed, in this context, Brock even uses the word technology in a fully Ellulian sense. In claiming to remake creation, autonomous technology seeks to wrest back control in the pursuit of a godless utopia:

> It makes sense to call those who still try to live in this way *technologists*. Ignoring the curse, they aim to overcome, prematurely to conclude and settle the human struggle with material disorder, so circumventing the claim that this victory is wrought only by God. . . . Both horror and technological activism make wonder at the givenness of creation impossible.[223]

However, beyond Ellul, Brock offers a theology of creation which funds the rediscovery of the moral claims "given material order" places upon us. This involves seeing our work, technological work included, as collaboration with God. "Our labor is nothing more than the finding and collecting of God's gifts; quite unable to create or preserve anything."[224] Brock's readings of the Tabernacle and Sabbath as denoting collaboration between humanity and God are bedrocks of this argument. "The goodness of making lies solely in being in the train of divine working and is marked by an awareness of its participants of this location in God's service to the world."[225]

Drawing on this identification of worship and work, he offers in a closing summary on "an ethos of dwelling in the house of the LORD."[226] In contrast to Ellul's account, Brock argues that creation's given material form can still be a bearer of God's grace. Likewise our ordinary work can be graced now, and although we do not yet know its eternal value, still God's gracious presence can be upon it now, and not only at its destiny. "The gospel reveals

221. Brock, *Technological Age*, 297–98.

222. Brock, *Technological Age*, 379.

223. Brock, *Technological Age*, 298 (my italics).

224. Brock, *Technological Age*, 297, citing Luther. See also Brock, *Technological Age*, 335–39, chapter 7.

225. Brock, *Technological Age*, 229.

226. Brock, *Technological Age*, 374–88.

as good news human ingenuity and the richness of creation's material form, insisting that the *two* can come together in the creation of good and beneficial techniques and mechanical artifacts."[227]

Eschatology cannot therefore work against a doctrine of creation, and it is the task of the church to proclaim both. There is a temptation for all forms of eschatology, secular and would-be Christian, to float free of creation's material form. The decisive link between Apocalypse and Creation is the Incarnation. Because the Word has entered our world in Jesus Christ, we cannot simply turn away from creation's material form on account of future transformation. *Desacralizing* technology is not to turn away from it or destroy it but to break it down into routines and practices, and to expose its inner workings, to see how they might tempt us away from God's reconciling work.

The challenge for us is infinitely harder than for previous generations, for as Brock argues (with Ellul), modern technologies are incommensurate with their premodern ancestors. As the power to manipulate creation has grown, so danger has crouched ever nearer our door:

> Understanding the problem this way, we can see that the answer to the properly theological question of technology is not to be against all technology but to be continuously wary of our own modes of power, perpetually ready to give them away and to become skilled at doing so in order to resist their perpetual temptation to become things we love rather than conduits of love. Christians must ask: How does this technology embody love for others?[228]

Indeed, this rigorous task of discernment may lead us to see that a given technology may indeed have a place in this reconciling work.[229] Sanctification implies the remaking of our minds:

> Having had the mythical utopia promised by mathematical rationality shattered by the reconciling Lordship of the God-man, Christians are those testing technological methods against

227. Brock, *Technological Age*, 381.

228. Brock, *Technological Age*, 235. So, for example, "The growth in the power to heal and to restore can only be applauded wholeheartedly by Christians as an unvarnished good. But as the power to manipulate grows, so does the temptation for technique to become an end in itself." Ellul too affirms that advances in medical science fits within the framework of healing, although he raises questions about their intrusiveness: "I am by no means hostile to medicine or surgery. I fully accept medical work, as long as it does not infringe on one aspect of God's work" (*Si* in *Défi*, 942).

229. See Brock, *Technological Age*, 225. Brock offers few concrete examples of deacralization, but see his discussion of the Internet, 273–88.

their love of the material creation and their bodies as gifts, in gratitude for the social connections that emerge from the divine mandate to reconciliation.[230]

Conclusion

In this chapter, we have seen that Ellul's creative proposal in *Théologie* is that Christian ethics must exhibit a concern for the ways technological power can deny the Incarnation. This is a good starting point. However, I have recorded three underlying and self-reinforcing problems in Ellul's ethical explorations.

Firstly, the tendency to supersede the Tabernacle narrative leads to a muted understanding of divine-human power-sharing in good work. Granted, as Northcott notes, there must be an abiding ambiguity in any fully *Christian* account of building. "In the Christian tradition, even more than the Jewish, the Son of man . . . has nowhere to lay his head and the body of Christ is not confined to any temple or sanctuary but incarnate in the presence of God in his people."[231]

And yet there is no essential contradiction because the Incarnation works a spiritual and material redemption, and the people of God can still carry with us the vision of the Tabernacle into our daily work.

Secondly, Ellul's potential misreading of the Sabbath command leads him in general to separate work and worship. Yet in a fully *Christian* theology of Sabbath, worship is integrally related to work, its vital impulse, as Brock outlines.

Thirdly, Ellul's technology criticism, although it marks a significant and timely challenge to the false utopianism of mathematical rationality, fails to provide a positive account of how digital technologies can be tested, not only in order to be useful, but in some sense also to be agents of God's reconciling work.

---

230. Brock, *Technological Age*, 381–82, drawing on Wannenwetsch.

231. Northcott, *Moral Climate*, 212

Conclusion

IN THE CONCLUSION TO this study I will summarize the main lines of my argument for a theology of Technique in the work of Jacques Ellul and highlight the resources for ethical discernment this offers. I will then briefly recapitulate the critiques I have leveled, before proposing areas for further exploration.

Summary of the Argument

This project began as an enquiry into the challenge of Christian mission in a time of rapid cultural change driven by information communication technologies. I contended that contemporary theological accounts of technology often uncritically frame it either within a naive notion of cultural mandate or an optimistic appropriation of eschatological hope. I have taken the work of Jacques Ellul as a fruitful and still contemporary model of engagement with the phenomenon he named Technique.

As we have seen, accounts of Ellul's project have tended to construe the dialectical relationship between his sociology and theology in terms of separate works of different genres. In my first chapter, drawing on the work of Frédéric Rognon, I sought to deconstruct this dichotomy, since it is to the detriment of a full understanding and a fruitful retrieval of Ellul's legacy. I argued, in conversation with recent readers of Ellul, that his work is best understood as a single project of bringing technology into confrontation with the Word of God. *Therefore, at the risk of betraying Ellul's fastidious concern for readers to attend to his entire work, I have shown particular concern for texts which exhibit an internal dialectic between sociology and theology, since these are, on my reading, programmatic of an internal dialectic between the Word and the world at the heart of his entire project.* I suggested that this detailed attention to the shape of Ellul's biblical theological engagement with Technique builds upon and complements recent attempts to understand and apply his work today.

In four consecutive chapters I explored the resources for a fine-grained account of Ellul's theology of Technique, not only in his most celebrated and translated work but also in a number of lesser known works and recently published works, arguing that a thorough exploration of Ellul's hermeneutical framework is essential to the task of assessing his concept of Technique. In chapter 2, I considered Ellul's perhaps best-known theological work *Sans feu ni Lieu*. I delineated how Ellul reads scripture, before proceeding to explore the twin poles of Ellul's theological account of Technique in this work: Cain and the Apocalypse.

What the narrative of Cain reveals, Ellul claims, is our rebellious human desire to run away from creation to build a new home for humanity, paradigmatically in the counter-creation of the city. The city, for Ellul, is the OT's characteristic and prescient way of speaking of Technique, marking it out as a deeply spiritual, and in Ellul's terms, sacred project, working against what was given in creation. This spiritual dynamic at the heart of the city/Technique is what Ellul denotes by the "spirit of power." Bringing René Girard's work on myth, power and the sacred into brief dialogue with Ellul, I then explored Ellul's understanding of Christ's work as a work of desacralization, leading towards the glorious hope of the New Jerusalem, the place where God judges and recapitulates even our works of counter-creation. Since the crowning act of history is a break with history, God's grace will have the last word. For Ellul, the Bible must be read back to front, and all Christian theology must thus be apocalyptic, for God's given future comes towards us.

In chapter 4, I outlined this "most radical hope" by attending in detail to Ellul's reading of Revelation. Here Ellul fleshes out the account he offered in *Sans feu* of the "spirit of power" by finding in the biblical text a detailed exousiology, an account of what the NT terms the "powers and principalities." *The genius of Ellul's interpretation is his "functional" approach to the powers which allows him to read the biblical category in terms of contemporary realities without recourse to a speculative angelology. Indeed, by interpreting social, political, economic and technological forces in terms of the biblical powers he wishes to explain why these forces are able to exert such otherwise inexplicable, spiritual power over our lives.* I argued here that what concerns Ellul above all are the powers of "Argent, Etat, Technique," although his particular concern and insight is the cardinal importance of Technique in the modern world, which, in his terms, is incommensurate to all previous forms of technical innovation. This alone marks him out as prescient, for from an early moment, he intuited the growing power of mathematical rationality over all our lives, and the tendency to erode reasoned judgment.

History is most decisively the arena of these powers, and yet the Apocalypse of Jesus Christ is Good News for it reveals the meta-historical moment of desacralizing the powers and reconciling human works of power to God by separating them from the spiritual forces which have dominated history. Moreover, despite his concern for a final discontinuity between the present and the new creation, the works of desacralization and reconciliation can be anticipated in the present time, and we are in this sense invited to begin to exorcise the powers of "Money, State, and Technology" now, and render their products profane, that is to say, necessary but entirely ordinary, and without ultimate power over us.

Having established that this dynamic of desacralization and reconciliation is the driver of Ellul's theology of Technique, I then delineated Ellul's apocalyptic account of both the Incarnation and Creation in two consecutive chapters. In chapter 4, I explored the dynamic of desacralization and reconciliation in Ellul's reading of the Gospels, paradigmatically in his meditation upon Jesus' confrontation with the Devil in Luke's account of temptation in the desert and his account of Christ's confrontation with and disarming of the powers on the cross. *For Ellul, imitating Jesus' non-power is the heart of Christian ethics. Moreover, his perhaps novel proposal is that Christian ethics must take Jesus' example seriously with regard to technological power.* However, once again, there is perhaps more in the Gospels than Ellul grants. As we saw, Yoder finds positive ethical content in Jesus' declaration of the Jubilee. Drawing upon the riches of historical scholarship (a resource to which Ellul sadly grants too little value),[1] Yoder builds his ethics around the Nazareth sermon (Luke 4:14–21), and Isaiah 61 behind it, demonstrating that Jubilee is interwoven into Jesus' teaching in the Gospels.[2]

In chapter 5, I undertook a close reading of Ellul's neglected doctrine of creation, concluding that Ellul's reading of the Sabbath best expresses his hope for reconciliation. The continuing seventh day is for Ellul an eschatological hope. It represents an essential continuity between God's original good creation, inaccessible to us, and the world after the rupture. *On his account, the human vocation is not to develop or improve creation, but to live within its perfection, freely. This is what we anticipate in keeping the Sabbath. But Sabbath is above all for Ellul God's initiative, uniting the original blessing and final reconciling action of God over all things.* The

---

1. At points in my engagement with Ellul's methodology, I argue that while Ellul rightly refuses the narrow focus of historical-critical method, nonetheless, his work must be accountable to a wider community of biblical scholarship. His work must equally be accountable to alternative readings of the sociological evidence, and therefore, it is with regret that we read his often polemical and cavalier dismissal of sociological writings which do not fit his framework.

2. See the recent report in Tearfund, *Restorative Economy*, for a detailed, alternative vision of economics outworking Jubilee principles.

Creator will judge, sift and reconcile the works we do in the course of history to his ultimate purposes.

Resources for Ethical Discernment: Desacralizing the Smartphone?

Having spent a good deal of time probing Ellul's theological engagement with Technique, in chapter 6, I argued that Ellul's model of desacralization and reconciliation offers a timely contribution to contemporary assessments of technology, which often gyrate between dark despair and undimmed hope. In this respect, I made clear that Ellul proposes neither the naive use nor the total rejection of technologies. Rather, I argued from a clearly dialectical text, *Théologie et Technique*, that Ellul sees the Christian ethical task in relation to technologies within the biblical framework of discerning the spirits (1 John 4). Granted, as we have seen, Ellul is far from the first or indeed the most celebrated exponent of ethics rooted in exousiology, or a theology of the powers. However, we might justifiably credit Ellul for the prescience to see that what makes Technique as a power qualitatively different from the other Ellulian powers of Money and the State is the power it offers to manipulate almost every area of life. For him, Technique is the most complete incarnation of the "spirit of power" and "the spirit of lies."[3]

I began in chapter 6 to employ Ellul's framework to elaborate some practices of Christian ethical discernment in a technological age, in part by attending to the rich resources Ellul finds in the history of the Christian West for desacralization today. In seeking to address the concerns of our day, I drew at length upon *Parole* and *Changer*, attempting to show how Christians might respond to digital technologies, at one and the same time both negatively and positively.

Given the parameters I set myself, I have not attended at length to particular examples and case studies in this primarily conceptual study. This research, in its theological focus, has lacked the detailed attention to contemporary sociological resources that marked Ellul's technological trilogy, and hence to some degree lacks "the element of incarnation," as Ellul would put it. However, the problem here lies partly with Ellul, for despite his engagement with concrete realities, he rarely gives examples of what alternative practices might look like, a major deficit.

Before we proceed to this critique, let us very briefly attempt to draw together by way of conclusion what reading Ellul might bring to contemporary Christian practices of desacralizing technology. To mark in concrete

3. See chapter 6 above; *Théologie et Technique*, 274–97.

terms what we might gain from Ellul's *functional* approach to the powers, by discerning the "spirit of power" and "spirit of lies," let us consider that most banal and ubiquitous of devices of a technological society today: the digitally-enabled mobile telephone, often called the Smartphone.[4] The polemical force of Ellul's exousiology would not rest on making ontological claims about evil, but would insist nevertheless that the Smartphone can *function* as Satan's mouthpiece and eye in the living room.

A Smartphone offers us the hope of a substantial communion with others, an inexhaustible wealth of "facts," "information," and "data" about the world and the prospect of making it a better and more connected place. And it does this by commanding our attention. As we began to explore in Ellul's polemical but prescient account of word and image in *Parole*, what we attend to affects, quite literally, the persons we become. The ever-expanding literature on neuroplasticity suggests that paying constant attention to screens impacts the structuring of our brains, especially in our most formative years: "Circuits that fire together wire together."[5] Although the new skills of "digital natives" such as "continuous partial attention" and "multi-tasking" were once lauded, the body of evidence now suggests that an attention constantly divided against itself cannot stand. Partial attention is parceled, scattered attention, unlivable in the longer term. To be able to live, to love, to speak, to listen, to work and to worship, we need to foster a holistic attention to the wider context, and we need to hold the technologically mediated word in tension with the face-to-face, incarnate word. This truism needs action rather than mere repetition, as the growing technological manipulation of the spoken word is only likely to increase as artificial intelligence develops.[6]

Commanding our attention, the Smartphone hence provides multiple opportunities for an ultimately thin communion, all the while providing "Big Data" companies who have no interest in us as persons to use our profiles for economic or political ends over which we have little control.[7] In overwhelming us with information, the spirit of lies flatters us with the possibility of "my

4. A smartphone—on my definition—is a mobile phone that functions as a portable computer, with a touchscreen interface, Internet access, and an operating system running downloaded applications. At latest estimate, there are over 3 billion smartphone users in the world (Holst, "Smartphone Users Worldwide").

5. See, e.g., Carr, *Shallows*, 116. A balanced picture is of course necessary, yet we would do well to attend quickly to the growing challenge of "Internet addiction."

6. Brock, *Technological Age*, 231.

7. "Social networks like Facebook can be highly influential, since their algorithms determine the news that appears in our feeds. Whether or not the 'trends' are actively shaped as a matter of policy, as some critics have argued, they can never be value-free" (Brandon, "Medium Is the Message," 4).

news," which is perhaps not as far from an invitation to "fake news" as respectable journalists would like to think. And as we all too quickly mass-shame, crowd-fund and engage in digital activism we would do well to remember Ellul's Kierkegaardian call to the individual in the mass society first to step out from the crowd, and thus evade the spirit of power.

Christians will own smart phones, and will no doubt think seriously about how to use them, but it is not an exaggeration to say that here we enter the perennial battlefield of God's people with idols, whose manifest "solidity" serves to mute God's voice.[8] Hearing God's voice in Scripture, in listening to the voices of others and in attending to creation's music opens up true connectedness in relationships: as Ellul would put it, "a new attentiveness to reality," to "the neighbor," and to "the event" of the Incarnation and its meaning in every other event.[9]

However, despite the prescience and almost infinitely suggestive character of Ellul's technology criticism, at the same time I noted in chapter 6 three question marks over his ability to propose alternatives. We will need to look elsewhere for substantial resources about how we might desacralize and therefore well use such devices as the Smartphone. Moreover, the question of technology as an agent of God's reconciling work lies very far from Ellul's purview. Therefore, in brief summary, it is important to raise some areas for further exploration.

Areas for Further Exploration

> And even if our gospel is veiled, it is veiled to those who are perishing. In their case the god of this world has blinded the minds of the unbelievers, to keep them from seeing the light of the gospel of the glory of Christ, who is the image of God. For we do not proclaim ourselves; we proclaim Jesus Christ as LORD and ourselves as your slaves for Jesus' sake. For it is the God who said, "Let light shine out of darkness," who has shined in our hearts to give the light of the knowledge of the glory of God in the face of Jesus Christ. But we have this treasure in clay jars, so that it may be made clear that this extraordinary power belongs to God and does not come from us. We are afflicted in every way, but not crushed; perplexed, but not driven to despair; persecuted, but not forsaken; struck down, but not destroyed; always carrying in the body the death of Jesus, so that the life of Jesus may also be made visible in our bodies. (2 Cor 4:3–10)

8. Brock, *Technological Age*, 230–31, citing Jer 10.
9. See 45 above, referencing *Présence*. See also Ps 139:1–12; 1 Cor 13.

We began this enquiry with the Apostle Paul's words in 2 Corinthians in order to frame my questioning of all methods of communicating and living the gospel in a technological society. As we conclude this study, we return to this text to hear echoes of what has preceded. The blinding of the minds (2 Cor 4:4a) is the Apostle's reference to the connections between the refusal of his hearers to believe and the refusal of Israel to listen to Moses in the Golden Calf narrative, a text Ellul notes as significant for the account of Technique. The uniqueness of the divine image and glory in Jesus Christ (v. 4b) marks another of Ellul's polemical notes within modern theology. The clear linkage of creation, incarnation and new creation (v. 6) is what we have found in Ellul's theological framework. There is no knowledge which is more dazzling or elemental than the knowledge of Jesus Christ. There is no Christian form of communion or communication that is not to be Christ-like.

Moreover, we note here in adding verses 7 and 8 that this knowledge is to be embodied and made visible not just in our hearts but also in our bodies, fragile clay jars, but still vessels for worship. The Apostle marks that this pattern of life is dialectical, involving the contradiction of death and resurrection.[10] This power comes from God; it is not from us, and yet it is visible in us. Moreover, as the Apostle continues in chapter 5, and the metaphors pile up, we glimpse the linkages between the temple of our bodies and the Temple which is God's work, God's dwelling place.[11]

In an often hostile culture, Jacques Ellul staked his life on the Incarnation of the Son of God. As he wrote in *Présence*, "God did not become incarnate only for us to undo that work."[12] And he did not only write about it but attempted to embody it. It would seem disloyal to critique him for his words, when he claimed that only a life lived in obedience to Christ could be fully incarnate. As Greenman, et al., note, "While Ellul's recommendations for action were sometimes oblique and abstract to a fault, we can learn something from the way that he was involved in the affairs of his times."[13] Yet we have not here been able to engage at length with his pastoral ministry, much less his ecological campaigning for the protection of the Aquitaine coast, his

10. As James Alison rightly observes, what is required is an "incessant desacralization" in the life of each person, for we live in a complex world in whose structures we are all implicated. "Almost nobody escapes from some or other involvement to some degree in what is later considered to be an evil, and this is because the apparently contradictory movement of desacralization and resacralization is at its simultaneous work in the lives of each of us" (Alison, *Living in the End Times*, 136).

11. 2 Cor 5:1–5. Wright comments, "Paul's language of tent should awaken overtones of the Temple and its rebuilding" (*Resurrection of the Son of God*, 368).

12. *Présence* in *Défi*, 24.

13. Greenman et al., *Understanding Jacques Ellul*, 157.

prodigious journalistic output,[14] or his long commitment to community-based youth work.[15] However, we began, citing Rognon, by acknowledging that just as translating someone is to traduce them, so reading someone is to betray them. What I have attempted here is a "faithful betrayal." We therefore proceed to some more critical findings.

A More Incarnate Methodology

We have noted at various points that Ellul's theology of incarnation is essentially polemical, highlighting well the flight from incarnation that is characteristic of a technological society, and we have considered at length this iconoclastic emphasis in his work.[16] In this respect, we can rightly claim that Ellul marks a prophetic warning, not only in what he says but in the dialectical methodology he employs. I have argued that this simultaneous attention to the Bible and human culture is his central legacy.

I hope it has been made abundantly clear in my argument that there are many fruitful interconnections between Ellul's so-called "theological" and "sociological" writings. At times, I have gone so far as to argue that Ellul's philosophical and theological presuppositions lead his sociology astray, as in the pervasive and uncritical use of the Kierkegaardian dialectics of truth-reality and means-end to understand Technique throughout his career.[17] Moreover, his rather curt theologically-driven dismissal of image-based technologies seems in part to stem from a dogged refusal to engage with sociological literature which might challenge his framework.[18] And again, his fundamental theological suspicion of power is also open to question, although it is harder in this case to trace whether the influence is from theology to sociology or vice versa, or most probably, a process of mutual reinforcement.[19] We note finally Ellul's continual return to the theme of political revolution, a concept only marginal within the history of Christian theological accounts of the church's ministry of reconciliation.

These challenges by no means disqualify Ellul's project; rather they demonstrate the increasing integration of sociology and theology in his inquiry into an unprecedented technological age. As Ellul becomes

14. See Ellul, *Penser globalement, agir localement.* "Think global, act local" is a slogan some accredit to him.

15. See, e.g., *Déviances et déviants.*

16. See chapter 4 above.

17. See 177–81 above.

18. See Mitchell's critique above, 208–9.

19. O'Donovan's critique above, 209–11.

increasingly aware, all theologies are ultimately sociologies, and all sociologies are ultimately theologies, even if at the outer extreme, they are a-theologies.[20]

However, to put my argument at its simplest, Ellul does not give us enough to go on for the task of reconciliation. Case studies and examples are few and far between in his writings and as Greenman, et al., note rightly in their assessment:

> Ellul aims to set his readers off on an adventure, in imitation of his hero, Karl Barth. That said, in these matters Ellul's reflections are stronger in their diagnosis and critique than in their articulation of responses and viable alternatives. As with other prophets, he is better at tearing down than building up. We are impressed by Ellul's critique, yet wish that he had developed more concrete alternatives to exemplify the practical steps involved in meaningful "iconoclastic" practices.[21]

The problem here is not merely that Ellul does not get down to details in his writings. The problem, I contend, is that Ellul does not have a fine-grained theological account of worship, bodies and work in order to shape an account of practice.[22]

A Better Account of Bodies, Worship, and Work

In chapter 6, I raised three particular concerns which bear summary here. Firstly, I asked whether Ellul misses the full canonical significance of

20. See my engagement with Ellul's "somber apocalyptic tableau," the "Death of God" movement, and the "betrayal" of the West (chapter 6, 194–197). Although a rapprochement between Jacques Ellul and Radical Orthodoxy seems rather unpromising, it is worth considering the degree to which this statement of John Milbank could be brought into dialogue with Ellul's approach in *Sans feu*. "As the Church is already, necessarily by virtue of its institution, a 'reading' of other human societies, it becomes possible to consider ecclesiology as also a sociology. But it should be noted that this possibility only becomes available if ecclesiology is rigorously concerned with the actual genesis of real historical churches and not simply with the imagination of an ecclesial ideal" (Milbank, *Theology and Social Theory*, 482). Ellul's ecclesiology is rather thin with respect to "real historical churches," but indeed, this has been said about radical orthodoxy.

21. Greenman et al., *Understanding Jacques Ellul*, 59.

22. We note here that 1 John has been subject to the critique that it asserts the incarnation without, so to speak, fleshing it out in alternative forms of life: "It is notable that the writer never says why it is a matter of such importance to faith that Jesus came in the flesh. So much in his theology, in particular his depreciation of the world, would point to the theology we now find him attacking" (Houlden, *Commentary on the Johannine Epistles*, 107).

Tabernacle/Temple for a fully Christian theology of technology; secondly, I queried whether his account of Sabbath typifies his curious tendency to emphasize the transcendent element of worship to the detriment of the bodily element; thirdly, as a result, I speculated whether Ellul fails to provide a positive account of how digital technologies can be placed under discernment, not only in order to be used, but in some sense also to be agents of God's reconciling work. Let us turn very briefly to each in turn, highlighting what further work might fruitfully be done.

We have already explored briefly Kidwell's account of the importance of the Tabernacle/Temple theme to a fully biblical theology. If the "Temple not built of human hands," the Body of Christ, can have "recourse to the same notion of craftsmanship" in the OT, and if understanding the OT offertory practices can renew our understanding of our offering today, we will need to consider what this might look like in practice, as Kidwell begins to explore.[23] What Ellul lacks, and what this study perhaps leads towards is greater attention to the professional lives of Christians in real-life churches.[24]

In thicker theological terms, Ellul's account of the image of God as essentially spiritual cuts the cord of a full account of bodily life. This is at one with his account of the Incarnation as a temporary moment, which neglects the ongoing incarnation of Christ in the life of the church.[25] There is potential here for contextual studies of concrete local churches, exploring how Christians are attempting to test and reconcile technologies to God's redemptive purposes for creation.[26] Moreover, there are opportunities for resources which seek to wean the church off a dependence on technical fixes in its practices of mission in a technological society.[27]

23. On renewing the practice of tithing or offering in relation to money, see Kidwell, "Drawn into Worship," 220–22.

24. The London Institute of Contemporary Christianity programs (see LICC, "Fruitfulness on the Frontline"; "Whole Life Worship") seek to help Christians see their professional lives within the framework of worship, offering a variety of liturgical resources. See also the ReFrame course (Garber et al., "About ReFrame") from Regent College, Vancouver, which takes the Temple as a key motif for our work, offering "case studies of Christians in various professions wrestling with how to apply their faith to their professional and personal lives."

25. This hermeneutic is made possible by the bodily nature of the Incarnation and the bodily form of the Church. In this sense, "the language of the human body is the language of God" (Radner, *Time and the Word*, 190).

26. The CODEC Research Centre for Digital Theology at St John's College, Durham, has offered pioneering research in this area.

27. See Keifert and Rooms on the need to discern the missionary task of the church without resorting to "technical fixes" (*Forming a Missional Church*, esp. on renewing attention to God's Word in exercising discernment). For similar perspectives on mission, but engaging with Ellul, see Frost and Hirsch, *Shaping of Things to Come*; Hirsch and Hirsch, *Untamed*.

We touch briefly now upon the second deficit, a corollary of the first, which was the lack of intimate connection between Sabbath and work in Ellul's account. We do not need to repeat this critique here. If Christians are going to live out the incarnation in daily life, they will need a pattern of spiritual life which relates work and worship. As Greenman, et al., again astutely observe, Ellul's constructive account of Christian ethics neglects the centrality of corporate worship, prayer, study, fellowship and friendship. "Ellul mentions few exemplars of the sort of authentic freedom he advocates, apart from Jesus. Readers of Ellul who are inspired by his vision of Christian freedom will need to supplement his writings with resources related to spiritual and moral formation if they are to exercise faithful presence in the modern world."[28]

In terms of this particular presence in the workplace, what is required here is not merely an account of the gathering of the church in set-piece worship and the impact it can have on Monday to Saturday, but an investigation into formative practices of Christians being Spirit-filled for daily work. There are many existing initiatives working along these lines, and inter-disciplinary reflection upon praxis would be a vital contribution scholarship can make to the renewal of work.[29] Volf excellently summarizes the challenge here:

> It would be inadequate to conceive communion with God's Spirit in worship merely as a background experience that influences work from the outside, so to speak. For worship only deepens the continuous presence of the Spirit in the life of the Christian. . . . A Christian does not work out of an experience of God's Spirit that belongs to the past (a past Sunday experience). She works through the power of the Spirit that is now active in her.[30]

Mathematical Rationality

Lastly, we come to the question of mathematical rationality. As Ellul begins to argue, the task of desacralization is not to reject technologies but in fact to render them ordinary, to discover how to use them. However, as we saw in chapter 6, Brock helpfully redresses and completes Ellul's critique, by

---

28. Greenman et al., *Understanding Jacques Ellul*, 142.

29. See, e.g., Transform Work UK, "What Do We Do?"; God at Work, "About."

30. Volf, *Work in the Spirit*, 141. For a practical outworking, see Herbert, *Pocket Prayers for Commuters*, or, more recently, any number of the new daily prayer apps, such as Jesuits in Britain, "Pray as You Go"; Loyola Press, "3-Minute Retreats."

adding that beyond simply reducing technologies to useful things, we may even re-receive them as a gift.[31]

I have no doubt whatsoever that artificial intelligence, nanotechnology and even Twitter can all be desacralized and find their place within God's work of reconciliation: not least in providing opportunities for digital discipleship and evangelization, *pace* Ellul. To say any less would be ungrateful for the gift of mathematical rationality: this entire thesis is deeply indebted to the rather mundane manifestation of "narrow artificial intelligence"[32] we find in innumerable Microsoft Explorer search filters as well as the heavy use of Google! Moreover, no doubt my very thought processes in attempting this account are a melding of my own intuition, reading and memory with "how the Internet is changing the way we read, think, and remember"[33]—a reflection both comforting and sobering. However, there is no going back from the digital age, and if Ellul has taught us anything, it is that we need to contend not with the world as we would like it to be, but with the real world of everyday experience as it is, as we bring it into dialogue as well as confrontation with the theological tradition.

What further research into this area could usefully examine would be the use of technology that is not merely pragmatic but even graced, inspired by the Spirit in both desacralization and reconciliation. For example, Christian computer scientist Andrew Basden provides an interesting example of desacralizing the exclusive claim of the number. "As a computer scientist, I find current languages expect us to represent the world as logic, numbers or 'objects.' But this does not respect the diversity of the world, such as its spatial or textual aspects. So I develop general algorithms and computer languages appropriate to each aspect. In this way I oppose 'reductionism.'"[34]

Guy Brandon has recently argued that advanced communication technologies can be "digitally remastered." Research is burgeoning into the theological implications of the grander claims of so-called "general AI."[35] This moreover is not only a Western concern but also a truly global challenge. We noted in chapter 6 the weakness in Ellul's claim to a "global sociology," and we will need to supplement his analysis with voices from

31. See above, 219–223.

32. For a brief account of "Narrow AI" and "General AI," see Cameron, *Robots Are Coming.*

33. This is the subheading of Carr, *Shallows.*

34. Basden, "Ethics of Information Technology," 3. In terms of the desacralization of hardware, an interesting example is the use of the Raspberry Pi single-board computers to teach basic computer science in schools in Britain and in the Southern Hemisphere (see Raspberry Pi Foundation, "About Us").

35. For example, Samuelson, *Artificially Intelligent.*

the majority world if we are to face the challenge of reconciling technologies to God's purposes. The exponential development of digital technologies in the Southern hemisphere, skipping over the phase of heavy
industrialization, provides an important arena for Christians who are in
the forefront of innovation.[36]

Conclusion

Why explore the writings of a writer over twenty years deceased when
considering the very epitome of a changing subject-matter: technology?
I have argued in this thesis that Ellul's model of confronting technology
theologically is a timely and significant contribution for the task of articulating Christian ethics today. For our truly global world is wrought with
the challenges of new technologies and it is harder than ever to resist what
Ellul calls us to resist: the luxury of the reactionary rejection of technology,
throwing up our hands in despair, or the luxury of a spiritualized escape
from bodily life, naively using technologies, without asking questions
about how we are used and how we are using others. This research has
offered a learning journey with a learned and remarkable guide in how to
read the Bible and culture together. What I have proposed is a constructive
engagement with Ellul for today.

I have tried to resist simply restating Ellul's arguments, for as a prophet
who wanted no honor, Ellul did not desire readers merely to repeat his warnings or fix his ideas.[37] He sought attentive readers who would be able to follow his dialectical method of engagement, to re-think his thoughts in new
situations.[38] If we can proceed to critique him, we should at least continue
to listen to him. For we ignore this prophetic voice, I fear the church will be
unable to navigate the digital revolution without a "wholesale capitulation
to the spirit of the age."[39]

---

36. There is an urgent need for good theological work to go hand in hand with
technological innovation, e.g., Ring and Vijayam, "Technology." See the report already
cited by CAFOD et al., *Wholly Living*.

37. As Nordon notes, the aim of Ellul's analyses was to change the course of events
rather than simply to be proven right (see the interview with Nordon in Rognon, *Générations Ellul*, 254).

38. "Reading Ellul takes patience. . . . His views are often idiosyncratic and are
marked by strong assertions. Even the most enthusiastic of Ellul's followers will admit
that he is prone to the typical hazards of prophetic writings, whether ancient or contemporary" (Greenman et al., *Understanding Jacques Ellul*, 146). The authors go on to
call Ellul "the C. S. Lewis of the social sciences."

39. Brock, *Technological Age*, 20.

Bibliography

Alexander, Jon, et al. *Think of Me as Evil? Opening the Ethical Debates in Advertising.* Wales: Public Interest Research Centre (PIRC); WWF-UK, 2011. Online. https://www.globalpolicy.org/globalization/globalization-of-culture/51171-think-of-me-as-evil-opening-the-ethical-debates-in-advertising.html?itemid=id.

Alison, James. *Living in the End Times: The Last Things Re-imagined.* London: SPCK, 1997.

———. *Raising Abel: The Recovery of Eschatological Imagination.* 2nd ed. London: SPCK, 2010.

Angel, Andrew R., and N. T. Wright. *Playing with Dragons: Living with Suffering and God.* Eugene, OR: Cascade, 2014.

Arnold, Clinton. *Powers of Darkness.* Downers Grove, IL: InterVarsity, 1992.

Atkinson, David John. *The Message of Genesis 1–11: The Dawn of Creation.* Leicester: InterVarsity, 1990.

Backhouse, Stephen. *Kierkegaard: A Single Life.* Grand Rapids: Zondervan 2016.

Banner, Michael C. *The Ethics of Everyday Life: Moral Theology, Social Anthropology, and the Imagination of the Human.* Oxford: Oxford University Press, 2014.

Barbour, Ian. *Ethics in an Age of Technology.* San Francisco: Harper, 1993.

Barth, Karl. *Christ and Adam: Man and Humanity in Romans 5.* 1956. Reprint, Eugene, OR: Wipf & Stock, 2004.

———. *Church Dogmatics.* Edited by Geoffrey William Bromiley and Thomas F. Torrance. Study ed. London: T&T Clark, 2010.

———. *The Humanity of God.* Richmond: John Knox, 1960.

Bartholomew, Craig G. *Where Mortals Dwell: A Christian View of Place for Today.* Grand Rapids: Baker Academic, 2011.

Barton, Stephen, ed. *Idolatry: False Worship in the Bible, Early Judaism, and Christianity* London: T&T Clark. 2007.

Basden, Andrew. "The Ethics of Information Technology." *KLICE Ethics in Brief* 13.6 (2009). Online. http://klice.co.uk/uploads/Ethics%20in%20Brief/Basden%20%20v13.6%20pub.pdf.

Bauckham, Richard, ed. *God Will Be All in All: The Eschatology of Jürgen Moltmann.* Edinburgh: T&T Clark, 1999.

———. *The Theology of the Book of Revelation.* New Testament Theology. Cambridge: Cambridge University Press, 1993.

Bauman, Michael. "Jesus, Anarchy, and Marx: The Theological and Political Contours of Ellulism." *Journal of the Evangelical Theological Society* 35.2 (1992) 199–216. Online. http://www.etsjets.org/files/JETS-PDFs/35/35-2/JETS_35_2_199-216_Bauman.pdf.

Baxter, Jonathan, ed. *Wounds That Heal: Theology, Imagination, and Health.* London: SPCK, 2007.

Beale, G. K. *The Temple and the Church's Mission: A Biblical Theology of the Dwelling Place of God.* New Studies in Biblical Theology 17. Downers Grove, IL: InterVarsity, 2004.

Benedict XVI. "Caritas in Veritate." Encyclical Letter, June 29, 2009. Online. http://w2.vatican.va/content/benedict-xvi/en/encyclicals/documents/hf_ben-xvi_enc_20090629_caritas-in-veritate.html.

Berger, Peter L. *The Sacred Canopy: Elements of a Sociological Theory of Religion.* New York: Anchor, 1990.

Berlin, Adele, et al. *The Jewish Study Bible: Jewish Publication Society Tanakh Translation.* Oxford: Oxford University Press, 2004.

Bimson, John J. "Reconsidering a 'Cosmic Fall.'" *Science & Christian Belief* 19 (2007) 77–86.

Blenkinsopp, Joseph. *Prophecy and Canon.* Notre Dame: University of Notre Dame Press, 1977.

Blocher, Henri. *In the Beginning: The Opening Chapters of Genesis.* Leicester: InterVarsity, 1984.

Boff, Leonardo. *Cry of the Earth, Cry of the Poor.* Ecology and Justice. Maryknoll, NY: Orbis, 1997.

Bookless, Dave. *Planetwise: Dare to Care for God's World.* Nottingham: InterVarsity, 2008.

Bourg, Dominique. *L'Homme artifice: le sens de la technique.* Paris: Gallimard, 1996.

Boyd, Gregory A. *God at War: The Bible & Spiritual Conflict.* Downers Grove, IL: InterVarsity, 1997.

———. *Satan and the Problem of Evil: Constructing a Trinitarian Warfare Theodicy.* Downers Grove, IL: InterVarsity, 2001.

Brandon, Guy. *Digitally Remastered.* Edinburgh: Muddy Pearl, 2016.

———. "The Medium Is the Message: The Spiritual Impacts of Social Media." *Cambridge Papers* 25.3 (2016). Online. http://www.jubilee-centre.org/medium-message-guy-brandon.

Brewin, Kester. *The Complex Christ.* London: SPCK, 2004.

Brock, Brian. *Christian Ethics in a Technological Age.* Grand Rapids: Eerdmans, 2010.

———. *Singing the Ethos of God: On the Place of Christian Ethics in Scripture.* Grand Rapids: Eerdmans, 2007.

Brock, Rita Nakashima, and Rebecca Ann Parker. *Saving Paradise: How Christianity Traded Love of This World for Crucifixion and Empire.* Boston: Beacon, 2008.

Brooks, Ed. *Virtually Human.* Nottingham: InterVarsity, 2015.

Brown, Colin. "Karl Barth's Doctrine of the Creation." *The Churchman* 76 (1962) 99–105. Online. http://www.churchsociety.org/docs/churchman/076/Cman_076_2_Brown.pdf.

Brueggemann, Walter. *Genesis.* Bible Commentary for Teaching and Preaching. Atlanta: John Knox, 1982.

Burdett, Michael S. *Eschatology and the Technological Future.* Routledge Studies in Religion 43. New York: Routledge, 2015.

Burridge, Richard A. *John.* Oxford: Bible Reading Fellowship, 1998.

Cameron, Nigel. *The Robots Are Coming: Them, Us, And God.* N.p.: CARE, 2017.

Caputo, John. D. *What Would Jesus Deconstruct? The Good News of Postmodernism for the Church*. Grand Rapids: Baker Academic, 2007.

Carr, Nicholas G. *The Shallows: How the Internet Is Changing the Way We Think, Read, and Remember*. London: Atlantic, 2011.

Carr, Wesley, ed. *The New Dictionary of Pastoral Studies*. London: SPCK, 2002.

Case-Green, Karen, and Gill C. Sakakini. *Imaging the Story*. Eugene, OR: Cascade, 2017.

Castells, Manuel. *The Rise of the Network Society*. Oxford: Blackwell, 1996.

Catholic Fund for Overseas Development (CAFOD), et al. *Wholly Living: A New Perspective on International Development*. London: Theos, 2010. Online. http://www.theosthinktank.co.uk/publications/2010/10/10/wholly-living-a-new-perspective-on-international-development.

Chase, Alston. *Harvard and the Unabomber: The Education of an American Terrorist*. New York: Norton, 2003.

Chastenet, Patrick, ed. *Comment Peut-on (encore) Être Ellulien au XXIe Siècle? Actes du Colloque des 7, 8 Et 9 Juin 2012*. Paris: La Table Ronde, 2014.

————, ed. *Jacques Ellul, penseur sans frontières*. Le Bouscat: L'Esprit du temps, 2005.

Chester, Tim. *Will You Be My Facebook Friend? Social Media and the Gospel*. Chorley, UK: 10Publishing, 2013.

Chitham, John. *The Temple: The Place of God*. Worthing, UK: Verité CM, 2011.

Christian, Brian. *The Most Human Human: A Defence of Humanity in the Age of the Computer*. London: Viking, 2011.

Christians, Clifford G., and Jay M. Van Hook, eds. *Jacques Ellul: Interpretive Essays*. Urbana: University of Illinois Press, 1981.

Christoyannopoulos, Alexandre. *Christian Anarchism: A Political Commentary on the Gospel*. Exeter: Imprint Academic, 2011.

Church of England, and House of Bishops. *Mission-Shaped Church: Church Planting and Fresh Expressions of Church in a Changing Culture*. London: Church House, 2004.

————. *Who Is My Neighbour? A Letter from the House of Bishops to the People and Parishes of the Church of England for the General Election 2015*. London: Church House, 2015.

Clausen, Ian. "Love or Nothing? Locating the Question of Modern Belief." *KLICE Ethics in Brief* 19.6 (2014). Online. https://static1.squarespace.com/static/5c9e3e63e8ba4496c1df9458/t/5cafod60652dea64b6860a3f/1554976096829/19.6+EiB+Clausen.pdf.

Clément, Olivier. *The Roots of Christian Mysticism: Text and Commentary*. London: New City, 1993.

Crystal, David. *Language and the Internet*. Cambridge: Cambridge University Press, 2001.

Curtis, Adam, dir. *All Watched Over by Machines of Loving Grace*. Written by Adam Curtis. 3 episodes. *BBC Two*, May 23, 2011.

Dasgupta, Partha. *Economics: A Very Short Introduction*. Oxford: Oxford University Press, 2007.

Davey, Andrew. *Urban Christianity and Global Order: Theological Resources for an Urban Future*. London: SPCK, 2001.

Davis, Erik. *TechGnosis: Myth, Magic + Mysticism in the Age of Information*. Updated ed. London: Serpent's Tail, 2004.

Davison, Andrew, and Alison Milbank. *For the Parish: A Critique of Fresh Expressions.* London: SCM, 2010.

Dawn, Marva J. "The Concept of 'the Principalities and Powers' in the Works of Jacques Ellul." PhD diss., University of Notre Dame, 1992.

———. *Keeping the Sabbath Wholly: Ceasing, Resting, Embracing, Feasting.* Grand Rapids: Eerdmans, 1989.

———. *Powers, Weakness, and the Tabernacling of God.* Schaff Lectures at Pittsburgh Theological Seminary (2000). Grand Rapids: Eerdmans, 2001.

———. *Reaching Out without Dumbing Down: A Theology of Worship for the Turn-of-the-Century Culture.* Grand Rapids: Eerdmans, 1995.

Dawn, Marva J., et al. *The Unnecessary Pastor: Rediscovering the Call.* Grand Rapids: Eerdmans, 2000.

Deane-Drummond, Celia, ed. *Re-ordering Nature: Theology, Society, and the New Genetics.* London: T&T Clark, 2003.

Dixon, Patrick. *Cyber Church: Christianity and the Internet.* London: Monarch, 1997.

Dunham, Paul. "The Meaning of Technology: A Theology of Technique in Jacques Ellul." EdD Diss., University of West Virginia, 2002.

Dunham, Trey. *Jesus and the City: A Theology of Technique in Jacques Ellul.* N.p.: CreateSpace, 2016.

Dunn, James D. G. *Romans 1–8.* Dallas: Word, 1988.

Dyson, Freeman. *Infinite in All Directions.* London: Penguin, 1988.

Ellul, Jacques. *Apocalypse: The Book of Revelation.* New York: Seabury, 1977.

———. *A temps et à contretemps.* Paris: Le Centurion, 1981.

———. *The Betrayal of the West.* Translated by M. J. O'Connell. New York: Seabury, 1978.

———. "Cain: The Theologian of 1969." *Katallagete* IV (1969) 4–7.

———. *Ce que je crois.* Paris: Grasset and Fasquelle, 1987.

———. *Changer de Révolution: L'inéluctable Prolétariat.* Empreintes. Paris: Editions du Seuil, 1982.

———, ed. *Conférence sur l'Apocalypse de Jean: [Suivi du texte de l'Apocalypse].* Nantes: Éditions de l'AREFPPI, 1985.

———. *A Critique of the New Commonplaces.* Translated by Helen Weaver. New York: Knopf, 1968.

———. *Déviances et déviants dans notre société intolérante.* Toulouse: Érés, 1992.

———. *Entretiens Avec Jacques Ellul.* Paris: La Table Ronde, 1994.

———. *The Ethics of Freedom.* Translated and edited by Geoffrey W. Bromiley. London: Mowbrays, 1976.

———. *Éthique de la liberté.* 2 vols. Geneva: Labor et Fides, 1973–74.

———. *Fausse présence au monde moderne.* Paris: Les Bergers et Les Mages, 1963.

———. *Histoire des institutions.* Paris: Presses universitaires de France, 2014.

———. *Hope in Time of Abandonment.* Translated by C. E. Hopkin. New York: Seabury, 1973.

———. *The Humiliation of the Word.* Translated by Joyce Main Hanks. Grand Rapids: Eerdmans, 1985.

———. *If You Are the Son of God: The Suffering and Temptations of Jesus.* Translated by Anne-Marie Andreasson-Hogg. Eugene, OR: Wipf & Stock, 2014.

———. *Islam et judéo-christianisme.* Paris: Presses universitaires France, 2012.

————. *Jesus and Marx: From Gospel to Ideology.* Translated by Joyce Main Hanks. Grand Rapids: Eerdmans, 1988.

————. *The Judgment of Jonah.* Translated by G. W. Bromiley. 1971. Reprint, Eugene, OR: Wipf & Stock, 2011.

————. "La Bible et la ville." *Foi et Vie* 48 (1950) 4–19.

————. *La parole humiliée.* Paris: Seuil, 1981.

————. *La subversion du christianisme.* Paris: Seuil, 1984.

————. "La Technique et les premiers chapitres de la Genèse." *Foi et Vie* 59 (1960) 97–113.

————. *La Technique ou l'enjeu du siècle.* Paris: Armand Colin, 1954.

————. *L'Apocalypse: architecture en mouvement.* Essais bibliques 44. Geneva: Labor et Fides, 2008.

————. *Le bluff technologique.* Paris: Hachette, 1988.

————. *Le défi et le nouveau: oeuvres théologiques, 1948–1991.* Paris: La Table Ronde, 2007.

————. *Le Vouloir et le Faire: Une critique théologique de la morale.* New ed. Geneva: Labor et Fides, 2013.

————. *L'Empire du non-sens: l'art et la société technicienne.* Paris: Presses universitaires de France, 1980.

————. *Les combats de la liberté.* Geneva: Labor et Fides, 1984.

————. *Les nouveaux possédés.* Paris: Mille et une nuits, 2003.

————. *The Meaning of the City.* Translated by Dennis Pardee. 1970. Reprint, Eugene, OR: Wipf & Stock, 2011.

————. *Money & Power.* Translated by LaVonne Neff. 1984. Reprint, Eugene, OR: Wipf & Stock, 2009.

————. *The New Demons.* London; Oxford: Mowbrays, 1975.

————. "New Hope for the Technological Society: An Interview with Jacques Ellul." *Et cetera: A Review of General Semantics* 40 (1983) 192–206. Online. http://www.jesusradicals.com/uploads/2/6/3/8/26388433/new-hope.pdf.

————. *On Freedom, Love, and Power.* Edited and translated by Willem E. Vanderburg. Toronto: University of Toronto Press, 2010.

————. *The Politics of God and the Politics of Man.* Translated and edited by Geoffrey W. Bromiley. Grand Rapids: Eerdmans, 1972.

————. *Pour qui, pour quoi travaillons-nous?* Edited by Michel Hourcade, et al. Paris: La Table Ronde, 2013.

————. *Prayer and Modern Man.* Translated by C. E. Hopkin. New York: Seabury, 1973.

————. *The Presence of the Kingdom.* Translated by Olive Wyon. Philadelphia: Westminster, 1951.

————. *Presence in the Modern World.* Translated by Lisa Richmond. Eugene, OR: Cascade, 2016.

————. *Propaganda: The Formation of Men's Attitudes.* Translated by Konrad Kellen and Jean Lerner. New York: Knopf, 1965.

————. *Propagandes.* Paris: Economica, 1990.

————. *Reason for Being: A Meditation on Ecclesiastes.* Translated by Joyce Main Hanks. Grand Rapids: Eerdmans, 1990.

————. *Sans feu ni lieu: Signification biblique de la grande ville.* Paris: La Table Ronde, 2003.

———. *Sources and Trajectories: Eight Early Articles That Set the Stage.* Translated by Marva Dawn. Grand Rapids: Eerdmans, 1997.

———. *The Subversion of Christianity.* Translated by Geoffrey W. Bromiley. Grand Rapids: Eerdmans, 1987.

———. "Sur la nature et la création." In *Mélanges André Neher,* edited by E. Amado Levy-Valensi, et al., 39–48. Paris: Librarie D'Amérique et d'Orient, 1975.

———. *The Technological Bluff.* Translated by Geoffrey W. Bromiley. Grand Rapids: Eerdmans, 1990.

———. *The Technological Society.* Translated by John Wilkinson. New York: Knopf, 1964.

———. *The Technological System.* Translated by Joachim Neugroschel. New York: Continuum, 1980.

———. *Théologie et technique: Pour une éthique de la non-puissance.* Edited by Yves Ellul and Frédéric Rognon. Geneva: Labor et Fides, 2014.

———. "Travail et Vocation." *Foi et Vie* 79 (1980) 9–24.

———. *An Unjust God? A Christian Theology of Israel in Light of Romans 9–11.* Translated by Anne-Marie Andreasson-Hogg. Eugene, OR: Cascade, 2012.

———. "Urbanisme et théologie biblique." *Dieu Vivant* 16 (1950) 109–23.

———. *Violence: Reflections from a Christian Perspective.* Translated by Cecilia Gaul Kings. New York: Seabury, 1969.

———. *What I Believe.* Translated by Geoffrey W. Bromiley. Grand Rapids: Eerdmans, 1989.

Ellul, Jacques, and Patrick Chastenet. *A contre-courant: entreti ens.* Paris: La Table Ronde, 2014.

Ellul, Jacques, and Didier Nordon. *L'homme à lui-même: Correspondance.* Vifs. Paris: Editions du Félin, 1992.

Ellul, Jacques, and François Tosquelles. *La Genèse aujourd'hui.* Éditions de l'AREFPPI, 1987.

Fasching, Darrell. "The Sacred, the Secular, and the Holy." *The Ellul Forum* 54 (2014) 7–9.

———. *The Thought of Jacques Ellul: A Systematic Exposition.* New York: Edwin Mellen, 1981.

Feenberg, Andrew. *Questioning Technology.* London: Routledge, 1999.

Finamore, Stephen. *God, Order, and Chaos: René Girard and the Apocalypse.* Paternoster Biblical and Theological Monographs. Milton Keynes: Paternoster, 2009.

Francis. "Laudato Si'." Encyclical Letter, May 24, 2015. Online. http://w2.vatican.va/content/francesco/en/encyclicals/documents/papa-francesco_20150524_enciclica-laudato-si.html.

Frost, Michael, and Alan Hirsch. *ReJesus: A Wild Messiah for a Missional Church.* Peabody, MA: Hendrickson, 2009.

———. *The Shaping of Things to Come: Innovation and Mission for the Twenty-First Century.* Peabody, MA: Hendrickson, 2006.

Garber, Steven, et al. "About ReFrame." Online. https://www.reframecourse.com/about.

Gathercole, Simon J. *The Preexistent Son: Recovering the Christologies of Matthew, Mark, and Luke.* Grand Rapids: Eerdmans, 2006.

Gill, David W. "A Conversation with René Girard." *The Ellul Forum* 35 (2005) 19–20. Online. https://journals.wheaton.edu/index.php/ellul/issue/download/60/60.

———. "The Enduring Importance of Jacques Ellul for Business Ethics." *The Ellul Forum* 52 (2013). Online. https://journals.wheaton.edu/index.php/ellul/article/view/405.

———. *The Word of God in the Ethics of Jacques Ellul.* ATLA Monograph Series 20. Metuchen, NJ: American Theological Library Association; Scarecrow, 1984.

Girard, René. *I See Satan Fall Like Lightning.* Maryknoll, NY: Orbis, 2001.

Girard, René, and Benoît Chantre. *Battling to the End: Conversations with Benoît Chantre.* Studies in Violence, Mimesis, and Culture. East Lansing: Michigan State University Press, 2010.

Girard, René, et al. *Evolution and Conversion: Dialogues on the Origins of Culture.* New York: T&T Clark, 2007.

Glaeser, Edward. *Triumph of the City.* London: Pan, 2012.

God at Work. "About." 2015. Online. https://www.godatwork.org.uk/about.

Goddard, Andrew. *Living the Word, Resisting the World: The Life and Thought of Jacques Ellul.* Carlisle: Paternoster, 2002.

Goldingay, John. *Genesis for Everyone.* London: SPCK, 2010.

Gorringe, Timothy. *A Theology of the Built Environment: Justice, Empowerment, Redemption.* Cambridge: Cambridge University Press, 2002.

Greenman, Jeffrey P., et al. *Understanding Jacques Ellul.* Eugene, OR: Cascade, 2012.

Hanks, Joyce M. *The Reception of Jacques Ellul's Critique of Technology: An Annotated Bibliography of Writings on His Life and Thought (Books, Articles, Reviews, Symposia).* Lewiston, NY: Edwin Mellen, 2007.

Harari, Yuval Noah. *Homo Deus: A Brief History of Tomorrow.* Vintage Popular Science. London: Harvill Secker, 2016.

Harink, Douglas Karel. *Paul among the Postliberals: Pauline Theology beyond Christendom and Modernity.* Grand Rapids: Brazos, 2003.

Harrison, Peter. *The Cambridge Companion to Science and Religion.* Cambridge: Cambridge University Press, 2010.

Hart, Archibald D. *The Digital Invasion: How Technology Is Shaping You and Your Relationships.* Grand Rapids: Baker, 2013.

Hauerwas, Stanley, and William H. Willimon. *Resident Aliens: Life in the Christian Colony; A Provocative Christian Assessment of Culture and Ministry for People Who Know That Something Is Wrong.* Expanded 25th anniversary ed. Nashville: Abingdon, 2014.

Herbert, Christopher. *Pocket Prayers for Commuters.* London: Church House, 2009.

Herman, Edward S., and Noam Chomsky. *Manufacturing Consent: The Political Economy of the Mass Media.* London: Vintage, 1994.

Heschel, Abraham. *The Sabbath.* New York: Farrar, Straus & Young, 1951.

Hirsch, Alan, and Debra Hirsch. *Untamed: Reactivating a Missional Form of Discipleship.* Shapevine. Grand Rapids: Baker, 2010.

Holloway, James, ed. *Introducing Jacques Ellul.* Grand Rapids: Eerdmans, 1970.

Holst, Arne. "Smartphone Users Worldwide 2016–2021." *Statista*, November 11, 2019. Online. https://www.statista.com/statistics/330695/number-of-smartphone-users-worldwide.

Hood, Neil. *God's Payroll: Whose Work Is It Anyway?* Carlisle: Authentic Lifestyle, 2003.

Houlden, J. Leslie. *A Commentary on the Johannine Epistles.* Black's New Testament Commentaries. London: A. & C. Black, 1973.

Howard-Brook, Wesley, and Anthony Gwyther. *Unveiling Empire: Reading Revelation Then and Now.* New York: Orbis, 1999.

Jackson, Tim. *Prosperity without Growth: Foundations for the Economy of Tomorrow.* New York: Routledge, 2017.

James, Oliver. *Affluenza: The Secret of Being Successful & Happy.* London: Vermilion, 2005.

Jamison, Christopher. *Finding Sanctuary: Monastic Steps for Everyday Life.* London: Weidenfeld & Nicolson, 2006.

Jeronimo, Helena M., ed. *Jacques Ellul and the Technological Society in the Twenty-First Century.* New York: Springer, 2013.

Jesuits in Britain (Society of Jesus Trust for Roman Catholic Purposes). "Pray as You Go." Online. https://pray-as-you-go.org.

Keifert, Patrick R., and Nigel Rooms. *Forming a Missional Church: Creating Deep Cultural Change in Congregations.* Cambridge: Grove, 2014.

Keller, Tim. *Counterfeit Gods: When the Empty Promises of Love, Money, and Power Let You Down.* London: Hodder & Stoughton, 2010.

Kelly, Gerard. *Get a Grip on the Future without Losing Your Hold on the Past.* London: Monarch, 1999.

Kidwell, Jeremy. "Drawn into Worship: A Biblical Ethics of Work." PhD diss., University of Edinburgh, 2013. Online. https://www.era.lib.ed.ac.uk/bitstream/handle/1842/9452/Kidwell2014.pdf?sequence=1&isAllowed=y).

Kierkegaard, Søren. *Upbuilding Discourses in Various Spirits.* Edited and translated by Howard V. Hong and Edna H. Hong. Princeton: Princeton University Press, 2009.

Lane, A. N. S., ed. *The Unseen World: Christian Reflections on Angels, Demons and the Heavenly Realm.* Grand Rapids: Baker, 1996.

Lavignotte, S. "Inclassable et iconoclaste." *Réforme (Spécial: centenaire de la naissance d'Ellul)* 3446 (2012) 4. Online. https://www.reforme.net/?s=ellul.

Lewis, Bex. *Raising Children in a Digital Age: Enjoying the Best, Avoiding the Worst.* Chicago: Lion Hudson, 2014.

London Institute of Contemporary Christianity (LICC). "Fruitfulness on the Frontline." Online. https://www.licc.org.uk/ourresources/fruitfulness.

———. "Whole Life Worship." Online. https://www.licc.org.uk/ourresources/wholelifeworship.

Lovekin, David. *Technique, Discourse, and Consciousness: An Introduction to the Philosophy of Jacques Ellul.* Bethlehem, PA: Lehigh University Press, 1991.

Loyola Press. "3-Minute Retreats." Online. https://www.loyolapress.com/3-minute-retreats-daily-online-prayer/about-3minute-retreats.

Lyon, David. *The Electronic Eye: The Rise of Surveillance Society.* Minneapolis: University of Minneapolis Press, 1994.

MacCulloch, Diarmaid. *A History of Christianity: The First Three Thousand Years.* London: Allen Lane, 2009.

MacDonald, Gregory, ed. *"All Shall Be Well": Explorations in Universalism and Christian Theology from Origen to Moltmann.* Eugene, OR: Cascade, 2011.

Mangina, Joseph L. *Revelation.* Brazos Theological Commentary on the Bible. Grand Rapids: Brazos, 2010.

Marlin, Randal. *Propaganda and the Ethics of Persuasion.* Peterborough, ON: Broadview, 2013.

Martin, James. *The Meaning of the Twenty-First Century: A Vital Blueprint for Ensuring Our Future.* London: Eden Project, 2006.

Marx, Karl, and Friedrich Engels. *The Communist Manifesto*. Rendlesham, UK: Merlin, 1998.

McAlpine, Thomas H. *Facing the Powers: What Are the Options?* 1991. Reprint, Eugene, OR: Wipf & Stock, 2003.

McGilchrist, Iain. *The Master and His Emissary: The Divided Brain and the Making of the Western World*. New Haven: Yale University Press, 2010.

McGrath, Alister E. *Christian Theology: An Introduction*. 2nd ed. Cambridge, MA: Blackwell, 1997.

Milbank, John. *Theology and Social Theory: Beyond Secular Reason*. Oxford: Blackwell, 1990.

Mitcham, Carl, and Jim Grote. *Theology and Technology: Essays in Christian Analysis and Exegesis*. Lanham, MD: University Press of America, 1984.

Mitchell, Jolyon. *Visually Speaking: Radio and the Renaissance of Preaching*. London: T&T Clark, 1999.

Moltmann, Jürgen. *The Coming of God: Christian Eschatology*. London: SCM, 1996.

———. *God in Creation: An Ecological Doctrine of Creation*. Gifford Lectures 1984–1985. London: SCM, 1997.

Moy, Richard, and Anna Drew. *Leadership and Social Networking: Updating Your Ministry Status*. Cambridge: Grove, 2011.

Moynagh, Michael, and Philip Harrold. *Church for Every Context: An Introduction to Theology and Practice*. London: SCM, 2012.

Mumford, Lewis. *The Myth of the Machine*. San Diego: Harcourt Brace Jovanovich, 1970.

Murray, Stuart. *City Vision: A Biblical View*. London: Daybreak, 1990.

Negroponte, Nicholas. *Being Digital*. Rydalmere, UK: Hodder & Stoughton, 1996.

Northcott, Michael S. *The Environment and Christian Ethics*. New Studies in Christian Ethics. Cambridge: Cambridge University Press, 1996.

———. *A Moral Climate: The Ethics of Global Warming*. London: Darton Longman & Todd, 2007.

Nouis, Antoine. *L'aujourd'hui de la Création: Lecture actualisée du récit des commencements*. Paris: Les Bergers et les mages, 2002.

O'Donovan, Oliver. *The Desire of the Nations: Rediscovering the Roots of Political Theology*. Cambridge: Cambridge University Press, 1996.

Parker, Russ. *Healing Wounded History: Reconciling People and Healing Places*. London: Darton Longman & Todd, 2001.

Pattillo, Matthew. "Christianity, Violence & Anarchy: Girard and Ellul." *The Ellul Forum* 35 (2005) 5–18. Online. https://journals.wheaton.edu/index.php/ellul/issue/download/60/60.

———. "Violence, Anarchy, and Scripture: Jacques Ellul and René Girard." *Contagion: Journal of Violence, Mimesis, and Culture* 11 (2004) 25–54.

Pinker, Steven. *The Language Instinct: The New Science of Language and Mind*. London: Penguin, 1995.

Polkinghorne, J. C. *Science and Theology: An Introduction*. London: SPCK, 1998.

Porquet, Jean-Luc. *Jacques Ellul l'homme qui avait (presque) tout prévu*. Paris: le Cherche Midi, 2003.

Prather, Scott Thomas. *Christ, Power, and Mammon: Karl Barth and John Howard Yoder in Dialogue*. Bloomsbury: T&T Clark, 2014.

Prior, Matthew. "Technique, Language, and the Divided Brain." *The Ellul Forum* 54 (2014) Online. https://journals.wheaton.edu/index.php/ellul/article/download /417/19.

Pullinger, David J. *Information Technology and Cyberspace: Extra-Connected Living.* London: Darton Longman & Todd, 2001.

Rad, Gerhard von, and John H. Marks. *Genesis: A Commentary.* Philadelphia: Westminster, 1972.

Radner, Ephraim. *A Brutal Unity: The Spiritual Politics of the Christian Church.* Waco: Baylor University Press, 2012.

———. *Time and the Word: Figural Reading of the Christian Scriptures.* Grand Rapids: Eerdmans, 2016.

Raspberry Pi Foundation. "About Us." Online. https://www.raspberrypi.org/about.

Reinke, Tony. *12 Ways Your Phone Is Changing You.* Wheaton: Crossway, 2017.

Ring, Shawn, and Joseph Vijayam. "Technology: Has Technology Exceeded Our Humanity?" *Lausanne Movement.* Online. https://www.lausanne.org/networks/ issues/technology.

Ringma, Charles. *Resist the Powers with Jacques Ellul.* Vancouver: Regent College Publishing, 2009.

Rognon, Frédéric. *Générations Ellul: Soixante héritiers de la pensée de Jacques Ellul.* Geneva: Labor et Fides, 2012.

———. *Jacques Ellul: Une Pensée en dialogue.* Geneva: Labor et Fides, 2007.

Rollison, Jacob. *Revolution of Necessity: Language, Technique, and Freedom in the Writings of Jacques Ellul and Slavoj Zizek.* New York: Atropos, 2016.

Sacks, Jonathan. *The Great Partnership: God, Science, and the Search for Meaning.* London: Hodder & Stoughton, 2011.

Samuelson, C. *Artificially Intelligent.* Cambridge: Jubilee Centre, 2019.

Scott, Peter. *A Political Theology of Nature.* Cambridge: Cambridge University Press, 2003.

Sheldrake, Philip. *Spaces for the Sacred: Place, Memory, and Identity.* London: SCM, 2001.

Sine, Tom. *Mustard Seed vs. McWorld: Reinventing Life and Faith for the Future.* Grand Rapids: Baker, 1999.

Sommer, Benjamin D. *The Bodies of God and the World of Ancient Israel.* Cambridge: Cambridge University Press, 2011.

Stark, Rodney. *The Victory of Reason: How Christianity Led to Freedom, Capitalism, and Western Success.* New York: Random House, 2006.

Stevens, R. Paul. *The Abolition of the Laity: Vocation, Work, and Ministry in a Biblical Perspective.* Cumbria, UK: Paternoster, 1999.

Strobel, Lee. *The Case for a Creator: A Journalist Investigates Scientific Evidence That Points toward God.* Grand Rapids: Zondervan, 2004.

Sykes, Stephen. *Power and Christian Theology.* London: Continuum, 2006.

Talbott, Stephen. *The Future Does Not Compute.* Sebastopol, CA: O'Reilly & Associates, 1995.

Tate, William. *Biblical Interpretation: An Integrated Approach.* Rev. ed. Peabody, MA: Hendrickson, 1997.

Taylor, John V. *The Christlike God.* London: SCM, 1992.

———. *The Holy Spirit and the Christian Mission.* London: SCM, 1973.

Tearfund. *The Restorative Economy: Completing Our Unfinished Millennium Jubilee.* Teddington, UK: Tearfund, 2015. Online. http://www.tearfund.org/~/media/ Files/Main_Site/Campaigning/OrdinaryHeroes/Restorative_Economy_Full_ Report.pdf.

Theissen, Gerd. *The Shadow of the Galilean.* London: SCM, 2001.

Tomlin, Graham. *The Provocative Church.* London: SPCK, 2004.

Transform Work UK. "What Do We Do?" Online. https://www.transformworkuk.org/ Groups/53537/Transform_Work_UK/About_Us/About_Us.aspx.

Turkle, Sherry. *Alone Together: Why We Expect More from Technology and Less from Each Other.* New York: Basic, 2011.

Um, Stephen T., and Justin Buzzard. *Why Cities Matter: To God, the Culture, and the Church.* Wheaton: Crossway, 2013.

Van Vleet, Jacob E. *Dialectical Theology and Jacques Ellul: An Introductory Exposition.* Minneapolis: Fortress, 2014.

Vanhoozer, Kevin J. *Remythologizing Theology: Divine Action, Passion, and Authorship.* Cambridge Studies in Christian Doctrine 18. Cambridge: Cambridge University Press, 2010.

Vanstone, W. H. *The Stature of Waiting.* New York: Morehouse, 2006.

Volf, Miroslav. *Work in the Spirit: Toward a Theology of Work.* 1991. Reprint, Eugene, OR: Wipf & Stock, 2001.

Walker, Simon P. *The Undefended Leader.* Carlisle: Piquant, 2010.

Walters, James. *Baudrillard and Theology.* London: T&T Clark, 2012.

Ward, Keith. *What the Bible Really Teaches: A Challenge for Fundamentalists.* London: SPCK, 2004.

Welby, Justin. *Dethroning Mammon: Making Money Serve Grace; The Archbishop of Canterbury's Lent Book.* London: Church House, 2017.

Wenham, Gordon J. *Genesis 1–15.* Waco, TX: Word, 1987.

Willard, Dallas. *The Spirit of the Disciplines: Understanding How God Changes Lives.* San Francisco: HarperSanFrancisco, 1990.

Williams, Rowan. *Being Disciples: Essentials of the Christian Life.* London: SPCK, 2016.

Windle, Brian. *Eight Innovations to Leading Millennials.* N.p.: Thrive, 2019

Wink, Walter. *The Powers That Be: Theology for a New Millennium.* New York: Doubleday, 1998.

Wolters, Albert M. *Creation Regained: Biblical Basics for a Reformational Worldview.* 2nd ed. Grand Rapids: Eerdmans, 2005.

Wright, Chris. *God's People in God's Land: Family, Land, and Property in the Old Testament.* Grand Rapids: Eerdmans, 1990.

Wright, N. T. *The New Testament and the People of God.* London: SPCK, 1992.

———. *The Resurrection of the Son of God.* London: SPCK, 2003.

———. *Scripture and the Authority of God.* London: SPCK, 2005.

———. *Surprised by Hope.* London: SPCK, 2004.

Wright, Nigel Goring. *A Theology of the Dark Side: Putting the Power of Evil in Its Place.* Carlisle: Paternoster, 2002.

Yoder, John Howard. *The Politics of Jesus: Vicit Agnus Noster.* 2nd ed. Grand Rapids: Eerdmans, 1994.

Zahl, Paul F. M. *Grace in Practice: A Theology of Everyday Life.* Grand Rapids: Eerdmans, 2007.

Žižek, Slavoj. *Living in the End Times.* London: Verso, 2010.

Made in the USA
Middletown, DE
07 May 2023

30185738R00146